4/95

D0824483

THE COLONIAL
ARCHITECTURE
OF MEXICO

THE COLONIAL
ARCHITECTURE
OF MEXICO

JAMES EARLY

UNIVERSITY OF NEW MEXICO PRESS

ALBUQUERQUE

For Ann

Library of Congress Cataloging-in-Publication Data
Early, James
The colonial architecture of Mexico/ James Early. — 1st ed.
p.   cm.
Includes bibliographical references and index.
ISBN 0-8263-1474-0
1. Architecture, Spanish colonial—Mexico.
2. Architecture—Mexico.
I. Title.
NA753.E27   1994
720'.972—dc20   93-42991
CIP

CONTENTS

ILLUSTRATIONS

Chapter IV

Chapter VII

Chapter VIII

 Preface

This is a book about the most notable post-Columbian architecture constructed on the American continent before the appearance north of the border of the buildings of Henry Hobson Richardson, Louis Sullivan, and Frank Lloyd Wright in the last decades of the nineteenth century. I am interested in the urban settings of colonial New Spain in which the buildings were placed, and in the spiritual and material aspirations of the people who commissioned, designed, built, and used them. The diverse and changing society of New Spain was remarkable and is remarkably little known in the United States. Alan Riding entitled his perceptive portrait of contemporary Mexico, *Distant Neighbors*. My study is of a remote colonial past rather than the present, but, like Riding, I aim to inform North Americans about our neighbors to the south.

Implicit in my narrative, though only occasionally made explicit, is the contrast between the familiar, modest colonial world of English North America and the grand, alien scene of colonial New Spain, ranging from Bernal Díaz del Castillo's account of his first view of Aztec Tenochtitlán to Alexander von Humboldt's description of the Valley of Mexico at the end of the colonial period.

For a reader familiar with English colonial architecture and life in North America, recognition of parallels and contrasts will be frequent. The grandeur of the religious edifices of New Spain, from the Gothic churches of the friars and the Renaissance cathedrals of the cities to the Baroque sacred chapels and Neo-Classical parish churches will suggest contrasting images. Among them might be the gathering of the members of a New England town in a simple house for meeting, such as the Old Ship which survives near Boston, the Hebrew worship of the Jewish community of Newport in their sober synagogue, and the services of modest splendor of the most prominent of Anglican congregations in King's Chapel in Boston and Christ Church in Philadelphia. Descriptions of life on a vast hacienda, in a festive and exploitive mining town, or in a nobleman's house in Mexico City might suggest the comparative modesty of plantation houses like Westover of William Byrd or Mount Vernon of George Washington, of little Williamsburg with its college and two public buildings, or of the city houses of prominent English colonists, whether the old wooden house of Paul Revere in Boston or the impressive new brick one of the Hammonds in Annapolis.

The differences between the colonial societies originated in part in the differences between the colonizing countries, expansive imperial Catholic Habsburg Spain and primarily Protestant, if not Puritan, England, still a secondary power in Europe. Of great importance as well was the difference between the native societies found by the colonizers—populous, complex, architecturally splendid Aztec-dominated Mexico—and woodland eastern North America inhabited, in the words of the leader of the Plymouth colony, William Bradford, by "wild beasts and wild men."

Many important characteristics were shared by both colonial societies. Among them are the people's sense of themselves as Christians, their impatience with officials sent out from Madrid or London, and the importance of business activities and the desire to rise in the world.

The book begins with two great programs of construction and the patterns of living associated with them, the hundreds of churches and conventos erected under the direction of friars to minister to the immense, though rapidly decimated, indigenous population and the numerous towns and cities laid out for the Indians and for the Spanish settlers. Subsequently, in the recreation of the cultural milieu of Baroque religious architecture, characteristic manifestations are described, such as the life in convents for nuns, both of the austere and the relaxed types, and the cults of the saints and the Virgin, the Mexican national cult of the Virgin of Guadalupe in particular. Later there is an account of the commercial prosperity of Mexico City, of the merchants and miners, of the great haciendas, and of the enormously rich families, both with noble titles and without. In conclusion comes a discussion of Neo-Classicism in architecture, of the royally chartered Academy of San Carlos, and of the lingering taste for Baroque dynamism in the works of the principal Neo-Classicists in Mexico.

The general history of architectural developments in the colonial cultural context is supplemented by discussions of notable and representative buildings. In these descriptions and histories concern is shown for the patrons commissioning the structures and for the symbolic and functional uses of the structures, as well as for the constructional methods and the formal qualities. The esthetic judgments are my own but I have tried to incorporate the available architectural scholarship, both of the last generation and of the last two decades.

A book of general scope is indebted to the work of many predecessors. Everyone working in my field stands upon the older works in Spanish of Diego Angulo Íñiguez, Manual Toussaint, Francisco de la Maza, and Justino Fernández, and in English of George Kubler, Elizabeth Wilder Weismann, and John McAndrew, whose *Open Air Churches of Sixteenth-Century Mexico* helped inspire my concern for the life surrounding the buildings of colonial New Spain. Important recent studies include, in English, a book by Robert Mullen—*Sixteenth-Century Dominican Architecture in Oaxaca*—and, in Spanish, an essay by Jorge Alberto Manrique and books by Martha Fernández and Guillermo Tovar de Teresa.

Sources for the cultural history of New Spain are manifold. They begin with the letters of Cortés to Charles V and the histories of Bernal Díaz del Castillo and Fray Toribio de Motolinía and continue through Octavio Paz's remarkable recreation of the seventeenth-century literary, intellectual, and religious world of *Sor Juana*, the greatest of Mexican colonial poets. A rather full account of my scholarly indebtedness appears in the suggestions for further reading appended at the end of this book.

My interest in the architecture of colonial New Spain was sharpened many years ago by the discovery of George Kubler's *Mexican Architecture in the Sixteenth Century* in the library of Gertrude Duby Blom's Na Bolom in San Cristóbal de Las Casas. The book's completion in Dallas was greatly assisted by the holdings in Mexican and Spanish works of the De Golyer Library of Southern Methodist University and generous helpfulness of its director, David Farmer, and of Kristen Jacobsen and its staff. My friends in the SMU Department of History, David Weber and William B. Taylor, have provided greatly appreciated psychic and scholarly support. The final text reflects significantly the patient questioning of my editor, Dana Asbury. Throughout the explorations and reexplorations of architectural sites in Mexico extending over a number of years and the subsequent work toward a clear and readable text, Ann Early was an indispensable colleague and critic.

I
ARCHITECTURE FOR THE
VICEROYALTY OF NEW SPAIN

Prologue: THE CITY OF MEXICO OF MONTEZUMA AND OF
CORTÉZ

Writing in his old age, Bernal Díaz del Castillo recalled the Spanish conquerors' initial view of the valley of Mexico. They were astounded at "all those cities and villages built in the water, and other great towns on dry land, and the straight and level causeway leading to Mexico City. . . . These great towns and temple crested pyramids and buildings rising from the water, all made of stone, seemed like an enchanted vision from the chivalric book of Amadis of Gaul. It . . . was . . . [a] first glimpse of things never heard of, seen or dreamed of before."[1] After forty some years he still remembered freshly the spacious lakeside palace in which he had been lodged before marching with Cortés to the capital, the structure shining with burnished stucco and decorated with marvelous paintings and extraordinary stone ornamentation. Its courtyards were covered with awnings of woven cotton. Its gardens were filled with roses and fruit trees and other sweet-smelling vegetation. The garden ponds attracted strange colorful birds, and canals permitted large canoes to enter from the lake. In November 1519 Díaz and his companions believed that they were discovering the last great wonder of the world. Recalling the scene after nearly half a century, Díaz was moved by the poignancy of loss, writing, "now all that I then saw has vanished, nothing remains."[2]

Unlike the English settlers of Massachu-setts, who found in the words of William Bradford no "inns to entertaine or refresh their weatherbeaten bodies, no houses or much less townes to repaire too" but only "a hideous and desolate wilderness, full of wild beasts and willd men,"[3] the Spanish conquerors of Mexico confronted a populous and powerful civilization, alien to Christian Europe, strange, dazzling, and shocking. The architectural splendors of the palaces and temple pyramids of the Aztecs, or Mexica, were obliterated in scarcely a decade, but other forms of art, culture, and living endured, despite modifications, for much of the sixteenth century. Traditional types of songs and instrumental music persisted, probably revived powerfully during the middle decades of the century. Preconquest manuscript painting continued in gradually Europeanized form throughout the century. Dances and various religious and institutional patterns of life have endured in the countryside into the present time, as has the traditional diet. The Indian peoples of Mexico have endured, though decimated by European and tropical diseases, calculated brutality and casual slaughter, and by the shocking dislocations of political and cultural upheaval. They and their traditional ways of living have shared in the shaping of modern mestizo Mexico.

Hernán Cortés and his followers were astounded by the great city of the Aztecs—called

1

Tenochtitlán by modern scholars, Temixtitan by Cortés, and Mexico by Bernal Díaz. Its splendor in its mountain-girt lake, its great size, and its effectiveness as a political and economic capital all impressed the sixteenth-century Spaniards. Decentralized Spain was without a great dominating city. Modest-sized Madrid would not be designated as capital for forty years. The Spanish court took to the road, traveling as far south as Granada and as far north as Valladolid. Tenochtitlán roughly doubled the population of the largest cities in Spain, Seville and Valladolid. Estimates place its houses at 30,000 to 50,000 and its people at 80,000 to 200,000. The "empire," or confederacy of communities called *altepetls* by the Indians, dominated by the Aztec capital was more populous than Spain, which impressed foreign visitors of the sixteenth century with its emptiness. Territories subject to the Aztecs stretched from the Gulf of Mexico to the Pacific Ocean comprising most of the high central plateau and extending far to the south past the Isthmus of Tehuantepec into present-day Guatemala. Asked by Cortés if he was subject to Montezuma, a local ruler responded, "Who was not a vassal of Montezuma?"[4]

Tenochtitlán had in 1473 incorporated another, older, city of the Mexica to its immediate north, Tlatelolco. Both settlements had originated on islands in Lake Texcoco, the largest of the chain of five shallow lakes which stretched from north to south over forty miles filling most of the valley. The combined city was, like Aztec civilization, quite young. Almost everything visible to the Spanish conquerors had been built in the preceding eighty years. A particularly notable technological achievement was the city's nine-mile-long dike which kept the salt water of Lake Texcoco away and gave some help against the flooding of the city and its several causeways, each extending a mile and a half or more across the lake. Also remarkable was the double-tubed aqueduct running over the lake from a spring on the sacred hill of Chapultepec. These works were constructed entirely by the power of human beings without the aid of metal cutting tools, the use of wheeled vehicles, or of horses or other large animals for pulling or carrying.

The two sections of the city, Tenochtitlán proper and Tlatelolco, had grown together, and had greatly extended themselves in other directions from their original islands by the digging of canals in the shallow, swampy lake bed and using the soil dug up to create between them new plots, really little islands of land, called chinampas. Streets and canals alternated in much of the city and building complexes often had entrances toward both a street and a canal. On some of the main thoroughfares walkers could converse with canoeists paddling flowers or produce in from the towns and cities on the edges of the lake. The three principal avenues of the Tenochtitlán section marked cardinal directions, leading from causeways on the south, west, and north sides of the city toward the gates of the centrally placed walled temple precinct. A fourth avenue ran directly from the lake shore to the east wall of the precinct. The wooden drawbridges over the canals and over water gaps in the causeways impressed the Spaniards with their size and strength. The city's design was shaped by its role as religious center, embodying myths which sustained Aztec society, and reflecting its inheritance from earlier Meso-American cultures.

Montezuma is known to have been a regular religious visitor to the remains of Teotihuacán, the largest of pre-Columbian sites, twenty miles northeast of the island capital. Although Teotihuacán had been abandoned for eight hundred years, its influence on Aztec architecture and city planning was powerful. Tenochtitlán imitated its great predecessor in taking its orientation from the bearings of its most important temple pyramid. The orientation of that pyramid reflected the rising of the sun during the spring equinox over the sacred mountain of Tláloc beyond the eastern shore of the lake. As a result the principal north and south avenues and the city as a whole were ordered on an axis slightly more than 7° east of north. For approximately half a mile from the temple precinct the streets were arranged precisely at right angles and at roughly 720-foot intervals.

The great pyramid constituted the center of the Aztec world. Rebuilt and amplified at least seven times, it was located above the place which marked Tenochtitlán as the divinely sanctioned home of the Aztec people, where a vision appeared of an eagle resting on top of a cactus and grasping a serpent, or in some versions a bird, in its beak. Beneath the cactus were rocks, caves, and springs and from them arose the ancient god of nature, Tláloc, to welcome the tribal deity of the Aztecs, Huizilopochtli, as his son. The pyramid supported twin temple shrines dedicated to the duality of these principal deities and in its own form represented both the legendary serpent hill, birthplace of Huizilopochtli and site of his slaughter as a newborn infant of his sister and virtually all of his four hundred brothers, and the rain-filled mountain of Tláloc, emblematic of the nurturing and destructive forces of nature. Huizilopochtli, whose emblem was the eagle, was god of warfare and tribute, and of the sky and the sun. Tláloc, associated with the jaguar, fierce prowler of the rain forest, was god of the earth, of sustaining water and vegetation, and of mountains, caves, and the underworld.

The Tenochtitlán section of the city was divided into four large districts by the four principal avenues leading out from the temple precinct. Each of these districts, Moyatlán, Teopán, Aztqualco, and Cuepopán had a temple and a market and was subdivided into four areas or barrios in which particular groups, called calpulli in Spanish, lived. These groups had a corporate and religious life centered in a temple and an associated school. The groups sometimes shared a common trade or ethnic or provincial origin.

The city consisted primarily of complexes of single-room buildings arranged around patios, each structure providing living accommodations for a single family unit of an extended family group. Some families had "roof houses" providing additional living space in a second story, reached by ladder or external stair. For those accustomed to the cramped, walled cities of late medieval Europe, Tenochtitlán seemed spacious. Except for the temple pyramids it was horizontal rather than vertical, and seemingly capable of continued expansion over the broad lake in all directions.

Next to the general layout of the city, the Spanish visitors of 1519 were most impressed by the many markets, the various buildings of Montezuma, and the splendid and shocking structures of the temple precincts. Tlatelolco was a community dominated by merchants, and its market was the greatest in the country. Cortés described it in a letter to his sovereign, Charles V, as being attended by 60,000 people daily, both from the city and the countryside. Colonnades surrounded the huge plaza on which it centered, twice as large as that of Salamanca, according to Cortés. The order of the vast market area was striking. Particular portions of the plaza and of neighboring streets were devoted to particular types of merchandise. A street specialized in herbs and medicines. Another was devoted to game where the Aztecs sold rabbits, deer, young ducks, turkeys, snakes without tails or heads, and small, barkless dogs which had been castrated and fattened for eating. Chocolate beans were greatly prized and were used as a substitute for money. A section of the market was filled with slaves for sale, some fastened to long poles by collars at the neck and others allowed to stand at ease. Cortés was amazed at the infinite variety of earthenware pots and vases, most of them glazed and painted. He noted the availability in the island market of bulky building materials, lumber, adobe, and stone, both rough and finished in various ways. Boards, beams, cradles, blocks, and benches of wood were all for sale in a particular quarter. The varieties of textiles ranging from those of rough maguey cactus and palm fibers to finely spun cotton were impressive. Cortés described the cotton mart as similar to but larger than the silk markets of Granada.

Aztec craftsmanship attracted the admiration of the Spaniards. Of particular fascination were precious objects which combined in the casting both silver and gold. Parrots cast to move their tongues, heads, and wings, and monkeys capable of moving their feet and heads and holding distaffs so naturally that they appeared to be spinning impressed the Spaniards as reflecting a skill beyond that of European smiths. Indian craftsmen in media unknown in Europe were similarly impressive, the stone smiths splitting and slowly transforming stones into knives, the featherworkers patiently placing, adjusting, removing, and replacing their varicolored feathers as the viewed them from one side and then the other, in sun and in shade and in half light until the match was perfect. Sometimes the featherworkers were so intent on creating a fully lifelike feather butterfly, or coyote, or flower that they would put off eating all day.

The market was governed by ten or twelve persons sitting as judges in a prominent structure in the plaza, rendering decisions upon disputes arising between buyers and sellers. There were also officials who constantly moved about the market area observing the sales and the measures used in selling. Fraudulent measures were broken.

Montezuma's many buildings inside and outside the city had a diversity which Cortés assured Charles had no parallel in Spain. Among the more notable were the pleasure palaces and gardens set among the great trees on the slopes of Chapultepec, a sacred site occupied by the Aztecs when they first entered the valley from the north. Of particular excitement to the Spaniards was a building housing human freaks and wild animals. In the upper rooms were albinos, dwarfs, and grotesquely crippled people and below were cages for snakes and for jaguars, mountain lions, and other formidable cats. The patio and adjoining areas contained birds of prey, eagles, hawks, and many varieties of falcon. Human oddities were familiar features of European courts, but zoological collections were extremely rare and unknown to the Spaniards. They praised a residence in the city having galleries supported by pillars of jasper and a spacious garden with overhanging arbors containing ten ponds, some of salt water for sea birds, others of fresh water for lake birds.

The principal palace, or *tecpan*, was located near the center of Tenochtitlán, just southeast of the temple precinct. Covering roughly six acres, it exceeded the size of any palace known to the Europeans. The lower story of the *tecpan* was devoted primarily to governmental activities. Particular halls were used by Montezuma's war council and by his special council. Courts met in other chambers. Officials from the barrios met every day in special rooms to receive their orders from the ruler. Above the first story were broad terraces and spacious living quarters for Montezuma, his hundreds of women, their servants and slaves.

The vast *tecpan*, which had twenty doors opening on the plaza and the adjoining streets, was organized around three interior patios. There were many large halls supported by wooden columns and approximately a hundred rooms measuring about twenty-five by thirty feet. The baths equaled the rooms in number. The ceilings were supported by huge cypress beams carved to suggest different types of trees. The Spaniards were impressed by the solidity of the system of construction which made no use of nails. They admired the Aztecs' use in their stone walls of a wide variety of materials, light stone, translucent stone (tecali), stones which suggested to European eyes jasper, marble, and porphyry, and a black stone shot with veins of ruby. The stuccoed adobe walls of the chambers were painted and decorated with mirrors of burnished stone and with hangings of cotton, rabbit fur, and the marvelous featherwork. The floors of polished wood were covered with straw mats and rugs of jaguar skins. Only the beds disappointed the Spaniards, consisting only of blankets laid over mats or loose straw.

The most spectacular architecture of Tenochtitlán, Tlatelolco, and the other cities of the Aztec tributary provinces was that contained in the temple precincts. This was an architecture of exterior shapes and surfaces, brightly colored, simple, and grand. It was organized to provide splendid theatrical settings for open-air ritual performances and for varied types of animal and human sacrifices. Ceremonies took place regularly at the end of each of the twenty-day Aztec months and at other periodic times of festival throughout the year. Great festivals of renewal, the New Fire Ceremonies, were celebrated at the end of the fifty-two-year cycles of the Aztec calendar. Many of the rituals were staged at night, with flaring torches and fires illuminating the darkness, or at dawn as the sky brightened to the east behind the great pyramid. Great drums, conch shells, and horns provided unearthly music. Costuming was magnificent, the victims frequently dancing and often arrayed as gods. Great plumes of feathers decorated their heads, and their bodies were clad in beautifully woven and ornamented cottons decorated with gold.

The temple precinct of Tenochtitlán was approximately 433 yards square and was separated from the city by a wall eight feet high ornamented at the top by serpent heads. Three double colonnaded gates opened to the avenues leading south, west, and north, and a fourth may have opened to the avenue leading east. Bernal Díaz recalled the paving of smooth white flagstones, and the whiteness, cleanliness, and polish of the whole. "There was not a straw or grain of dust to be found anywhere."[5] The enclosure contained living quarters for the priests, a school for the children of Aztec aristocrats, a court for the quasi-sacred American ball game, and a number of diverse religious structures. The whole was dominated by the huge teocalli, a stepped pyramid, which supported the shrines of the rain god, Tláloc, and the Aztec tribal deity, Huizilopochtli. At its base, decorated with an alternating hedge of snakes and serpent heads, the pyramid measured approximately 110 yards from north to south and 88 from east to west. Tall, twin stairways of 113 or 114 steps led up the west face of the pyramid to the broad terrace on which were placed the twin temples. Montezuma invited Cortés and other Spaniards to visit these shrines and to enjoy the view which the height of approximately one hundred feet provided. They exulted in the magnificent prospect of the city, the lake, and its causeways, and the sparkling cities of the shore and the great mountains beyond.

The shrines were less to their liking. The exteriors were dramatic. Both were surmounted by tall crested roofs carrying elaborate stucco ornamentation. A waving wreath of shells decorated the shrine to the north, which was colored watery blue and white for Tláloc. The larger shrine to the south dedicated to Huizilopochtli was painted red and decorated ominously with carved skulls which were painted white. This shrine was topped with a crest of butterflies, emblematic of the god and suggestive of the sun and fire.

The interiors were dark, confining, with elaborate carvings of monsters and other frightening and ugly figures. Each shrine contained a huge statue, or "idol," larger than human size, which Cortés could bring himself to praise as having "marvelous grandeur." Bernal Díaz gives us an extensive description.

They said that the one on the right was Huichilobos, their war god. He had a very broad face and terrible eyes. And there were so many precious stones, so much gold . . . stuck to him with paste . . . that his whole body and head were covered with them. He was girdled with huge snakes made of gold and precious stones, and in one hand held a bow, in the other some arrows. . . . Around Huichilobos' neck hung some Indian faces and . . . objects in the shape of hearts, the former made of gold and the latter of silver, with many precious blue stones.[6]

This image and the almost equally powerful one of Tláloc, "surrounded by little devils with snakes' tails,"[7] have been lost. But two statues survive traditionally associated with Huizilopochtli's mother, Coatlicue, but possibly representing Cihuacóatl, a monstrous goddess associated with caves and the underworld and embodying the terrifying, destructive aspect of Tláloc. The better preserved of these was unearthed in 1790 and rapidly reburied in horror and fear of its skirt of writhing snakes, its staring skulls, and its grim double head of great fanged serpents; it can provide us a partial sense of the shock given sixteenth-century Spanish Christians by these religious figures.

Close to the shrines were braziers cooking the hearts of three human victims whose organs had been jerked beating from their slashed rib cages earlier that day. The shrines themselves strongly smelled of the nauseating stench of human blood thickly splashed and caked on the walls and the floors. To the Aztecs the human blood represented sacred sacrifice essential to sustaining the cosmos and the social order. Sacrificial blood helped maintain the divine movement of the sun across the heavens and helped sustain the fundamental dualities of sky and earth represented by the twin shrines of the pyramid, sun, and maize-bearing soil, day and night, and the seasons of dryness and of rain. Additionally, in the Aztec view, divine sacrifice reinforced the tribal myths helping maintain an ordered society and the supremacy of Tenochtitlán in the Meso-American world. To the Spaniards the blood and the ritual cannibalism which followed the sacrifices were horrifying. The ascetic Aztec priests, clad in black, with huge, deformed, self-mutilated ear lobes and hair caked in tangles of dried blood, were regarded quite literally as agents of Satan. The Spaniards called the Aztec temples "mosques," which reflected the centuries-long crusade of Christians against Moslems in Spain, in an effort to relate the unknown to the known, attempting to assimilate to their human understanding a pagan religion centered on mass human sacrifice and cannibalism which seemed to them beyond the limits of what is human.

Despite the prudent advice of his chaplain, Fray Bartolomé de Olmedo, Cortés, characteristically, attempted while standing before the most sacred shrine in Mexico to persuade Montezuma to renounce his religion. Later after he captured Montezuma Cortés forbade human sacrifice. According to the conquistador Andrés de Tapia, and an account descending from another conquistador Alonso de Ojeda, Cortés attacked the statue of Huizilopochtli, leaping with an iron bar high enough to pry off its golden mask. Subsequently he had the great idols removed, the shrines washed of blood, and images of the Virgin and St. Christopher, or, possibly of the crucifixion, placed where the idols had been. This dramatic appropriation of the Aztec holy place for Christian worship was, Cortés wrote to Charles V, acceded to by Montezuma and other leading Aztecs after he told them of the one God, creator of all things. Cortés probably misinterpreted their feelings. His compulsive acts of Christian evangelism may have weakened the psychological control he exerted on Montezuma and initiated the series of disasters which led to the forced retreat from the city.

Much as the Spaniards feared and detested the rituals performed on the teocallis, they could not resist admiring their size and splendor. Later, after the capture of the city, Cortés was tempted to preserve an example or two as memorials to Aztec achievements. In the end he was unable to suppress his fear that preservation might foster the persistence of blind and bloody superstitions. Motolinía, the Franciscan missionary, wished to preserve their memory after their destruction. Writing in 1535, he described them at length so that Spanish immigrants of the future would know of them, "for memory of them is almost dying out."[8] He described the great pyramid in Mexico City as much higher than the new church of the Franciscans, the first vaulted structure in the country. In retrospect he recalled the look of the countryside in the middle 1520s. The devil, he wrote, was not content with the teocallis in the major cities.

> In every town and in each of its outlying districts, nearly a mile out, they had other small courtyards with three or four temples. . . . On every little hill or ridge there would be one or two and along the roads and in the cornfields many other little ones [,] . . . all whitewashed, so that they showed up clearly and looked very large, it seemed as if all places were full of houses [of the devil].[9]

Tenochtitlán and Tlatelolco were wholly destroyed by the Spaniards and their enormous contingents of Indian allies who were eager to cast off Aztec dominance. The initial six months' visit in the capital ended in the disastrous retreat of the *noche triste*, June 30, 1520. But Cortés regrouped his forces and allies, now possibly numbering as many as 200,000, subdued cities in the backcountry and around the lake, and began the final siege the following May by stopping the flow of water through the aqueduct. During the next three months, the allied forces used brigantines, constructed in pieces in Tlaxcala, carried over the mountains by Indian bearers and assembled on the shore, to seize control of the lake. They advanced over the causeways and systematically leveled the buildings of the city in order to prevent their use in defensive fighting and to secure material to fill the canals so that the terrifying horses could be ridden with maximum effectiveness against the Indians on foot.

Cortés wrote to Charles of his reluctant decision to destroy the city which he described as the most beautiful thing in the world. Always concerned with the thoughts and feelings of his opponents, Cortés hoped to discourage Aztec resistance through destructiveness. "In order to make them feel it the more," he later wrote, "I commanded my men to set fire on those big houses in the plaza, where the Spaniards and I had previously been quartered." "Although it distressed me, I determined to burn them, for it distressed the enemy very much more."[10] The total destruction of the city was not effective in breaking the Aztec spirit of resistance. The defenders encouraged themselves by jeering, prophetically, at the Spaniards' Indian allies telling them to go on burning and destroying because they'd have to rebuild the city regardless of which side was victorious in the struggle. The Aztecs surrendered amidst the piled corpses of their friends and families only after the Spaniards captured their young ruler Cuauhtemoc, Montezuma's second successor, and had destroyed the whole city except for a small area of chinampas on the eastern lake fringe of Tlatelolco.

The surrender took place on the day of San Hipólito, August 13, 1521. The Spaniards then retired to the lakeside city of Coyoacán and ordered Cuautemoc to have the surviving Aztecs clear away the dead, repair the pipes of the aqueduct, and restore all the bridges and causeways. At about the beginning of the new year, and after some months of hesitation because of the swampiness of the site and its distance from essential supplies of food and other necessities, Cortés decided to restore the Aztec capital. He wrote to his sovereign, Charles, from Coyoacán on May 15, 1522, that it had seemed best to rebuild the city "for the peace and security of all these parts."[11]

The restoration of Tenochtitlán-Mexico was both symbolic and practical. The imposing capital of the Mexica-Aztecs would be rebuilt to function as a new capital for the Spaniards because it "had once been so renowned and of such importance. . . . the capital and center of all these provinces." And, declared Cortés "so it shall be henceforth."[12]

Cortés used Indian labor for the reconstruction, creating the pattern for subsequent architectural activity throughout the country. He freed the second-ranking Aztec official, the *cihuacóatl*, put him in charge of Indians and construction, and appointed him leader of one of the four sectors of the city. He gave another sector to Don Pedro Montezuma, son of the dead ruler. Christian churches were constructed on the sites of the pagan pyramids at the center of each of these peripheral areas, which became Indian barrios. Extending his effort to obtain Mexican goodwill, Cortés made Aztec nobles the lords of streets and islands of the city, giving them authority but not as much as they had before lest they become dangerous to his rule. The central portion of the city

was reserved for Europeans, but Tlatelolco, like the outlying areas of Tenochtitlán, was assigned to Indians. Immense numbers were attracted by the liberties and immunities granted in the city, so many, writes Francisco López de Gómara, secretary and historian of Cortés, that there was scarcely room for them to stand for two or three miles around. The ruler of Texcoco led his people in the work, carrying his building materials in a jaguar skin. Other laborers came from towns obliged to furnish labor to Spaniards in the system of encomienda. Father Motolinía likened the rebuilding of the city to one of the plagues visited by God upon Egypt.

> So many were the people engaged in the work that a man could scarcely make his way along some streets . . . , broad as they are. In the construction some were crushed by beams, others fell from heights, others were caught beneath buildings which were being torn down in one place to be built up again in another. . . . The Indians do the work, get the materials at their own expense [often from the now discarded temple pyramids], pay the stonemasons and the carpenters, and if they do not bring their own food they go hungry. They carry all the material on their backs and drag the beams and big stones with ropes, and as they have no machinery and plenty of people, they used four hundred men to transport a stone that required one hundred. It is their custom to sing and shout as they work, so great was the zeal, which, in the early days they brought to the building of the town.[13]

The skill of the Indian masons was admired by Europeans who wondered at their carefully shaped walls, the beauty of which was not in the ornamentation but in the fine construction. The stones were laid so closely that it was difficult to detect the seam between one stone and another. Some of the old canals were reopened and others were newly cut through dry ground to recreate the Aztec alternation of streets and canals. Some canals were as large as fifteen feet wide and six feet deep. Canoes continued to bring to the city fresh produce, corn, hay for animal fodder, wood, and lime and stone for construction. Some of the canals would remain in use well through the eighteenth century. The major avenues and the rectilinear plan were preserved. In late 1523 or early 1524 Alonso Garcia Bravo, a stone mason and "a very good geometer"[14] who had created a fortified settlement near the port at Vera Cruz, was asked to plan the Spanish section at the center of demolished Tenochtitlán. Taking as his basis the four major avenues of the Aztec city, he traced a grid of seven streets in both directions, plazas, and building lots. Some newly built European towns of the late Middle Ages had ordered gridironlike plans, and the Italian theorists of the Renaissance founded their ideal cities on Vitruvian models. Nevertheless the rebuilt city of Mexico with its great size, its broad straight streets, its orderly low houses set on blocks 600 to 700 feet long and 300 to 400 feet wide, dazzled European visitors. Among them were Robert Tomson, an Englishman, in 1555, the future founder of French Canada, Samuel de Champlain in 1599, the Neapolitan world traveler Giovanni Francesco Gemelli Carreri in 1697, and the Prussian scientist Alexander von Humboldt in 1803.

Apart from its rectilinear plan, three elements of the old city were retained in modified form: the market plaza of Tlatelolco, a street of large houses leading west to the west causeway, and an ensemble of structures surrounding the central plaza of Tenochtitlán. That huge square, today's Zócalo, measured roughly 750 by 1,000 feet and incorporated a market plaza and a portion of the former temple precinct. Both the great Aztec palaces, which had faced each other across the plaza were marked for reconstruction by Cortés. He appointed a Spanish mason, Martín de Sepúlveda, master of works. His Indians from Coyoacán, claimed in encomienda, provided the labor and secured the materials. Four hundred worked for two days to carry the stone for a staircase. One hundred and ten worked daily throughout 1532, living in a separate compound, arriving by noon on Monday and leaving after noon on Saturday.

The scale of construction was immense, in accord with the memory of the demolished *tecpans* and with the ambitions of Cortés for the city and country he had conquered and was refounding. An appraisal of 1531 mentions nearly seventy thousand square yards of walls of *tezontle*, a volcanic stone. Both buildings were planned from the start for combined administrative and residential use. The first completed structure was on the site of the *tecpan* of Montezuma's father, Axayácatl, which had been the residence of the Spaniards in 1519. This building, which later became the city home of Cortés's descendants, was occupied by the conqueror in the periods he was in the city between 1523 and 1528 when he left for Spain. In addition to residential apartments it contained an audience chamber, an arsenal, two kitchens, many workshops, and shops for merchants along the street.

Much of the structure had two stories. The exterior walls of *tezontle* had castlelike towers at the corners. Following both Aztec and Andalusian precedents, there were interior courtyards. These were surrounded by covered walks with roofs supported by either colonnades or arcades of brick and stone depending upon their importance. Windows were an innovation in Mexico and though a surviving sketch portrays only a few, we know that five carpenters were steadily employed making window and door frames. Six thousand nine hundred and six giant beams were cut from the great stands of cedar then covering hillsides throughout the Valley of Mexico, apparently to support the ceilings of this palace alone.

The palace opposite, on the site of the *tecpan* of Montezuma, was begun later and built in stages. In its original L-shape it was not ready for occupancy until 1531. Later it grew to surround three large patios as had Montezuma's structure. The grand entrance on the plaza was not completed until 1551. Cortés's son Martín sold the building to the Spanish crown in 1562 for a palace for the viceroys. Subsequently a rioters' fire destroyed much of the structure. The present National Palace extending the full eighth of a mile length of the east side of the Zócalo, is its direct descendant.

Apart from the towered palaces of Cortés and the first Cathedral of Mexico, which would be placed in the plaza, the most striking features of the area were shops of the merchants set in the ground story of the great houses and in colonnaded porticoes (portales). From its beginning the new Mexico City continued the tradition of Tenochtitlán by being a city of commerce as well as a city of government and of religion. Three great markets were held weekly, that of San Hipólito on Monday, that of Santiago on Thursday, and that of San Juan on Saturday.

A particular concern in the early years was security. A reason for the choice of the island site of the city, subordinate only to the wish to retain the prestige of Tenochtitlán, was its defensibility against the millions of potentially rebellious Indians. In addition, Cortés seems to have believed that the island situation would make more easy his personal control of the unruly Spaniards. Tenochtitlán had had no fortified walls and only the one fortified gate on the south causeway. The Aztecs bore no arms in the capital. By the end of the sixteenth century, Mexico City would amaze European visitors by its lack of fortifications, but in its early years its appearance reflected the uneasiness of a small group of Spanish conquerors amidst an overwhelmingly numerous and potentially threatening native population.

A wall of houses, a *casa muro*, was begun, extending along the avenue toward the west causeway, to provide protection should another retreat like that of the *noche triste* be necessary. In addition, there may have been an initiation of a wall of houses around the periphery of the Spanish section, or *traza*, to provide protection like a circle of wagons on the nineteenth-century North American prairie. The houses of Cortés and of at least nine other Spaniards were provided with fortified towers. Cortés's older house also had battlemented walls with two openings for the firing of artillery pieces. The nearby house of Pedro Alvarado—larger perhaps even than his leader's and containing loopholes for archers—was placed so as to cover the approach to Cortés's structure.

In his letter to Charles of October 15, 1524, Cortés proudly described the fortified dock and hangar, or *Ataranza*, which he built on the eastern shore of the city to protect the brigantines in order to secure his control of the lake and also "the whole city should the need arise. . . . I have seen none to equal it," he wrote, "the part which lies toward the lake has two very strong towers with embrasures where necessary. Both these towers jut out beyond the curtain wall and are connected to it by a wall also with embrasures. Extending back from these two towers is a building of three naves where the brigantines are kept, with gates between the towers, opening onto the lake. . . . At the end facing the city is another very large tower with many rooms up and down for defending or attacking the city."[15] The completion of the *Ataranza* preceded the occupation of the city by the Spaniards. Once it was finished, Cortés wrote, everything seemed "secure enough to . . . settle inside the city so I moved in with all my people, and the building sites were distributed among the settlers." With characteristic hyperbole Cortés assured his "Sacred Majesty" that "within five years this will be the most nobly populated city which exists in all the civilized world, and will have the finest buildings."[16]

The *Ataranza* and the other fortified structures of Mexico were never needed for battle. They did function to symbolize Spanish strength. In a few years they were dismantled. After the Mixton war against Indians to the northwest in the 1640s, there were no serious interruptions of the peace and general stability of the central area of New Spain. Not until the tumultuous times of the revolutionary struggles of the nineteenth and early twentieth centuries would wars and conquering armies again come to the foreground of Mexican concern.

II
FRIARS AND INDIANS:
THE ARCHITECTURE OF EVANGELISM

An event critical in the shaping of the new Spanish Mexico was the arrival of twelve Franciscan friars in mid-June 1524. The famous twelve were not the first priests or even the first or most eminent Franciscans to reach New Spain. Their being sent out from the mother country and their reception by Cortés, however, ensured the vigorous initiation of a great campaign to bring Christian salvation to the Mexicans. It also led directly to the construction of approximately four hundred friaries and friary towns by the end of the century. The twelve missionaries, road weary from their over 200-mile barefoot trek over the mountains, were met by a delegation from the city. Cortés leapt from his horse, knelt before them, and attempted to kiss their hands or, at least, their habits. Cuautemoc and the other Aztec leaders who had accompanied the Spaniards were shocked at the sight of the regal conqueror on his knees kissing the dusty robes of the jaundiced-looking, barefoot friars. One of the twelve, Fray Toribio de Benavente, the historian of the first years of Mexican evangelism, adopted as his name, Motolinía, a Nahuatl word for poor he heard the Aztecs using to express their impression of the Franciscans. In adopting the word, designating himself as the poor man, Fray Toribio was emulating his spiritual father, St. Francis, a nobleman who had delighted in being called *il poverello*, the poor one.

Francisco López de Gómara wrote the earliest description of Cortés's reception of the twelve from information probably provided by the conqueror himself. He stressed Cortés's humble devoutness and his determination to provide a dramatic and lastingly influential example for the Indians. It is likely that Cortés—who asked both Charles V and the general of the Franciscans, Fray Francisco de los Angeles, to send friars to Mexico—was also concerned to favorably impress the powerful order, influential in Spain and destined to be of great importance in America. His relations with the Franciscans remained close throughout his life. A later sixteenth-century Franciscan historian of Mexican evangelism, Fray Gerónimo de Mendieta, would portray him as a providential hero, a new Moses who led the Indians from idolatry as the original had led the Jews from Egyptian captivity.

Three prominent Franciscans from Flanders had been sent to Mexico by Charles V, himself, nine months before the Twelve: Juan de Aora (Jehan der Auwera), rumored to be of Scottish royal blood; Juan de Tecto (Johan Dekkers or de Toict), formerly prior of the friary in Ghent and professor of theology in the Sorbonne; and a lay brother, Pedro de Gante (Peeter van der Moere or Petrus de Mura), a Flemish nobleman believed by some to have been a close relative of the Emperor. The three set out to master Nahuatl, the language of much of the central plateau. Juan de Tecto began a catechism, later completed by Pedro de Gante, which was written in Spanish phonetic approximations of Nahuatl sounds. The Franciscans subsequently extended the use of Nahuatl to Indians to the north and south of central Mexico to foster conversion. Juan de Tecto and Juan de Aora drowned in 1526 while returning from Cortés's disastrous expedition to Honduras. Pedro de Gante lived until 1572 devoting almost half a century to teaching and ministering to the Indians.

The Spanish Franciscans, near contemporaries of the great sixteenth-century saints, Ignatius Loyola, Teresa of Avila, and John of the Cross, were members of the Observant branch of the order, Friars minor of the Observance, which was shaped by the recent reforms of Cardinal Cisneros and attempted to follow strictly the example of St. Francis in subsisting wholly on charity. Many were influenced by the recently printed writings of the twelfth-century apocalyptic theologian, Joachim of Floris, who had predicted a third, ultimate, spiritual age when the whole world would be freed from imperfection and a purified church would be created, led by true men of the spirit (monks or friars). The Franciscan followers of Joachim, and Christopher Columbus himself, were convinced that the last spiritual age described by Joachim had been initiated by God's providential disclosure of the New World with its pagan millions awaiting conversion. Columbus, who identified the American Indians with the pagan multitudes of Asia, saw his voyages as opening an ocean bridge for missionaries to hurry to the conversion of the last Gentiles. Many Franciscans believed that Spain had been assigned a particular providential role. The Catholic kings, Ferdinand and Isabel, had completed the Christian reconquest of Spain and had converted many Spanish Moslems and Jews. Their descendants were to complete God's plan and prepare for the end of the world by converting the Gentile Indians, whom some identified with the lost tribes of Israel. The belief in the impending end added particular urgency to the work of conversion.

Apocalyptic thinking was not the only belated medieval strain in the age of discovery. Spanish civilians in their obsession for gold seemed deranged to the Indians, but Spanish Franciscans were comparably driven to reach and maintain an ideal poverty. They avoided horses, ate coarse food, dressed in garments of the cheapest blue dye or rewoven from threads salvaged from used habits. They delighted in the Indians' lack of interest in material things, regarded them as wonderfully appropriate converts to a church of sanctified poverty. Their Indian church attempted, like the churches of their contemporaries, the earliest Protestants, to emulate the simplicity of the primitive church of Christ. To them the Indians seemed puppylike in their innocence, pitifully in need of Franciscan protection from ravenous lions, the Spanish conquistadors. The friars dreamed of a millennial kingdom in the New World removed from avaricious Spanish laymen, an Indian commonwealth fostered by paternal friars, a golden age characterized by innocence and poverty.

Early sixteenth-century Spanish idealism was nourished by contemporary writers as well as by medieval theologians. The Dutch humanist, Erasmus, was widely influential in the Spanish court and church. The *Utopia*, written in Latin by his English friend St. Thomas More, had a remarkable influence in Mexico. Vasco de Quiroga, judge of the supreme administrative court, the Audiencia, and later Bishop of Michoacán, founded two hospitals on the Utopian model of Christian socialism.

The Franciscans were soon joined by members of two other orders of mendicant friars. Of twelve Dominicans who arrived in the summer of 1526, only one or two priests and one lay brother remained alive in Mexico at the end of that year. Seven others joined them in 1528. Seven Augustinians followed in the late spring of 1533. The numbers of all three orders were augmented slowly; by 1536 there were only about sixty friars in New Spain. In 1559 after the completion of the major work of the conversion and well into the massive campaign of building friaries and churches, the Franciscans had 80 houses and 380 religious personnel, and the other two orders each had just half as many houses and just over 200 religious personnel.

The few converted the multitude. Fray Martín de Valencia, leader of the Twelve, asserted that each had baptized over 100,000 Indians. On one day 15,000 Aztecs were reported to have been baptized by two friars who would have gone on to baptize more had they not become so tired that they were no longer able to lift their arms. Pedro de Gante claimed to have converted 6,000 through a single sermon and to have persuaded all the men to renounce their extra wives that morning so that Christian marriages could be performed in the afternoon.

Gerónimo de Mendieta described a ceremony combining baptism and marriage performed in a morning for 3,000.

> The Indian men were lined up in rows, each paired with his woman. . . . A priest administered oil . . . and then without getting out of order, they marched with lighted candles up to the font where another priest baptized them. . . . Once baptized they went out in the order in which they had come in, following the cross carried by the other religious singing litanies with the Indian singers of the church . . . and then the priest who had given them oil began to give them chism. The priest who had just baptized them . . . took their hands and administered the Sacrament of Marriage.[1]

The priests then said mass for the newly baptized and married.

Such mass administration of the sacraments entailed skipping careful preparation and full doctrinal instruction. It allowed the few priests to make wonderful speed in conversion. Friars' estimates, probably overly generous, placed total conversions at 1,500,000 by 1531, 6,000,000 by 1541, and 9,000,000 by 1543.

The friars followed the conquistadors in the rapid enlarging of the territories subject to the Aztecs. The powerful Tarascan kingdom to the west, which had resisted Aztec domination, submitted peacefully but was invaded by Cristóbal de Olid and despoiled by Nuño de Guzmán. The Franciscans followed, quickly attempting to provide some compensation for Guzmán's atrocities. They were ready to organize the area as a separate

subprovince for their order as early as 1535, three years before Vasco de Quiroga was appointed bishop. In 1529, the leading Dominican, Fray Domingo de Betanzos was invited to Guatemala by the ferocious conquistador Pedro de Alvarado. Fray Domingo walked 1,000 miles through broken country from Mexico City with a single companion believing that a friar should not ride a horse. By the late 1530s, the friars entered the mountainous and semidesert areas populated by nomadic hunters, to the north, and northwest as far as the Pacific. Christianization of Maya Yucatán was under way by midcentury. Evangelization of the Pueblo Indians of New Mexico began in 1581.

The friaries, or conventos, constructed in Mexico by the three mendicant orders provided for the communal worship of the friars but, unlike traditional European monasteries, were not designed for contemplative withdrawal from the world. Except for major centers such as Mexico City and Puebla, the conventos normally housed no more than four or five friars. These small groups were responsible for the evangelical activities of the convento and for a series of half a dozen, or in some cases as many as thirty, *visitas*, small churches or chapels established in the villages surrounding the town in which the convento was located. Each *visita* was visited regularly by an itinerant friar—a barefoot precursor of the Methodist circuit rider.

Like other activities of the Spaniards, the conversion, the creation of Indian parishes, and the construction of churches and other friary buildings was heavily dependent upon Indian cooperation and upon the structure of preexisting Indian society. The Christian God of the conquerors was readily accepted in most communities as worthy of worship. His prowess had been demonstrated in the conquest. The first efforts of the friars were concentrated on the leaders of Indian society, on the local rulers, the *tlatoque*, whom the Spaniards called *caciques*, using a Caribbean Indian term, and especially their sons. The work of evangelization was physically arduous. Fray Gerónimo de Mendieta contrasted clerical duties in Spain, where after a sermon priests felt in such a sweat that they'd change their clothes, with those in Mexico. Every day in America a single friar

> would count the people in the morning, then preach and sing Mass, and after that baptize both children and adults, confess the sick no matter how many, and then bury any dead there might be. . . . There were some (and I knew them) who preached three sermons in different languages one after the other, and then sang Mass, and did everything else that had to be done, all before having anything to eat.[2]

The first friaries were established in Mexico City and in major Indian cities such as Tlaxcala, Texcoco, Cholula, and Cuernavaca. The important community of Huejotzingo was relocated by the Franciscans. Normally conventos were established at the centers of substantial Indian communities. They were often placed on the site of the principal temple and close to the dwelling of the ruler and the market. The centers were called *cabeceras*, head towns, by the Spaniards, and the outlying villages, where the friars had *visita* churches or chapels built, were called *sujetos*. But European-type hierarchical organization was alien to Indian thinking and no hierarchical distinctions were made between those who lived near the center of the community and those who lived on the outskirts. All the constituent groups, the *calpulli*, were regarded as virtually equal components of the whole. In areas where there was no substantial center, the friars frequently induced the people to live together in a new Indian town. Indian farmers, who frequently lived beside their remote corn patches, widely scattered on the mountain slopes, were "congregated" in Christian communities. Residents of a particular area, members of a particular *calpulli*, might be located in their own barrio within a newly formed town.

As the first Mexican church council of 1555 declared, evangelism would be more easy and effective if the Indians were brought together so that "they can be given the Holy Sacraments and be instructed in matters necessary for Salvation, and be succored in their sicknesses and be helped, when the time comes, to die in a proper Christian manner." Sixteenth-century Spaniards were town and city dwellers who believed that civilized human conduct was fostered by urban living and that godly behavior was apt to follow urbane human behavior. Forced collections of Indians from their wild mountains into orderly towns made them "worthy to be called men" and prepared them for the message of salvation. An unforeseen result of the resettlement was to make the indigenous people even more vulnerable to the spread of the killing diseases carried to America by the Europeans.

As James Lockhart has explained, in all the Indian communities, whether congregated or not, the friars used and adapted their activities to the traditional Indian communal structures. The ordinary people, *macehales*, remained subject to their hereditary rulers, the *caciques*, and to the members of the upper classes, *principales*. After the mid-sixteenth century when a Spanish-type political organization was imposed, consisting normally of a governor, two judges or *alcaldes* and a half dozen or more *regidores* who constituted the *cabildo*, or municipal council, responsible for judicial and political administration, the ruler and members of the traditional ruling classes filled these places. Representation of the *calpulli* seems also to have been incorporated into the new pattern of government. Although secular Spaniards were excluded from the Indian communities lest they prove poor examples of Christianity, the friars were dependent upon the cooperation of the non-resident *encomenderos* who had made arrangements with the *caciques* and the *principales* to secure the tribute and draft labor which the community was obligated to supply. In most instances the friars easily gained the support of the encomendero and the Indian leadership. The Christian parish and its church replaced the recently demolished temple as the principal symbol of the community's identity and prestige. The *cacique* and other leaders directed the traditional methods of collecting tribute and drafting labor to answering the needs of the resident friars and the church. They also encouraged the general populace to convert to Christianity and to attend mass and other Christian rites and ceremonies.

With rare exceptions Indians and part-Indians—mestizos—were excluded from the priesthood before the eighteenth century. They were essential, however, to support the work of the friars. Native stewards, who gained substantial prestige within their communities, were essential to the operation of the churches. They managed their assets and directed many of their activities, working in close cooperation with the friars and serving as the principal intermediaries between the Spanish clergy and the people of the communities. *Visita* chapels had to be maintained and operated by stewards between the friars' visits. Indians served as acolytes, readers, sacristans, musicians, porters, gardeners, and cooks. All these activities were prestigious and during the sixteenth century exempted those who performed them from tribute obligations.

Frequently saints' names were added to traditional community names and the Virgin and the patron Christian saints came to fill the roles vacated by the ethnic gods formerly worshipped by the communities and by their constituent *calpulli*. Pagan ritual life was replaced by festivals celebrating the patron saints and the important days of the Christian calendar. Late in the century Christian cofradías, or sodalities, began to develop importance as replacements for the ritual kinship groups of pagan times. They helped assure their dues-paying members of spiritual security in the afterlife and reinforced their communal identity in this one.

Writing for Spaniards in the 1560s, Doctor Vasco de Puga explained that in establishing themselves in a town the friars first laid out a large expanse of gardens and patios before they began the church and friary buildings. In the 1520s and early 1530s rapidly built structures were improvised of wood and adobe, often with thatched roofs. By the 1540s a standard plan for conventos had developed. The permanent structures which survive in such impressive quantity in central Mexico and Yucatán were begun between the early 1540s and the 1560s and, given their size, their numbers, and the conditions of construction, were completed with surprising speed.

The standard plan consisted of three elements: a large forecourt now called an *atrio* but most frequently called a patio in sixteenth-century writings; a substantial church normally running west to east; and a residential structure normally of two stories placed on the south side of the church and organized in rooms opening on

a central cloister. The convento normally was located on the east side of the town plaza and was often placed on a platform as much as ten, and, in at least one instance twenty-five, feet above the level of the streets. The *atrio* was walled and entered through an arcaded gateway on the axis of the church and frequently through one or more side gateways. In form the *atrios* approximated a square. In dimensions they were large, averaging 250 feet to a side. Some ran to 500 or even 600 feet to a side and could hold 40,000 people. Though designed for Christian purposes and traceable to some rare Christian precedents, the *atrio* was recognized by visitors as a striking Mexican phenomenon. There were clear similarities to the walled temple precincts of the Aztecs and to their customary religious rituals which were performed in the open air (Fig. 2.1).

Centrally placed in the *atrio* was a monumental cross. The famous cross of the Franciscan convento in Mexico City, cut from tall cypresses of Montezuma's gardens at Chapultepec, reached nearly 200 feet and was visible over the roofs of the city from the causeways and even from some of the cities along the lakeside. Surviving stone crosses, usually 6 or more feet high, retain something of the plastic power of Aztec sculpture.

At the four corners of many *atrios* were small stone chapels, rectangular in plan and containing an altar which was visible through one or more arched entrances. These chapels were called *posas* from the verb *posar* describing a friar's pausing at the altar as an outdoor religious procession moved around the *atrio*. Father Motolinía has described the enthusiasm of the Indians for the pageantry of the processions organized on the feast days of Christ and the Virgin and of the principal saints of their towns, processions which echoed the religious processions of their pagan past. The churches would be decorated with green branches and flowers. Triumphal arches were constructed of garlands and roses. "The Indian lords and principal men, adorned and dressed in their white tunics and blankets embroidered with feathers, and with bouquets of roses in their hands,"[3] danced and sang in their native tongues appropriate hymns which had been translated by the friars.

An almost universal feature of the *atrio* was an open chapel, open to the view of the Indi-

15

2.1 Plan of ideal atrio in use, from Diego de Valadés, Rhetorica Christiana, *from John McAndrew,* The Open Air Churches of Sixteenth Century Mexico; *photographed from copy in the Peabody Museum, Harvard.*

structurally and stylistically varied, and in some ways the most impressive, architectural creations of sixteenth-century Mexico. The types include simple chapels placed in the arcaded entrances to the convento building; chapels placed in porticos projecting into the *atrio* and normally fronted by an arcade of three to five arches; structurally complex buttressed buildings with varieties of Gothic ribbed vaulting; large and small barrel vaulted chapels with Renaissance ornamentation; and a few extraordinary examples which combined openness to the *atrio* with shelter for large numbers of Indians in many columned structures, which seem based on the friars' memories of the great mosques of Mohammedan Spain.

In addition to their use for feast day processions and religious plays, for Sunday masses and the zestful communal singing which followed, the *atrios* served daily as open air religious schools and as places for varied ministry to the Indians. Fray Diego de Valadés, mestizo son of a conquistador father and an Indian mother, included a picture of an ideal *atrio* in his *Rhetorica Christiana* (Perugia, 1579), the first book published in Europe by a Mexican. The *atrio* bore some relationship to that of San Francisco in Mexico City, where according to Pedro de Gante, five or six hundred were taught daily. Among the activities portrayed are friars teaching girls, boys, women, and men in separate groups in *posas* in the four corners. Fray Pedro de Gante and another friar are shown teaching about the creation of the world and other topics by means of pictures. Other friars are teaching groups how to write and are teaching about Christian doctrine, penance, and marriage. Still other friars are active in baptizing, serving communion, marrying, ministering to the sick, and conducting a funeral. These diverse activities are related by dotted lines to an image of the Holy Spirit of the Christian Trinity and to a symbolic church at the center of the *atrio* carried by twelve Franciscans, preceded by St. Francis and followed by Fray Martín de Valencia, and identified as "the first to bring the Holy Roman Church to the New World of the Indians."

Subsequent to the laying out of the *atrio* and improvising a provisional open chapel and, perhaps, a provisional church, the friars initiated

ans standing, kneeling, and squatting on their heels in the *atrio*, and providing shelter for the Host and those celebrating mass. As Motolinía explained, writing about 1540, the number of people was large and the churches too small to accommodate them. The chapels outside in the atrio were arranged in such a way that all the Indians could attend Mass every Sunday and feast day, and the churches were used for masses during the week. Usually open chapels were erected earlier than the churches or the living quarters of the friars. One was constructed in Puebla on the Tuesday following Easter Sunday of 1531, the day the city was founded. The earliest open chapels frequently were thatched huts. The permanent structures which followed constitute the most the construction of permanent masonry buildings. In the major towns of central Mexico this was the work primarily of the two decades following 1540. Roughly thirty-five major conventos survive in the central area and others remain in Yucatán. Disappointingly little is documented regarding the designing of these buildings. It is clear that the friars had no assistance from trained architects. As late as 1550 Antonio de Mendoza, the first viceroy, in his instructions to his successor lamented many errors in construction which had resulted from the absence in New Spain of even a single person with real architectural proficiency. We wonder not at the errors but at the achievement, at the number and quality of buildings the untrained friars succeeded in having built, especially because they had to proceed in most instances without architectural drawings sent from Spain or, until well after midcentury, architectural books.

Massive walls, thick vaults, homemade heaviness overall, and general absence of sophisticated finesse are readily understandable consequences of the conditions shaping the friars' methods of design and construction. What is surprising is the structural inventiveness, the grandeur, and the decorative charm of the best structures. The Franciscan belief in austerity and poverty might have seemed to rule out any sort of architectural display. Characteristic were the provincial statutes of 1541, which were particularly praised for their emphasis on Franciscan poverty by the reforming Pope Paul III, himself the builder of the massive and sumptuous Farnese Palace in Rome. The statutes stated that

> the buildings erected for the residence of the friars shall be very, very poor, in accordance with the wishes of our father St. Francis; and the conventos shall be so planned as to have no more than six cells to the dormitory, eight by nine feet . . . the dormitory corridor shall be no more than five feet wide, and the cloister shall not have two stories and shall be but seven feet wide.[4]

The Franciscans were more successful in maintaining poverty in their lives than in their architecture. They had ample labor available and in central Mexico sufficient materials for building, and they were nostalgic for the great Christian architecture of medieval Europe. They also were very conscious of the impressive pagan religious architecture familiar to the Indians, having seen it or having been told of it—recall Father Motolinía's concern that the great temple in Mexico City was much higher than the new vaulted church of the Franciscans. The friars were apt to rationalize their fondness for impressive architecture by convincing themselves that the weak nature of the Indians needed outward display to attract it to the subtle inner things of the spirit. To continue and sustain the conversion they felt compelled "to ornament and make a show of the churches."[5] One type of display intended to impress the Indians was the fortresslike convento, constructed with battlemented *atrio* walls and a tall, powerfully buttressed church, topped by what resembled a military parapet. Such castlelike structures recalled the huge towered houses of Cortés and other conquistadors in Mexico City. Both the secular and the religious types were designed to convey a forbidding impression of Spanish and Christian might.

The Augustinians, the most lavish of mendicant builders, felt less compulsion to poverty. Father Matías de Escobar, writing in the early eighteenth century, recalled the golden age of the Augustinian province in Michoacán and the great builder Father Diego de Chavez. Father Diego had argued for architectural lavishness by saying that God himself had been responsible for the expenditures for the tabernacle and had inspired Solomon in his erection of the temple on which so many talents had been spent. These expenditures for tabernacle and temple were to house the ark of the covenant in which manna, the precursor of the sacrament, was kept. If God had countenanced such sumptuous buildings for the prefigurers of the sacrament, how much greater should be the expenditure "to guard the true Manna, Christo Sacramentado?"

The Dominicans did their best to keep pace with the Augustinians in erecting impressive structures. Their first church drew a letter of reproof from the queen because the first bishop of Mexico City, Juan de Zumárraga, found it more lavishly beautiful than its use justified. Both orders were warned by the king against accumulating valuable property. We can be amused by mendicant attempts to justify architectural splendor. We are also grateful for the splendid results of their extravagance. Architecture is not created by those who build simply for use. A rigorously austere architecture which is truly distinguished is exceedingly rare.

The friars' models for their ambitious new conventos came from their memories of the European buildings they had lived, worshiped in, and loved. The mixing of architectural styles characteristic of sixteenth-century Mexican religious construction resulted from those inexact memories of amateur architects. Spain, the main source of their models, was notable in the early sixteenth century for architectural diversity. Gothic and Renaissance styles were foreign importations and they were used in Spain alternatively or sometimes side by side in the same building, not according to a clear stylistic chronology. Both were modified by the persistence of the Mudéjar, the continued use of Moorish building techniques and the lingering affection for Moorish ornamental surfaces. Mexican buildings, deriving from memories of Spanish designs, freely mix the medieval and the Renaissance, the Moslem and the Christian, subjecting all to the sometimes subtle, sometimes readily apparent, modifications of the Indian craftsmen.

The friar historians of the sixteenth and early seventeenth centuries testify to the role of Indian workers in constructing the conventos. Their pious idealism may have led to some exaggeration of the enthusiasm of the Indians in welcoming the friars to their town and in competing with each other in making their church bigger and better, and ornamenting it as much as possible. But without doubt Indian communal pride reinforced the Christian pride of the friars. Both the Indian rulers and the ordinary people who made up the drafts of construction laborers saw their church as the visual embodiment of their community. Friars would come and depart but the church would remain in their town to demonstrate its worthiness and their own merit as its people. In some instances individual Indian laborers were recalcitrant and a whipping post for laggard workers and religious backsliders was a stan-

dard piece of *atrio* furniture. In one extreme instance the Augustinians built two jails for particularly reluctant workers in a modest town on the south slope of the volcano Popocatépetl. An informative account of the process of construction, which illustrates the persistence of sixteenth-century type evangelism in remote areas well into the eighteenth and even into the early nineteenth century, appears in Francisco Palou's life of Fray Junipero Serra. Father Palou, a fellow missionary of Father Serra, famed for his later founding of the upper California chain of missions, describes their arrival in Santiago de Jalpan in a remote area on the northern fringe of central Mexico, the Sierra Gorda, in 1750. The friars had been taught the Indians' Pame language and had translated prayers and the text of the catechism for their use. The total population of a thousand was soon baptized. To encourage Indian confessions Father Serra himself confessed publicly before everyone at high mass on festival days. After Christian practices were well established, he suggested the construction of a masonry church large enough to hold the entire town. Father Palou writes:

He proposed his devout plan to all those Indians, who gladly agreed to it, offering themselves to haul the stone (which was at hand) and all the sand, to make the lime and mortar, and to serve as helpers in carrying it to the masons. This work was begun and carried out during the entire dry season when the Indians were not needed for work in the fields. In a period of seven years a church was built, fifty-three yards long and eleven wide, with its corresponding transept and dome. . . .

With this activity they became skilled in various trades as stonemasons, carpenters, ironworkers, painters, gilders, etc. Likewise in his fervent zeal the Reverend Father Junipero did not forget to withdraw women from idleness, for he employed them in tasks befitting their sex, such as spinning, weaving . . . etc.[6]

In the 1530s and 1540s the initial training of Indian masons, carpenters, and other skilled craftsmen was necessary. Preconquest architecture was impressively massive and remarkably decorative but it required few subtle architectural skills. The extremely limited number of European craftsmen who came to New Spain usually remained in the capital. The most skilled cadres of Indian workers lived there or in neighboring communities such as Texcoco or Xochimilco. Some crews of Indian craftsmen became itinerants, directing the huge numbers of unskilled laborers available. At Yanhuitlán in the 1570s the Dominicans employed 6,000 Indian workers, using shifts of 600 each in sequence. The Franciscans frequently sent Indians for training to a school of craftsmanship directed by Pedro de Gante at the Franciscan convento in Mexico City. The Augustinians brought the teachers to the Indians, employing European craftsmen at a school in their convento in Tiripitío in Michoacán. The Dominicans had a similar school in Yanhuitlán.

Sixteenth-century accounts are unanimous in their praise of Indian adeptness in learning European techniques. Father Mendieta compared native masons to monkeys in their ability to imitate Spanish craftsmanship and praised their ability to "make and decorate round, segmental, and terciate arches, rich doorways and windows, and whatever arabesque and grotesque decoration they have seen."[7]

The residential buildings, the conventos proper, often the first built permanently, allow us to sense the developing architectural skills of the Indian craftsmen. Almost universally placed on the sunny, protected southern side of the church, except in warm low regions where they were often on the shadier north, the conventos were given little exterior embellishment. The two-story mass facing the *atrio* received major architectural emphasis only in the arcaded *portería*, or entrance, which led to the lower cloister walk. This sheltered walk and the one above were used for prayer and meditation. Usually decorated with fresco paintings, they ran at right angles around a square, or nearly square, cloister garden containing a central fountain and formally disposed European flowers such as roses, lilies, and carnations. A limited number of doors on three or four sides gave access from the walks to the interior of the building. On the ground level the side opposite the church housed the refectory, where the friars ate in silence listening to readings from religious texts. Nearby was a kitchen. In a wing of the building close to the church was placed the

sala de profundis, the chapter room, named from the first Latin words of Psalm 130 which was read to conclude the meetings held there. Only rarely, as in the refectory at Augustinian Actopan (Fig. 2.17), were these rooms given particular architectural expression. A stone stairway led to the upper level that contained, usually on the south or east sides, the modest rectangular cells of the friars. The cells had windows, and in some instances window seats, overlooking the convento gardens of native, Caribbean, and European vegetables and fruit trees. The convento library was also located on the upper level.

The principal architectural expression of the convento buildings appeared in the inner facades facing the central cloister garden. Older examples, reflecting the limited skills of the earlier Indian craftsmen, are crude and heavy. Relatively small rounded openings are cut through the mass of rubble walls to provide light for barrel-vaulted cloister walks. The facades are punctuated vertically by simple rectangular or edged buttresses, which alternate with the double-tiered rounded openings and assist in supporting the vaults. Later the openings were decorated with cut-stone arches and rib vaults replaced the low barrel vaults. Cloister walks covered with wooden ceilings sometimes had elaborate Moorish patterning in the four corner bays and cut stone replaced rubble in the walls. These cloisters were more architecturally sophisticated and cheaper to build because they required much less masonry and much less lime for the mortar. The facades facing the court were reduced to screens of columns, capitals, arches, and a greatly reduced area of masonry above and between the arches. Such economy of means was possible because Indian masons had been sufficiently trained in European architectural skills. Care was taken to minimize the expenditure of these precious skills. The numbers of cuttings were minimized. Columns were cut in a single piece. The carefully cut stones for an arch were as large, and as few, as possible. Some shallow segmental arches which require less masonry were used in small cloisters. Pointed Gothic arches were used by the Augustinians for the lower arcades at Actopan (Fig. 2.16) and Ixmiquilpan. Ultimately the classical taste for semicircular arches prevailed.

Although many of the early provisional churches had central naves and flanking aisles and a particularly interesting group of these three-aisled churches survives from the middle of the century, the standard church of all three mendicant orders consisted of the unbroken space of a single nave. In Europe the mendicant orders traditionally built large open churches emphasizing the importance of preaching to the people more than the ritual activities of the religious community. Medieval churches of a single nave were well known in southwestern France and several were built in sixteenth-century Spain. Limitation to a single interior space represented the austere simplicity which the Franciscans wished to exemplify in their new Indian church, conceived as the true successor of the primitive church of the first Christians. The Augustinians, in Yuriria in west-central Mexico, and the Dominicans, in Oaxtepec, near Cuernavaca, and in several churches in the south in Oaxaca and Chiapas, built cruciform churches, but the majority of the churches consisted of a great unified volume of interior space. The ratio of length to width was approximately four or five to one. Lengths ranged from about fifty to over seventy yards, widths from ten or fifteen to, in rare cases, over twenty yards. Heights come fairly close to doubling the widths.

Exteriors were tall and boxlike. Roofs were seldom visible above the top of the walls. Architectural expression was provided primarily by the buttresses punctuating the side and rear walls, the castelated parapets, and the simply organized facades. A minority of the churches had one or two towers; angled buttresses at the ends of the facade were more common. Many facades consisted simply of a tall blank wall decorated by a somewhat classical portal and above it a window to allow afternoon light to penetrate to the choir balcony where the friars recited their canonical offices. The exceptional lower facade of Augustinian Acolman (Fig. 2.20) was organized in the plateresque style of the Spanish Renaissance with a classical order and statues in niches. North doorways were often given particular architectural ornamentation.

Walls were very thick, usually of rough rubble and measuring from about five to ten feet through. Thickness was necessary because of the crude construction of rubble or, even, of rammed earth contained between cut-stone facings. The weight and thrust of vaults was an additional reason for heaviness in the walls of cautious amateur designers.

An Indian parishioner entering the Renaissance-type portal of the church would first pass under the choir balcony through a wide low space frequently covered by splendid late-medieval rib vaulting. Then the height of the nave would reveal itself. A few churches, largely Dominican, had lateral chapels along both nave walls. Most had high flat walls cut by a few small windows, unglazed and sometimes filled with waxed cloth. Roofing might be supported by long timber beams as in Aztec construction, sometimes with wonderfully intricate Moorish ceilings. The more ambitious structures usually had some type of vaulting. Augustinian naves were customarily barrel-vaulted. The Franciscans preferred a sequence of four square bays of domical-rib vaults, and, in at least fifteen instances, constructed rib vaults throughout both the church and the cloister. The most elaborate late Gothic vault patterns, stars, flowers, and crystals, were placed at the east end over the chancel or sanctuary. The vaults themselves were normally constructed of foot-thick rubble masonry, rather like concrete, instead of carefully cut stones. The patterned ribs of cut stone, brick, or plaster were attached to the surface of the vaults like decorative moldings. They greatly lightened the overall appearance of the vaulting. Barrel vaults were sometimes frescoed as were walls, especially within the chancel. Black and white predominated but some other colors were used.

The walls of the spacious nave narrowed in a polygonal, usually trapezoidal, sanctuary, often set off by a tall framing arch. The parishioner could approach the sacred area of the mass and its richly furnished altar by mounting a flight of three, five, or seven steps. But a communion rail kept the laity at a distance. Against the rear wall behind the altar rose a many tiered retablo containing religious paintings and colored statues set in a gilded framework of Renaissance architecture. The sanctuary, sometimes including part of what was structurally the nave and sometimes entirely structurally distinct, occupied roughly a fifth of the entire interior. Together with the choir balcony it occupied from a third to half of the space.

FRANCISCAN HUEJOTZINGO

Huejotzingo was one of the original four communities chosen in 1524 as centers for evangelization by the Franciscans before they organized a convento in Mexico City. The Huejotzinca were an important tribe numbering, according to early sixteenth-century estimates, between one hundred thousand and four hundred thousand. Former allies of the Aztecs, they had gone over to their enemies the Tlaxcalteca and had furnished warriors to the Spaniards for the conquest of Mexico. The Huejotzinca's traditional territory was just over the mountains from Mexico City on the eastern slope of the range of volcanoes separating the valleys of Puebla and Mexico, with a principal settlement and ceremonial center located on an elevated site protected by steep canyon walls.

A letter of 1560 from the Huejotzingo cabildo to Philip II, which asks relief from heavy demands for tribute, stresses the immediate and unanimous welcome given the first Franciscans and Christianity by the community and the im-

mediate destruction of the temples and the representations of the old gods. This letter probably reflects the desire to curry favor more than to relate events accurately. In any case the Huejotzinca complied with Fray Juan de Alameda's moving the center of their community in about 1529 to the present level site of Huejotzingo, roughly fifteen miles northwest of Puebla. This was one of the earliest Spanish acts of resettlement.

References to building activities of the early years are scanty. The friars seem to have erected or adopted some religious structures at the canyon site. The first church at the new site was probably wooden-roofed and three-aisled. Both Fray Toribio Motolinía and Fray Martín de Valencia, the leader of the Twelve, served as guardian, or prior, of Huejotzingo before the present structures were built.

These structures resulted from a building campaign initiated in the middle 1540s, perhaps in 1544, shortly before the greatest of colonial epidemics, possibly of measles, which some estimate reduced the Indian population of New Spain from approximately fifteen million to about three million. Many conventos, like the Aztec temples before them, rest on massive platforms. The first work at Huejotzingo was the construction of a platform for the whole complex raising it nine steps above the town. During the next decade, despite the disruption of the epidemic, work was completed on the walls of the *atrio*, 120 meters square, on its two entrance gates, and on the four *posas* in the corners. The residential building, the convento proper, probably was begun about 1548, and the church of San Miguel a year or two later. The date 1550 is carved on one of the *posas*. A chapter meeting was held in Huejotzingo in 1558 suggesting that the convento was then completed sufficiently to be inhabitable. A document of 1564 informs us that the main and north entrances of the church had then been finished, that the walls of the sanctuary were completed, and those of the nave were three-quarters up. The church and convento were finished by 1571 after twenty-five years of construction during which the town's population, shrinking since the conquest, declined by more than half to between twenty-five and forty thousand. Work may have been interrupted in the early 1560s and there are some in-

2.2 *Huejotzingo, plan of church and convento building, from Richard Perry,* Mexico's Fortress Monasteries, *p. 97.*

21

2.3 *Huejotzingo, posa. See also Plate I.*

2.4 *Huejotzingo, portería (entrance to convento building).*

dications that the cloister, at least, was completed in more modest fashion than it was begun.

The four virtually identical *posas* are among the supreme achievements of Mexican ar-

chitecture, combining geometrical clarity of design with wonderfully inventive yet carefully controlled ornamentation. Square in plan, seventeen feet to a side, each *posa* consists of a rectangular block higher than it is wide surmounted by a pyramid slightly steeper than an equilateral triangle. The sides facing the *atrio* are pierced by archways half their height and half their width. The arches are ornamented with a chain pattern and supported by clusters of colonnettes with medieval capitals and bases.

The upper portions of these sides are occupied by a rectangular frame or frieze containing four shields, or escutcheons, carrying strangely stylized images of a Franciscan emblem, the blood flowing from the five wounds Christ received on the cross. These friezes are bordered by a sharply edged flat band. Below them the zones surrounding the arches are framed by a molding of impressive sculpted vigor in the form of another Franciscan emblem, the cord. These knotted cords, which show the influence of the Manueline style of late Gothic Portugal, constitute the shape of a Mohammedan decorative frame called an *alfiz* and contain on each side a flying angel carrying an instrument of Christ's passion. The angels recall Romanesque relief sculpture. At the top of the arch is another shield, carrying a monogram of Mary and surmounted by a cross and a crown, which pushes through the chord and the flat frame into the area of the upper frieze.

The rising sides of the crowning pyramids are set slightly back from the edges of the rectangular lower mass of the *posas*. Stylized palm crests are placed at the corners to mask the transition between the rectangular blocks and the rising edges of the pyramids. These edges are ornamented by medieval-type moldings which lead the eye up to the crosses which originally surmounted all the *posas*. Memento mori in the form of carved skulls and bones mark one of the faces on the pyramidal top of the posas on the north side of the *atrio*.

The outstanding expressive feature of the two-storied convento building is its double-arched entrance, or *portería*. The left arch is decorated by a powerful representation of a double chain, and, in the right, each stone carries an abstract pattern suggesting a crystal or a flower.

2.5 *Huejotzingo, facade.*

2.6 *Huejotzingo, center of facade, portal and window.*

The stubby half-columns supporting the outer ends of the arches seem Romanesque, resembling the colonnettes of the *posas*, but the massive, strangely divided, banded, braided, and fluted

central column follows no single recognizable European model.

The steep fortresslike church of San Miguel was faced with carefully cut ashlar masonry which seems to have been taken from a preconquest structure. The thick walls are filled with rough rubble and rammed earth. The side and rear walls are punctuated by tall, narrow, stepped buttresses topped by crenelations that seem the inverse of the triangular Moorish ones, with perforations at their centers which project above the tops of the walls. At the front corners of the church, buttresses are set at oblique angles to provide support for the vaults of the choir balcony and roof, to constitute a frame for the facade, and in their diagonal spread, to reach out an invitation to enter.

Except for a broad flat band running a few feet below the parapet, the upper zone of the facade is undecorated. An impressive ornamental composition fills the middle of the lower two-thirds of the front, framing the entrance and the window, which lights the choir balcony. Renaissance, medieval and Moorish motifs are freely combined into a harmonious whole. The frame of the portal is defined at its outer sides by tall, thin, fluted columns which stop just short of the horizontal molding that divides the lower zone from that of the window. The doorway is set deep in the facade in a sharply incised, slanting Moorish–late Gothic inner frame which is topped by a nearly flat, pointed, many curved arch. The edges of the inner frame are defined by moldings rising from strange bases, which foreshadow the slanting columns of the Baroque. The moldings resemble Romanesque colonnettes as they rise along the sides of the doorway to triple-banded capitals. Above the capitals the molding is transformed into a soft, almost squishy element, looking like toothpaste squeezed from a tube, echoing the pattern of the sharp edge of the curving and pointed frame above, as it wriggles across the entrance to culminate at the center in a pinched tip.

At the sides, horizontal accents are provided by three decorative bands running out across the plain outer frame of carefully cut masonry. They originate, oddly, from intermediate points half a stage below each of the triple bands of the capitals of the colonnettes. The elements above the incised multicurved arch are straight-forward, consisting of seven medallions with the monogram of Christ, two lower ones flanking the upper edges of the incised frame, and a row of five above. A twisted Franciscan cord, less vigorous than those on the *posas*, defines a narrow rectangle in the area above the medallions.

The arched choir window in the zone above the doorway is set deeply in the wall. Within the wall, well back from the surface, is

an arch supported by Gothic colonnettes and capitals. The outer arch is recessed slightly from the surface of the facade and is defined by a restrained Renaissance molding and set within two restrained rectangular Renaissance frames; the outer is set on medieval bases. The inner of these frames approaches the plane of the facade and the outer projects slightly beyond it. A third outer rectangular molding is made from a twisted Franciscan cord thickly applied to the surface of the

2.7 Huejotzingo, north portal.

2.8 Huejotzingo, general view of the interior (nave facing chancel).

2.9 Portal to the sacristy. (The photograph is of a copy in the Viceregal Museum, Tepotzotlán.)

facade. At the sides strange two-tiered forms are placed above the outer corners of the frame of the portal zone and seem to support flanking escutcheons containing the five wounds of Christ and the three nails of the cross and decorated by twisted swirls of Franciscan cord. Above the ornamented zone is a plain horizontal band and a horizontal strip of Franciscan cord.

A decorative ensemble more extravagant than that of the facade surrounds the now-walled-up portal on the north side of the church. The design, like that of the main portal, is divided into an upper and a lower zone. Here a relatively austere upper arched opening, which is larger than the portal, may have been intended for an open chapel. Jambs at the sides, of European medieval design, were completed to what would have been the springing of an arch and then were abandoned. The opening was walled up. The arch of the north portal below is contained in an *alfiz*, which has, in its upper corners, shields with the five wounds, and is bordered by a molding decorated by small floral medallions. The arch is ornamented by three bands. Its inner face is profiled by a waving pattern of projections and indentations, possibly derived freely from the classical dentil molding. The arch proper carries a chain pattern, modeled after the emblem of the great Burgundian and Hapsburg Chivalric Order of the Golden Fleece of which Charles V was grand master. The outer band, which extends into the area of the *alfiz*, is a softly flowing cord or vegetative stem supporting alternating stylized palm sprouts and palmettes. The organic feeling of this lush band is also prominent in the remarkable asparaguslike columns and quasi-capitals which flank the doorway. The influence of Portuguese Manueline style may be felt. The columns are horizontally marked by braided basketlike segments above the bases and below the capitals. The fluted central sections are interrupted by escutcheons. The columns create a remarkable visual counterpoint with the broad quasi-pilasters set behind them, whose capitals complete the frame of the *alfiz*, substituting the Pearls of Castile for the small floral medallions. The pilasters are decorated with three strongly bordered panels of stylized floral ornament. The fluted vertical sections of the columns are placed so that they cross

in front of the strong horizontal accents of the two intermediate borders of the panels of floral ornament on the pilasters. In the middle of the column the escutcheon is set against the central floral panel of the pilaster so that it is framed by the strongly emphasized horizontals and verticals of borders. The vertical movement of the column leading up to its asparagus top is interrupted below and above by the horizontals of the borders behind it and, in between, by the lower and upper edges of the escutcheon in front of it. Still another strong horizontal accent runs behind the column at the level of the pearls of the capital of the pilasters, here set against the division between the upper braided segment and the "capital."

The ensemble of exterior ornamentation at Huejotzingo—the *posas*, the entrance to the conventual building, the main and north portals—is unique in the inventiveness of its blending of motifs drawn from a broad range of European sources: medieval, Renaissance, Moorish, and Portuguese of the age of Manuel I. Indian craftsmen, working under the direction of the Franciscans, fused the differing European motifs into a series of strikingly varied decorative compositions. Nothing in the decorative vocabulary of Huejotzingo is Indian but the skill in carving and the sureness of the design suggest the power of early sixteenth-century Aztec sculptural ornamentation.

The interior of the church is a handsome example of the characteristic Franciscan single-naved construction with only one feature that shares in the decorative inventiveness of the exterior. Immediately inside the western entrance is a choir balcony supported by late Gothic stone-ribbed vaulting. At the distant eastern end of the nave there is a polygonal sanctuary. The four domed vaults of the ceiling are decorated with patterns of plaster ribs which spring from the half-columns marking the divisions of the bays along the nave walls. The relatively simple middle vaults have octagons at their centers. The vault over the choir, like that under it, has a four-petaled design. The multiribbed design over the sanctuary consists of four petals which are set within a square of flowing sides and which as they join at the center are transformed into a flowing octagon. In the south wall the framing of the doorway from the nave to the sacristy resembles in a restrained way the inventive ornamentation of the exterior. A flattened archway is edged by a thin medieval molding and framed by a broad rectangular gateway set on architectural bases and terminated at the top by a cornice ornamented by medallions suggestive of flowers with swirling petals. The gateway proper carries, within plain borders, patches of stylized floral ornamentation set within a deeper pattern created by an interwoven vine design. The bases are decorated by a

2.10 *Huejotzingo, main retablo.*

band of slightly larger floral rectangles set between rounded moldings.

At the end of the vista from the entrance down the nave is a gilded altar screen, or retablo, attached to the rear wall of the sanctuary. This towering four-tiered work is signed by Simon Pereyns, a Fleming and the leading painter and retablo designer of New Spain, and dated 1586. Pereyns completed the major paintings himself and employed Pedro de Requena to carve the principal statuary. Installed a decade and a half after the completion of the church, it is its most European work of architectural design. Modeled on Spanish Renaissance retablos such as that of the

church of Santa Clara in Briviesca, it consists of a four-tiered main panel with an arched top and slanting three-tiered wings. Colored statues of saints set in half-columned niches frame the central panel and the wings. The columns of the lowest tier are Doric, decorated in the Spanish plateresque manner, and those above are Ionic, of increasing decorative complexity. Figures and scenes carved in low relief occupy the central tier of the main panel, ranging from God the father in the arched top to St. Francis receiving the stigmata in the third level. A representation of St. Michael Archangel, the titular patron of the church, is missing from either the fourth or the second level. A Neo-Classical tabernacle occupied the two lower levels until some time after 1934.[8] Religious paintings by Pereyns, some copied from engravings of works of Martin de Vos, occupy the inner sections of the tiers of the wings and the decorative segments above them. Outstanding among the sculptural works, carved by Pedro de Requena, are the panel of St. Francis receiving the stigmata, for which Rehena was paid 150 pesos, and the four panels representing the busts of the twelve apostles which are set below the tiers of columned niches.

Such a complex and costly work, taking at least two and a half years to complete and involving the labor of diverse craftsmen—carvers, painters, gilders, and carpenters—demonstrates Franciscan enthusiasm for architectural expression. The austerity of Motolinía seems to have been forgotten.

AUGUSTINIAN ACOLMAN AND ACTOPAN

Acolman and Actopan were major sites occupied by the Augustinians in the area north and northeast of Mexico City. Acolman, now in open fields a few miles from pre-Columbian Teotihuacán and a regular stop for tourist buses, had in Aztec times been related politically to the major lakeside city, Texcoco. The Augustinians replaced the Franciscans in Acolman in 1539. Actopan, serving Otomí Indian communities further to the north, was occupied not quite ten years later. Construction of the present buildings at both sites was begun about 1550. A possible exception is that part of the residential building containing the cruder cloister at Acolman. One of the earliest to survive in Mexico, it may date from the Franciscan occupation. The entire male population of Acolman assisted in the construction of the church. Some stone was transported from a temple of Quetzalcoatl in the vicinity. Fray Andrés de Mata, who had been in Italy, initiated construction at Actopan. Patrons of the work there were Don Juan Inica Actopan and Don Pedro Izcuicuitlopelco, Indian leaders of the principal communities in the area.

Distinct *atrios* are not now apparent at either site. The one at Acolman is terraced after partial excavation of the flood silt which buried the church floor and facade to a depth of six feet. That of Actopan, originally 950 by 600 feet, over three times the area of Huejotzingo, has been largely absorbed into the town. Across the road from the convento at Acolman is a remarkable *atrio* cross (Figs. 2.11–2.13) which reflects the persistence of features of Aztec sculptural style. The cross suggests both the cross and the body of Christ on the cross with the horizontal elements suggesting arms and hands and a calm, lifesize, bearded face projecting from the intersection. At the base is a strange image of the Virgin, stern faced, not grieving, suggestive of the fierce goddesses of the Aztecs. Below her is a round, toothy skull and what appear to be the remains of a diminutive dragon.

Both conventos have open chapels. The modest one of Acolman (Fig. 2.12) faces the *atrio* from the second story of the residential structure, flush with the facade of the church. The arched opening, hollowed from the wall and decorated with a crude *alfiz*, creates a simple raised proscenium for the celebration of the mass. The magnificent open chapel at Actopan (Fig. 2.13), set well back from the front of the church on its north side, is covered by a great barrel vault fifty-seven feet across, broader than all the church vaults in Spain except that of the Cathedral of Gerona. The thrust is stabilized primarily by modest rooms on either side. The underside of the vault was painted in a red and black coffer-and-cross design, probably derived from an illustration in Sebastiano Serlio's *Third Book of Architecture*. The front edge of the arch, the archivolt, was treated with an odd delicacy which emphasized decoration of surface rather than the structural sturdiness of a classical barrel vault. Until recently the lower portion of the chapel was closed by the graceful swooping silhouette of an eighteenth-century baroque wall.

The walls are painted with twenty-five scenes colored in blues, yellows, reds, and browns and based primarily upon European religious illustrations but given naive force by the indigenous artists. Monstrous jaws of hell, personifications of sins, and scenes of the torments of the damned, including what seem to be references to the ritual cannibalism of the Indians, cover the side walls. Upon the end wall on either side of the space once occupied by the retablo are scenes from Genesis, ranging from the Creation of Eve, to the Flood, and the Destruction of Babylon, the latter possibly suggestive of the ruin of Tenochtitlán. Above, filling the semicircle shaped by the great vault, is a rendering of the Last Judgment with the fires of hell forming its base and images of the saved poised above a rainbow at the top.

Both convento buildings were entered through arcaded *porterías*. At Acolman five undecorated flattened arches are separated by simple buttresses (Fig. 2.12). The three arches at Actopan are decorated with a triumphal arch pattern (Fig. 2.14). Cut-stone masonry is used instead of the plastered rubble of Acolman. Tall Corinthian pilasters take the place of the simple buttresses. The arches spring from fluted and filleted bases, and the individual stones (the voussoirs) of the face of the archivolt are incised to form coffers. The coffering continues in the barrel vaults formed as the arches cut through the thick wall.

Acolman is notable for having two cloisters. We know that in 1580 it contained a grammar school, twenty-four friars, and five priests to minister to the Indians. The earlier cloister is of rough rubble masonry, barrel-vaulted with buttresses at the lower level and roofed with wood above. The arches below are relatively flat, and rectangular piers have been reconstructed on the second story. The subtly constructed second cloister (Fig. 2.15), wooden roofed at both levels, is constructed of soft-brown ashlar masonry. The arches, softly semicircular, and the columns and piers, with richly varied capitals and

2.11 *Acolman, atrio cross. See also Plate II.*

2.12 *Acolman, church and convento building.*

2.13 *Actopan, the open chapel.*

bases, suggest Romanesque rather than Renaissance influence. The sides of the lower arcade are divided by central piers into two units of two arches each; narrower arches in the second story are grouped in units of three above the units of two. At Actopan the rhythm is two-to-one, with, at the upper level, two rounded Renaissance-type arches supported by simple columns placed over each arch below. The lower arches are pointed Gothic arches, rare in Mexico, and are separated by paneled buttresses which support the ribbed Gothic vaults of the lower cloister walk. Diagonal passages leading from the cloister walk to the chapter room, the refectory, and elsewhere in the convento are an interesting and puzzling feature of the construction at Actopan. Unique in Mexico is the coffered vault of the refectory. Octagonal coffers are sunk into a major section of the barrel vault which sheltered the friars as they ate silently, listening to readings of one of the community from a pulpit placed two-thirds of the way along the wall inside the cloister walk. The coffered sec-

tion of the vault has been painted in Renaissance coffering patterns in black and orange against a white ground, and recently another portion of the vault has been wallpapered to match.

A prominent feature of the convento building at Actopan is a large squared vaulted staircase in a corner of the cloister walk adjoining the church. The walls are painted in dry fresco with representations of saints, prelates, and Augustinian theologians. The paintings, primarily in black and white, with a few details in color, are placed in painted architectural settings defined by decorated columns and arches and separated horizontally by bands of classical ornamentation. North European prints were a primary source for the decorative scheme. Italian and Spanish influences are also probable. Other paintings of par-

2.15 *Acolman, second cloister.*

2.14 *Actopan, view of portería, tower, and facade from the east-southeast.*

2.16 *Actopan, the cloister.*

2.17 *Actopan, the refectory.*

ticular interest at Actopan include a landscape, portraying activities of the Augustinians, which is in the chapter room; an expressive representation of Christ tied to the column, which is at the end of an upper corridor; and a monogram of Christ, surrounded by flowers and linked by flowing ribbons to winged angels in the four corners, on the tower-room vault.

The churches at both Acolman and Actopan have thick walls of rubble without the facing of carefully cut stones used at Huejotzingo. At Acolman the original buttresses were unadorned

and modest in size, stopping well below the top of the walls, which are ornamented by a sprightly faceted row of small merlons. On the north side, unsupported by the convento building, the buttresses proved insufficient to support the vaults and were subsequently reinforced by an alternate series, broader, lower, and diverse in size and shape. The present overall composition of the wall has a picturesque charm unintended by the original designer. The buttresses at Actopan are tall, unadorned up to the top of the wall, and terminating above it in forms suggesting fortified gate houses. The strong vertical accents of the buttresses provide an expressive contrast to the horizontal massing of the long church. The northwest corner of both churches is given additional support. At Acolman there is a lower and cruder version of one of the diagonal buttresses of Huejotzingo (Fig. 2.12). At Actopan the side wall thickens into a massive flat buttress which ascends smoothly to the top of the wall where its front edge slopes pyramidally upward behind the pedimented frontispiece at the top of the facade.

Although the church facades of Augustinian Acolman and Actopan much more clearly reflect Renaissance designs than did slightly earlier Franciscan San Miguel Huejotzingo, they have prominent nonclassical elements. San Agustín Acolman has a skyline broken by fortresslike crenelations and, in the center, a small pedimented projection cut through with three arched openings to hold bells (Fig. 2.12). San Nicolás Actopan has a dominating Moorish tower (Fig. 2.14) placed slightly back from the facade, between the church and pilastered arcade of the entrance to the convento. The tower is square and is decorated on each face as it rises above the body of the church by a broadly arched window and a castellated termination formed by small crenelated gatehouses at the corners and a crenelated parapet in between, and perforated below by a shadowed row of four small arched openings. A larger crenelated gatehouse, set back from the faces, rises at the center of the tower to constitute its summit and support a cross.

When it is glimpsed at an angle from the area in front of the entrance to the convento, Actopan's pedimented frontispiece seems pasted to the sturdy body of the church, overlapping part of the tower, a Renaissance afterthought added to an essentially medieval structure. Perhaps in an effort to secure some overall unity, the frontispiece was decorated above the roofline of its classical pediment with medieval crenelations akin to those placed above the other walls of the church between the more forceful small gatehouses atop the buttress. Despite deliberate contrasts between the surface of the wall and areas of suggested depth, the facade seems thin. The pediment at the top lacks vigor because it is defined by overly delicate moldings.

The principal ornamented features are those usually emphasized in sixteenth-century church facades. At the middle level is an arched window to the choir balcony, framed by vigorous half-columns and a classical entablature. The principal zone below is distinguished by a Mannerist interplay between classical orders of differing heights, an interplay between three differing semicircular forms which echo the curve of the arched window above, and an interplay between elements placed in front of the plane of the fa-

2.18 Actopan, view of the church from the west-southwest.

cade, those which suggest that plane, and those which suggest depth. A large outer frame set forward from the front wall is created by two pairs of tall quasi-Corinthian half-columns which rest on double bases and which surround a vertical tier of four tall, narrow, empty niches. An inner frame created by pairs of short Corinthian columns on single bases and surrounding two empty niches occupies the lower half of the larger frame. The upper half of that frame contains discrete medallions set against precisely cut masonry in the spandrels of a large three-tiered coffered arch, which recedes from the frontal plane back to a deep-set coffered archivolt surrounding a more deeply set tympanum. These rounded forms are placed directly over the coffered arch of the doorway, which also has medallions set in its spandrels. The lower order of columns framing the doorway

30

clearly projects out from the recessing coffered arch and the more recessed, shadowed tympanum above, but its outer entablature folds in to follow the recessing of the coffered arch as it slants toward the tympanum. The recession of the arch may recall Bramante's illusionistic suggestion of a barrel-vaulted apse in Santa Maria presso San Satiro in Milan. Here the suggestion is not of a full barrel vault but of substantial depth in what is a shallow facade. Although the formal decorative composition at Actopan is less assured than

2.19 Actopan, central facade.

the deft Gothic-Mohammedan design of Huejotzingo, it is a remarkably ambitious effort in sophisticated manipulation of the Renaissance vocabulary of decorative forms by a friar designer, or designers, with no professional architectural collaborators, and a crew of Indian craftsmen who had to be taught an alien tradition of construction.

Contrary to esthetic experimentation at Actopan, the designer of the facade at Acolman (Fig. 2.20) took few risks. Probably executed by a Spanish craftsman, the design is an assured example of the flattened Renaissance style the Spanish call plateresque, similar to the ornament on silver plate. An inscription declares "This work was completed in the year 1560, in the reign of the king Don Felipe our Lord, son of the Emperor Carlos V, and under the government in

New Spain of his illustrious Viceroy, Don Luis de Velasco, with whose favor it was constructed." As at Huejotzingo the ornamented choir window and portal are set against a panel occupying the lower two-thirds of the church front. Here the panel is clearly distinguished by its excellent ashlar masonry and defined by a classical cornice at the top of the ornamented zone. The window and portal are more clearly integrated in a unified patterned design which seems glued to the surface of the ashlar panel. The zone of the portal below is richly occupied by decorated moldings, medallions, decorated paired composite columns, and statues of Saints Peter and Paul in niches supported by angel consoles and shaded by elaborate canopies. The thickly ornamented round arch of the doorway is repeated by a larger outer arch decorated by fruits and vegetables.

Areas of plain wall surface are hard to detect amid the rich ornamentation of the zone of the portal, but they are esthetically important in the area of the facade above the entablature. Here the various elements, the richly ornamented arched window, the flanking escutcheons, the projections forming unifying connections with the columns and arches below—candelabra, children carrying baskets of fruit, and the niched figures of young Jesus and flanking child musicians—all gain from being contrasted with plain masonry.

Much of the church interior was modified in the eighteenth century, but the sanctuary with powerfully expressive ribbed vaults is dated 1558. The frescoes in black, white, and orange, like those of the stair at Actopan, portray saints and prelates, here seated on thrones rather than placed in painted architecture. European prints again furnished models for the Indian painters.

The broad nave of Actopan, almost fifteen meters across, is covered in characteristic Augustinian manner with a simple barrel vault. Also typical of Augustinian construction is the concentration of decorative ribbed vaulting in the area of the sanctuary and on the underside of the vault of the choir balcony.

Because of their thick walls and heavy vaults, the lack of glass, and perhaps because of the brightness of the Mexican sun, windows were small and well-separated in sixteenth-century churches. Franciscan windows tended to be placed in regular sequence along the nave walls. Augustinian windows were less regular, often arranged so as to provide extra light for the sanctuary where the customary ribbed, domed vaulting permitted more freedom in fenestration than the barrel vaulting of the nave. Actopan is exceptional in its strong concentration of light on the sanctuary and in its use of windows of varied abstract shapes, triangles, rhomboids, circles, and ellipses.

A DOMINICAN CLUSTER: TEPOSCOLULA, COIXTLAHUACA, AND YANHUITLÁN

Dominican evangelical activity was concentrated along a chain of missions which developed from Fray Domingo de Betanzos's thousand-mile trek south from Mexico City to Guatemala. Along that route particular emphasis was given to the Zapotec Indians of the valley of Oaxaca and to the Mixtecs, who had lived since at least the seventh century in a number of city states located in small valleys among the mountain ridges of northern Oaxaca. The Mixtecs, celebrated for their illustrated manuscripts and their ornaments of gold and gems, had fallen under Aztec domination in the mid-fifteenth century. Coixtlahuaca, their principal city, paid, as tribute to Montezuma, twenty-five gourds of gold dust annually, more than any other community, and, more red cochineal dye than all other places together. Teposcolula and Yanhuitlán were important cities in neighboring valleys of the Mixteca Alta, the high country of the Mixtecs. Dominicans were active in the area as early as 1529. Friaries were established at Teposcolula and Yanhuitlán in 1538; the one at Yanhuitlán was abandoned because of conflicts with the civilian encomendero and reestablished in the same year that Coixtlahuaca was founded a decade later. The initiation of building activity in all three sites may be related to the assignments of Fray Francisco Marín. Construction of Teposcolula and Yanhuitlán seems to have been continued under the direction of Fray Antonio de Serna. Fray Marín is described by the sixteenth-century Dominican historian Fray Agustín Dávila Padilla as a person who drew plans for conventos and churches and

2.20 Acolman, central facade.

who supervised their construction. The Dominicans were pleased to employ professional Spanish craftsmen, and it seems likely that lay designers influenced the later work at Coixtlahuaca and Yanhuitlán, at least. The important Spanish architect, Roderigo Gil de Hontañón, known for his work on the cathedrals of Segovia and Salamanca, and the facade of the University of Alcalá, was long associated with the Dominican order and seems to have influenced Dominican construction in New Spain, probably through plans and sketches dispatched across the Atlantic.

The community of Teposcolula, like Huejotzingo, was shifted by the friars from a higher site to one in a valley. In the middle years of the century, it prospered as a center of the new Spanish silk-raising industry. The modest church of San Pedro and San Pablo and the residential buildings have suffered and been altered over the years. The only interesting surviving portions of the construction begun during Fray Marín's initial stay, from either 1538 or 1541 until 1546, are the *portería* to the convento; the Santa Gertrudis chapel with its powerful low arches and great, squat, twisting columns; and the layout and facade of the church. In plan San Pedro and San Pablo follows the precedent of an earlier Dominican church at Oaxtepec, south of Mexico City, in having a transept added to its single nave. Overall it consists of four nave bays, the transept and crossing section, and a rectangular apse. The facade is an early example of a favorite Dominican scheme. Two towers are set in front of the central portion of the facade so that they seem to press in upon it. The towers are adorned with statues in niches set between Doric half-columns on the lower story and Ionic pilasters above. These orders, placed closer to the inside than the outside of the towers so that they leave a border of plain wall at the outside corners, seem to form a continuous visual unit with the similar orders flanking the doorway, and the choir window of the central facade recessed behind them. The statues, three-quarters round, are, like their supporting pedestals, built into the wall. The smooth rectangular face and low arch of the *portería* frame are flush with the wall of the south tower. The double arched portal to the residential quarters, set deep with the arched frame, is a delightful example of an Indian craftsman's modification of European decorative forms, the style called *tequitqui*.

Fray Marín left Teposcolula and arrived in Coixtlahuaca, only about twelve miles away by air, in February 1546. During his stay of a year and a half, he probably had the large platform constructed to raise the low site which was then bordered by a river. It is likely that he designed and oversaw the building of an open chapel for the ten thousand inhabitants. In addition he may have designed the church and convento and supervised the laying of the foundations. Coixtlahuaca would not formally be accepted as a Dominican establishment until the intermediate chapter meeting held in August 1548, eleven months after he had left for Oaxaca.

The church was planned without transepts but with four shallow chapels (Fig. 2.22) on each side of the nave set between buttresses, which support the four ribbed vaults required to cover an area considerably narrower than the twenty meters of width of the church at floor level. Like San Pedro and San Pablo of Teposcolula, the facade of the church at Coixtlahuaca is recessed between two towers, here massively plain (Fig. 2.23). The decoration of the two lower stories, which, although not completed until 1576, may be based on designs made during Fray Marín's stay, deftly

2.21 Teposcolula, general view.

mixes a wide assortment of motifs drawn primarily from Renaissance architectural motifs.

In the lowest horizontal level the portal is framed by a strange triumphal arch design, with an order of coffered pilasters which frame four superposed pairs of niches. At the mezzanine level, placed just above the powerful coffering of the portal, is an oddly delicate pediment bordered with tiny dentils and containing an escutcheon decorated with the double Hapsburg eagles. The panel above, which crowned the original design, is filled with a medieval rose window surrounded by two rings of coffers and a powerful outer ring of scallops. The vertical organization of the facade is dominated by the strips of raised niches running up each side. Above the four superposed pairs of niches flanking the portal, are one pair at the mezzanine level, and three superposed at the level of the rose window. The eight tiers of paired arches may be derived from an illustration in Serlio for the triumphal arch of Janus, which had similar flanking arched units. The overall effect of the central facade is plateresque, shallow light and shade catching ornament applied to the surface. The deliberate contrast between the elaborate central facade and the plain flanking towers foreshadows many of the finest Baroque designs of eighteenth-century Mexico.

The open chapel (Fig. 2.24), square with trapezoidal sanctuary, was formerly decorated with a star vault. It is located toward the rear of the north side of the church, almost parallel with the polygonal apse which it resembles in plan. The vault was supported by six diagonal buttresses, one at each of the rear corners, one along each of the sides at the point where the square joins the polygon, and one inside each of the front corners. The front buttresses were originally conceived as flying buttresses supported by free-standing columns and open arches. Perhaps because of an earthquake, the daring combination of airy Renaissance arcade and complex medieval star vault was abandoned and all arches, except the segmental one spanning the entrance to the chapel, were filled and reinforced with additional masonry.

After a short stay in Oaxaca, Fray Marín was back in Teposcolula in the early fall of 1548. Either during the next two years or during a subsequent stay between 1553 and 1555, he must have initiated work on the remarkable open chapel which seems clearly related to the original plan for Coixtlahuaca. The chapel, also combining Renaissance arches with a late Gothic star vault, is placed on the north side of the church in line with its recessed facade (Fig. 2.21). The plan is complex and ingenious (Fig. 2.25). A rectangle 140 feet long is faced by five arches forty feet high, and divided into two ranges of bays of identical depth by a second, lower, arcade running across the middle of the rectangle. The second arcade is interrupted as it approaches the center of the rectangle by a hexagon, two sides of which coincide with the front and rear walls. The four other sides of the hexagon, which face the interior of the rectangle, are supported by arches on free-standing columns similar to the frontal arch. An

engaged arch set into the rear wall of the rectangle framed the altar and retablo for the congregation assembled in the *atrio*. Two diagonal buttresses intersect both the front and back walls of the rectangle at the corners of the hexagon to help support the heavy and complex star vault covering it. The front buttresses (Fig. 2.26), about thirty feet deep, more than twice the depth of those at the rear, are necessary because of the open arcaded construction of the front. They are designed as flying buttresses, incorporating arches

2.22 *Coixtlahuaca, interior.*

which are supported by free-standing columns as they intersect the arcade of the facade of the chapel. The massive outer piers are lightened in appearance by surface patterning of Renaissance panel designs and coffers. The vault at Teposcolula has now fallen, but it was largely in place when first seen in 1926 by Manuel Toussaint, the principal rediscoverer of Mexican sixteenth-century architecture. The earlier design at Coixtlahuaca did not endure until its completion. Its daringly intricate successor, despite earthquakes and neglect, sustained its vault for nearly 375 years.

In September 1550 Fray Francisco Marín arrived in Yanhuitlán, which had been abandoned by the Dominicans in 1541 and revived in 1548. Yanhuitlán later became the center of Dominican activity in the region, containing a school for the study of the Mixtec language and one for the training of native craftsmen. The encomendero,

2.23 Coixtlahuaca, facade.

Gonzalo de las Casas, son of the man whose hostility had driven the friars away, was an avid supporter of the work of construction. Fray Marín and his four to eight colleagues and successors availed themselves for twenty years of work crews of four hundred to six hundred from a pool of six thousand Indians to build the massive platform which supports an atrium measuring 350 by 500

feet and to construct the church and convento (Fig. 2.27). The wall shared by the church and convento was ten feet thick.

In plan the church of Santo Domingo Yanhuitlán, is simpler and more unified than those of Teposcolula and Coixtlahuaca. There is neither transept nor internal lateral chapels but only a great nave which narrows and lowers slightly as it terminates in an unusual round apsed sanctuary with rib-coffered vault and stately retablo (Fig. 2.28). The dimensions are inspiring, 200 feet in extent, nearly 60 feet in width, and fully 100 feet from the floor to the crest of the vaults. The four domed nave bays are constructed of good ashlar masonry and decorated by handsome octagon-centered patterns of ribs supported by corbels. The choir balcony is not supported by a vault but by powerful segmental arches (Fig. 2.29). The fine dark cedar ceiling covering the area below the balcony is of the Moorish type called *artesonado*, employing an alternating pattern of intricately carved recessed hexagons and diamonds, both framed by borders carved to represent cords and containing rosettes, those in the hexagons in the form of charmingly minute pineapple pendants.

At the other end of the nave, the sanctuary is framed by a tall arch decorated on its upper levels on either side by a figure of a saint, Peter and Paul respectively, and a winged archangel, surrounded by swirling webs of stucco strapwork ornamentation. Set in the apse beneath a network of coffering is a folded screen retablo soaring more than fifty feet and containing alternating tiers of paintings and sculptural figures set between twisting Salomonic columns. This Baroque work is a modernized version of a retablo constructed under the direction of Sevillian painter Andrés de la Concha. Gonzalo de Las Casas had brought de la Concha to Yanhuitlán directly from Spain in 1568. He remained for some years taking the leading role in the school for Indian craftsmen and establishing a workshop for the production of retablos for other conventos, such as the original one at Coixtlahuaca. De la Concha's paintings and the statuary from the sixteenth-century works were incorporated in the existing Baroque retablos of Coixtlahuaca and of Yanhuitlán.

The sober massive exterior at Yanhuitlán

2.24 Coixtlahuaca, the open chapel.

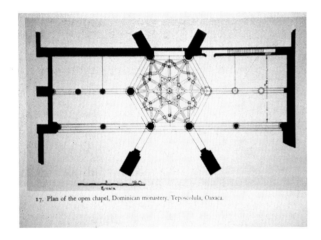

2.25 Teposcolula, plan of the open chapel, from Manuel Toussaint, Colonial Art in Mexico, p. 28.

is faced with carefully cut stones. The north flank, now shored up at either end by massive stepped buttresses cut through by arched passages, was originally designed with tall simple pier buttresses. It has arched windows containing medieval tracery but without glass, and a handsome plateresque portal, related to that at Coixtlahuaca. The portal incorporates a medieval window, a Renaissance shell tympanum, a coffered doorway, and two classical orders, the outer one tall and freely invented and the inner almost academically Corinthian.

The facade loosely resembles Coixtlahuaca in its plain towers and decorated recessed central facade. Instead of a harmonious combination of widely diverse decorative motifs, the central facade of Yanhuitlán presents in its three lower stories a consistent Renaissance design, perhaps derived from retablos like the one designed by Andrés de la Concha for the interior. Remnants of an earlier facade have been discovered behind the present one, which may have been constructed after 1600. Its central tier is occupied at ground level by an arched portal, at the second story by a panel of relief sculpture, and at the third by a recessed rectangular window. In the

2.26 Teposcolula, open chapel, view from the right.

2.27 Yanhuitlán, distant view of the church in the valley.

flanking tiers, tiny statues in framed niches are set between the shafts of paired columns, Doric at the portal stage, Corinthian at the level of the relief panel, with Ionic pilasters at the top. Crowning the facade are later additions, a gracefully curving and angled parapet, and, upon the right tower, a sober belfry stage. The retablo-type central facade of Yanhuitlán was destined to become the norm in colonial New Spain.

2.29 Yanhuitlán, artesonado ceiling under the choir.

2.28 Yanhuitlán, vault.

2.30 Yanhuitlán, facade.

III
Towns and Cities for the Spaniards

Concurrently with the massive effort of the friars in establishing towns for Indians to further the work of evangelism, a number of cities were constructed for European habitation. The Spanish created new towns and cities on a scale unimagined by Europeans since the breakdown of the Roman Empire. For them, perhaps more than for other sixteenth-century people, the urban community symbolized and made possible civilized Christian life. The laying out of cities according to a plan similar to the rectangular grid of Mexico City was normal. Within a few decades the new American cities acquired many of the amenities and the social and religious institutions of contemporary Spain. Dioceses were established and secular clergy were sent to augment the regular orders. Schools and hospitals were founded under religious auspices and convents were established for women to supplement the friaries for men. The Inquisition was established to enforce the orthodoxy and the morality of the European population. A *consulado*, or guild, was organized for the principal merchants of Mexico City, and guilds for craftsmen proliferated.

The need to provide for European means of transportation by horse, mule, and wheeled vehicle led to extensive road building in order to speed communication over the substantial distances between ports, cities, and mining areas. The long dry seasons made water projects necessary, notably substantial arched aqueducts. The periodic flooding of Mexico City in wet seasons led to a massive effort to divert water from the lakes to rivers outside its enclosed valley.

Except in times of flood the capital in America prospered and acquired economic power beyond that exercised by any city in Spain. Civic pride and civic aspiration were expressed by the construction of immensely ambitious cathedrals, not only in the capital and the newly founded Puebla nearby, but in remote regional centers with minuscule European populations such as Guadalajara in the west and Mérida in Yucatán.

Cortés had initiated the founding of new urban communities in order to get himself appointed Captain General and Chief Justice by the new town council in the name of the royal authority. The first municipality he established was Veracruz on the shore of the Gulf of Mexico. All his subsequent actions were taken as agent of the Spanish throne, not of Diego de Velásquez, the governor of Cuba who had dispatched the expedition. Private initiative in the name of the distant sovereign determined the lasting patterns of Mexican urbanism, which were established before the creation of regular royal institutions. In 1573 Philip II would sign official "Decrees on Population" prescribing in very considerable detail the layout to be followed in establishing new towns.

But the official decrees were published after most of the important communities had been founded. They confirmed a pattern of urban design that had been customary for almost half a century. As early as 1525 Cortés had formulated a general plan for new communities, writing to Hernando de Saavedra who was to establish towns in the jungles of Honduras,

> following the plan I have made, you must mark out the public places, just as they are shown: the plaza, church, town hall and jail, market and slaughterhouse, hospital.... Then you will indicate to each citizen his particular lot, as shown on the plan. . . . You will make sure the streets are very straight, and accordingly will find people who know how to lay them out.[1]

In the following year Charles V signed an order declaring that urban plans include a plaza from which the streets originated and that they be laid out regularly by the use of a measuring rod and line so that they could be extended as the town grew.

Cortés kept Charles V informed with his remarkable letters and acted in the Spanish interest as though he were a royal governor. He and the other conquistadors also prepared to establish themselves as feudal magnates securing substantial grants of Indian labor, the only readily apparent source of wealth in the country. As Bernal Díaz del Castillo noted, they came to serve God and the King, and also to get rich.

Charles V and the officials of his court had scant enthusiasm for the development of anything in the New World that resembled the medieval feudal and corporate structures that limited royal authority in Europe. The insatiable Hapsburg need for funds caused apprehension regarding the spread to Mexico of the West Indian system of encomienda, the granting of Indian labor as tribute to individual Spaniards. The first royal officials sent to New Spain were treasury officials charged with ensuring that the King received his fifth share of the spoils of the conquest. Next to be appointed were the officials of the First and Second Audiencias, courts with administrative as well as judicial authority, in some ways similar to

the county courts of many American states. The arrival in 1535 of the first viceroy, the distinguished aristocrat Antonio de Mendoza, continued the process of limiting the powers of Cortés and establishing royal control over both Indians and Spaniards. Ultimately Cortés was eased aside with the title of Marqués del Valle de Oaxaca, with vast tracts of land extending from the valleys of Mexico and Toluca south through the valley of Oaxaca to the Isthmus of Tehuantepec and with well over a hundred thousand Indian tribute payers. He was ultimately deprived of any role in the government of the country he had conquered. On the back of his last letter to Charles V, asking in advanced age for repayment for his services, someone wrote, "There is no reply."[2]

As early as 1526 the royal authorities began subdividing the Viceroyalty of New Spain into provinces with their own governors. In 1548 western Mexico, organized as New Galicia in 1530, was given a separate audiencia, first located in Compostela and then in Guadalajara. Towns not granted in encomienda or whose grant had been revoked became royal territory and were placed under alcaldes mayores. Córregidores were appointed as district governors with jurisdiction over important Spanish towns. Encomienda was limited to a single extension beyond the death of the original grantee. Royal tribute was assessed in private encomiendas as well as in crown territories.

Concurrent with political organization was the ecclesiastical organization of the country. In 1524 Cortés had asked Charles V for Franciscan and Dominican friars, denouncing as punishment for our sins the characteristic behavior of Spanish bishops who wasted resources donated to the church by lay people on pompous display and "other vices"[3] and on establishing hereditary estates for their children. Despite Cortés's warning against the demoralizing effect prelates would have upon newly converted Indians, the emperor soon appointed the first Mexican bishops, selecting Juan Garcés, a Dominican, for the diocese of Tlaxcala-Puebla and Juan de Zumárraga, a Franciscan, for the diocese of Mexico City. In the 1530s and 1540s other dioceses were created in Antequera (modern Oaxaca), Michoacán, and Guadalajara. The earliest bishops were admirable men, most of them members of the mendicant orders. Secular clergy, who served as parish priests for the Spanish population, arrived in gradually increasing numbers. Perhaps inevitably, conflicts developed by the middle decades of the century between the friars and the secular clergy regarding jurisdiction in particular towns, the question of Indians paying tithes to the bishops, and other matters. Philip II gave the bishops some control over the regular orders, but the friars retained much of their authority in many parts of Mexico well into the eighteenth century.

The founding of the city of Puebla, originally named Puebla de los Angeles, by the Second Audiencia in the spring of 1531 resulted from the wish to create a model for Spanish life in the new country. The First Audiencia seems to have conceived the idea of a new city for Spaniards, and Juan de Salmerón, *oidor* or judge of the Second Audiencia, took the lead in establishing it. Motolinía gives credit to the friars writing that he and his associates wished to provide for the settlers an alternative to waiting in idleness until they were awarded the service of Indians in encomienda. If the settlers could be persuaded to become farmers, devoting "themselves to tilling the fields and cultivating the land in the Spanish way. . . . They would lose their longing to return to their native country and would grow to love the land where they had their estates and were actively engaged in producing a livelihood."[4] A site was chosen in unsettled country near a small river not far distant from such major centers of Indian population as Cholula, Huejotzingo, and Tlaxcala. Not originally on the regular route to the coast, Puebla would become a principal stopping point on one of the highways constructed later from Veracruz to Mexico. Forty prospective townsmen were collected at Easter time, and they were joined by great numbers of Indians from the neighboring communities who carried materials to build straw huts to shelter them while they worked in constructing the town. They marched to the site "with their banners, singing and playing upon bells and others with groups of boy dancers."[5] A provisional plan for the town was laid out by a Spanish stonemason, and houses for all the settlers were completed by the Indians within a week. During the first rainy season the site was flooded and the inadequacy of its drainage became apparent. The following year the town was moved to the west bank of the river, and a new urban plan was devised that gave permanent form to the city. As in the rebuilt Tenochtitlán and a number of late medieval towns on both sides of the Pyrenees, a gridiron pattern was adopted. Puebla and other new towns shared the regularity that greatly impressed foreign visitors to Mexico City. The houses were of one or two stories and generally uniform in design, while the streets were all 14 1/2 yards in width. One house that was constructed out of line with the plan was ordered demolished and rebuilt. The axes of the gridiron were arranged so that the prevailing winds would not sweep directly down the streets. Each block measured 200 by 100 yards with the long side stretching east to west. The plaza, located at the right-angled intersection of the central streets, measured 217 by 128 yards and was surrounded by colonnades of wood. A fountain was located in the eastern half of the plaza, and the western half was left open for use as a market and for festivals and sporting events. The original cathedral was placed on one side of the plaza. Constructed between 1536 and 1539 by Indians from Calpan, it was three-aisled and thatch-roofed, with a wooden ceiling supported by two rows of handsome black stone pillars. Houses of government officials, prominent citizens, and merchants, which also served as places for political, legal, and business activities, were located on the remaining sides of the plaza.

Although there was some uncertainty regarding its future in the early years, by the middle of the sixteenth century Puebla had become the second city of New Spain, fulfilling the hopes of its founders. Its population at that time consisted primarily of people of modest means, farmers, merchants, shopkeepers, and artisans.

Other towns for Spaniards that would become regional centers were planned and constructed in similar fashion: Villa Real (modern San Cristóbal de las Casas) in southernmost Chiapas in 1528; Antequera (modern Oaxaca) in 1529; Guadalajara on its final site in 1542; and about the same time Valladolid (modern Morelia) in Michoacán and Mérida in Yucatán. Thirty towns in all were classified either as ciudad or villa before

1574. The largest had as many as five hundred Spanish families and the smallest only a handful. Guadalajara, the capital of New Galicia with its own audiencia, had only a few more than fifty families in 1569, and as late as 1605 consisted of a gridiron of twenty streets of one-story buildings. The cathedral then in use had walls of adobe, and the building of the audiencia was the only structure that had a second story.

Mexico City developed into the capital Cortés had envisioned. His city had approximately 125 European houses. By the late sixteenth century there were at least 1,500, and possibly as many as 4,000 Spanish inhabitants. In addition, as many as 80,000 to 100,000 Indians lived in the four barrios that lay outside the ordered plan of the European city. Viceroy Mendoza had directed a revision of the plan in 1546 which reflected his knowledge of the chapters on the embellishment of cities in the treatise on building of Leon Battista Alberti.

A glowing description of the splendors of Mexico City in 1554 is provided by Dr. Francisco Cervantes de Salazar, humanist professor of the newly founded University of Mexico, in his *Dialogues for the Study of the Latin Language*. In one of the *Dialogues* two residents tour the city with a visitor from Spain providing running commentary on the sights and responding to his observations. Their comments anticipate those that continued to be made for a quarter of a millennium until the time of Alexander von Humboldt early in the nineteenth century. Admiration is first expressed for the width and straightness of the streets and for the uniformity of the houses, limited to two stories as a protection against earthquakes and to permit the free circulation of air to disperse the noxious vapors of the swampy lake. The size of the plaza, and its surrounding buildings and mercantile colonnades, drew fulsome praise. The imposing structure shared by the viceroy and the audiencia was the building begun by

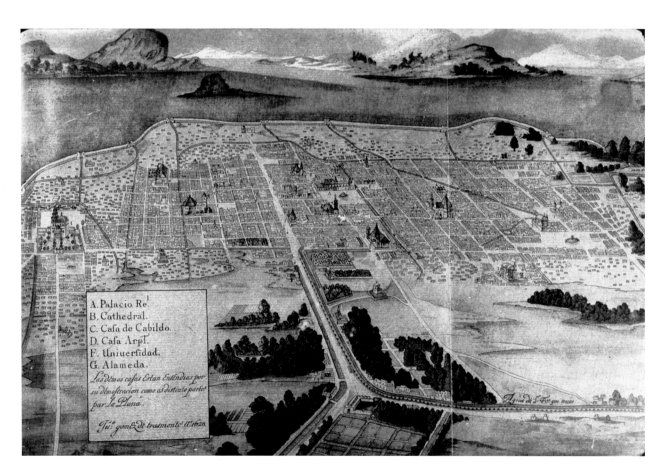

3.1 Mexico City, bird's eye view in 1628, by Juan Gómez de Trasmonte, detail.

42

Cortés on the site of Montezuma's *tecpan* and seemed large enough to hold an army, to be "another city not merely a palace."[6] The first cathedral, three-aisled and roofed with tramped earth, was begun in 1524 and finished by Bishop Zumárraga about 1532, and struck the visitor as unworthy of the city, "so small, so humble, and so lacking in adornment."[7] It would endure, subject to continual repairs, in the midst of the plaza until 1624. The conventos of the Dominicans and the Franciscans, and that of the Augustinians then under ambitious construction, were visited and described. In the tour of San Francisco particular attention was devoted to Pedro de Gante's mosquelike open chapel of San José de los Naturales (St. Joseph of the Natives), supported by tall sloping columns of wood and arranged so that the "crowd of Indians, great as it is, who press in here from everywhere on feast days are able to see without obstruction and hear the priest as he performs the Holy Sacrifice."[8] Within thirty years of the reconstruction of the city an impressive array of institutions had been established. The speakers mentioned separate schools for girls and boys of mixed blood, offspring of liaisons between Spaniards and Indian women, and the nearly twenty-year-old College of Santa Cruz at Tlatelolco, where Indian youths were given a humanistic education and taught to speak and write Latin. The faculty of the college at different times included two French Franciscans with doctorates from the University of Paris, the great students of Aztec culture Bernardino de Sahagún and Andrés de Olmos, and an Indian scholar, Antonio Valeriano. Valeriano served as governor of an Indian barrio of the city (San Juan Tenochtitlán), spoke and wrote graceful Latin as well as Spanish and Nahuatl, and collaborated in the Sahagún's investigations and, probably, in his writing. At the western edge of the city in the general vicinity of the Convento of San Francisco, the sightseeing trio paused to admire the handsome triangular commercial structure, the Shops of Tejada, named for its builder. Two sides containing identical shops were fronted by long porticoes that were supported by colonnades. Each shop included compact living quarters consisting of an entryway, a sizeable hall, a servant's area, a kitchen, and two dining rooms, and on the second

story above the porticoes amply windowed bedrooms. The rear side faced a canal and provided for the landing of goods at two wharflike structures that were connected to the building by flights of stone steps. Beyond the ordered Spanish section of the city, the three men noticed an outlying Indian barrio with its huts low along the ground. The visitor commented on the absence of orderly arrangement and one of the residents responded, "Such has always been their way of living," so soon had imperial Tenochtitlán been forgotten.

In 1580 the city contained almost a fifth of the Europeans in the country. In addition to approximately 100,000 Indians in the barrios, there were unnumbered mestizo offspring of what were usually informal unions of Europeans and Indians. Mestizos were occasionally assimilated in the Spanish community, often lived with the Indians, but, exasperatingly, frequently lived apart from either society, having no regular employment or property, paying no tribute, acting as trouble-making parasites and disturbing Indian pueblos. Blacks, ultimately to be wholly assimilated into the Mexican population, were a conspicuous segment of the city's population in the sixteenth century. Black slaves were held by individuals such as Bishop Zumárraga and by the government. They worked as herders, artisans, weavers, construction workers, and outside the city in mines, on sugar plantations, and as overseers of Indians. Numerous blacks were free. One was reported to control the labor of a village of one thousand Indians; others became vagabonds, making trouble for peaceful citizens and feared by the government.

Dr. Cervantes de Salazar's sightseers commented on a street inhabited by craftsmen "such as carpenters, blacksmiths, locksmiths, weavers, barbers, bakers, painters, stonemasons, tailors, shoemakers, armorers, makers of candles, makers of bows, sword cutlers, makers of biscuits, inn keepers, [and] lathe turners."[9] European artisans and building craftsmen had been gradually growing in numbers since the days of Martín de Sepúlveda, a mason who had supervised construction of the houses of Cortés and the first cathedral and had been regarded as too important to the city to be allowed to participate in subsequent campaigns of conquest. A Portuguese mason, Diego Díaz of Lisbon, Master of Works in the early 1530s, later claimed to have taught all the Indian masons the skills of European stone cutting.

Indian artisans were responsible for almost all the architectural work done for the friars outside the city, and they provided strong competition for the Europeans in the city. Bernal Díaz del Castillo named three painters and carvers, Marcos de Aquino, Juan de la Cruz, and El Crespillo, comparing them favorably with Appeles, the legendary painter of ancient Greece, Michelangelo, and Alonso Berruguete, the leading sculptor of sixteenth-century Spain. Native craftsmen not only demonstrated great skill, they undercut the wages of the Europeans. A visiting Englishman, Henry Hawkes, noted in 1572 that "Indians will do work so good cheap that poor young men that go out of Spain to get their living, are not set on work."[10]

In response the Europeans attempted to control the market by establishing medieval-style guilds. One for painters and gilders was approved by the viceroy in 1557, and another was authorized eleven years later for craftsmen in wood—carpenters, wood-carvers, joiners, and violin makers. Guild members could establish standards for their craft, train apprentices, examine them, and admit them to the guild as masters. They could limit the number of practitioners and indirectly, to some extent, determine prices. Indian craftsmen were not admitted to the guilds but were allowed to produce carved flowers, birds, and animals. Saints were to be portrayed by Europeans alone. Despite the regulations of the guilds, Indian artisans continued to find work and to be employed by European masters. The 1570 Ordinances of Gilders declare "that no one who is not a Master should gild any . . . object whatsoever." Yet a contract of 1585 discloses that "Marcos de San Pedro, Indian, gilder"[11] agreed to gild the great retablo of Huejotzingo for its designer, the Master of Painting Simon Pereyns.

Parish priests and male and female members of religious orders had assumed significant roles in the city's life by the last quarter of the century. In 1590 there were seven conventos for men and seven for women. Both the Augustinians and the Franciscans had two male establishments.

There were single conventos for the Dominicans and for two orders recently arrived, the Carmelites, the order reformed by Saint Teresa of Avila, and the Jesuits. Before the end of the century the Mercedarians, the Order of Our Lady of Mercy, established themselves in Mexico City. One of the Mercedarians, Fray Bartolomé de Olmedo, had been chaplain for the army of Cortés, and they would eventually establish twenty-three conventos in the country.

Tertiary sisters, or beatas, who were associated with the Franciscan order but had not taken full vows and were uncloistered, had been in the city as early as 1525 teaching Indian girls. In 1528 the empress, in response to a request from Cortés, sent sixteen women, nine of them nuns, to extend the educational program. Six more arrived with Cortés's wife two years later. The women teachers were enthusiastically welcomed and given as charges the daughters of prominent Indian families. Later several of the beatas were discovered to be proponents of "illuminism," a form of interior religious belief known especially in Seville that seemed to conservatives dangerously unorthodox, akin to Lutheranism. Bishop Zumárraga complained to Prince Philip in 1544 that the girls educated by these women were lazy and not interested in serving husbands. He asked that only cloistered nuns be sent "who would not flaunt their lack of obedience and roam out in the world." Spanish nuns founded the royally supported convento of La Concepción in the early 1540s. Young women of leading Creole families and granddaughters of Montezuma were admitted, and nuns from this convent founded others in Mexico City including the Regina Coeli (1573), Jesús María (1580), La Encarnación (1594), Santa Inés (1600), San José de Gracia (1610), and Nuestra Señora de Balvanera (1619). Conceptionist conventos were also founded in Puebla and Mérida. By the end of the seventeenth century there were in the capital, in addition to the seven Conceptionist establishments, four convents for women associated with the Franciscan order, and one or more associated with the Dominicans, the Jeronimites, and the Carmelites.

The terrible epidemics, which periodically obliterated so many Indians that Fray Bernardino de Sahagún feared they would soon be extinct, speeded the erection of many hospitals. Cortés endowed the still-existing Hospital de Jesús of Mexico City as early as 1525. Two famous Utopian hospitals of Santa Fé were organized by Vasco de Quiroga, a judge of the audiencia and later Bishop of Michoacán. Other hospitals were supported by Bishop Zumárraga and the second viceroy, Luis de Velasco. Many were founded by the Franciscans and Augustinian orders. Zumárraga's successor, Archbishop Montúfar, declared in 1554 that hospitals were the most important institution in Mexico, and a year later the first synod of the Mexican church ordered that hospitals be built alongside the churches in all Indian villages.

In 1580 the city had seven hospitals, six for Spaniards and one for Indians. The hospital for Indians handled two to three hundred patients in eight rooms. The staff included two physicians, two surgeons, five chaplains, and a considerable number of attendants. The proceeds from a theater were a major source of support for the hospital. The Congregation of San Hipólito, an order of lay persons, was founded by a former convict, Bernardino Alvarez, to support hospitals. Its principal hospital in Mexico City, established in 1567, cared for the mentally ill, priests of failing health, and aging conquistadors. The congregation also operated schools. It established two hospitals in Veracruz and others in Oaxtepec, Jalapa, Perote, Puebla, Oaxaca, Acapulco, and Querétaro in New Spain and others in Guatemala, Havana, and the island of Dominica. Support came from donations, royal subsidies, and the profits of sugar mills. A similar order from Spain, the Hospitalers of San Juan de Dios, arrived in Mexico in 1603. By the middle of the eighteenth century they were operating twenty-six hospitals. The Bethlemites, founded in 1650, also opened hospitals in Mexico. The Jesuit order, which reached the city in 1572, founded several educational institutions, including those later consolidated into the Colegio Maximo de San Pedro y San Pablo that educated many of the leaders of the society of New Spain. By the end of the seventeenth century the Augustinians, the Dominicans, the Franciscans, and the Mercederians were all operating colleges that provided pre-university education for boys.

A university, discussed in the first of Cervantes de Salazar's *Dialogues*, had opened in 1553, as a pontifical and a royal institution. Governance was patterned on the University of Salamanca, and chairs were established in medicine and in Indian languages as well as in theology and law. The quality of education available to Mexicans preparing for careers in the church and in the learned professions approximated that of Spanish universities. Viceroy Mendoza and Bishop Zumárraga had brought about the founding of a printing shop which was opened in 1535 by Johann Gromberg, a native of Germany. Volumes bearing its colophon survive from 1539. Early publications consisted primarily of grammars and devotional and theological books. Evangelical works appeared in several Indian languages. Of the 109 known examples published before 1572, 80 were written by Franciscans and 69 were in Nahuatl.

The "Holy Office," or Inquisition, was formally established in the city with the arrival in 1571 of its first head, Dr. Pedro Moya de Contreros, who later was appointed archbishop. Inquisitorial powers had previously been exercised by Franciscan and Dominican friars and by Bishop Zumárraga and Archbishop Montúfar. Dismay at Zumárraga's sentencing of the Indian leader of Texcoco to be burned in 1539 for scoffing at Christianity, attacking Spanish authority, and resuming ancestral religious practices led to Indians being declared exempt from the powers of the Inquisition. Despite its independence from regular political and ecclesiastical authorities and its intimidating secrecy, the Inquisition was accepted without protest by the populace at large. Relatively few were prosecuted apart from outsiders; captured heretics, that is, English and other foreign Protestants; and Portuguese Jews who, despite ostensible profession of Christianity, secretly practiced their old religion. Among the offenses investigated were witchcraft, bigamy, blasphemy, and priests soliciting sexual favors from women in the confessional.

The use of judicial torture to establish guilt or innocence, dismaying to the modern sense of what is fair and right, was normal practice in courts of law at the time everywhere in Europe. The great public theatricals of the *autos-da-fe* (acts of faith), which were staged every few years, attracted almost everyone in the city. By the seventeenth century a very elaborate ceremony had developed. The sentencing was preceded by two processions. On the eve of the *auto da fe* the Knights of Calatrava marched at the head of the assembled nobility of the city who were followed by the Dominican friars singing their responses. Among them was their black-garbed prior wearing the cross of the "Holy Office." The Dominicans spent the night at the scaffold praying and protecting the cross. At six in the morning the convicted, costumed in conical caps and sleeveless yellow *sambenitos* which fell to the knees and were inscribed with red crosses indicative of the degree of guilt, were marched to the scaffold, wax taper in hand. They were preceded by several companies of troops and followed by the great crosses and the clergy of all the city's churches. At the rear came the civil servants carrying their black wands of office and leading a saddled horse that carried a box wrapped in scarlet taffeta holding the records of those to be sentenced. Virtually all of the small minority of victims who were sentenced to be burned were killed quickly with the garrote before being set afire. Other sentences ranged from rowing in the king's galleys, or being publicly beaten while being marched "through the usual streets" at the tail of a horse, to spending some months in menial service in a convento.

The historical development of New Spain was permanently altered by the unexpected discovery in 1546 of massive deposits of silver just as the early dreams of riches had faded. The occasion was casual, unlike the desperate search for the lost treasure of Montezuma or the wild expedition of Francisco Vásquez de Coronado north into the present United States in quest for the legendary Seven Cities of Cíbola. A small body of soldiers led by Juan de Tolosa, a Basque, stopped for the night beneath a steep hill in the country of the Zacatecos, untamed nomadic Indians. In return for some trading trinkets the soldiers were given samples of silver ore. By the spring of 1550 a sprawling, disorderly mining camp had been established at Zacatecas, 375 miles northwest of the capital, well beyond the civilized area of the central plateau. Prospectors rushed up from all parts of New Spain, leaving the Guadalajara-Compostela area of New Galicia half deserted. Diggings were claimed and rapidly abandoned;

taxes were evaded and claims were jumped. The town layout bore no resemblance to the formal gridiron of Mexico City and Puebla. Houses and lanes were strung along sloping terrain by the sides of a small stream running between two steep hills. The haphazard linear pattern of the temporary camp was preserved in the city, which remained the greatest of Mexican mining centers until after the middle of the eighteenth century.

The need for roads to Zacatecas from the Guadalajara area and then for a highway from Mexico City led to an extended building campaign. Road building had become a major Spanish enterprise necessitated by the introduction of wheeled vehicles and large European animals of burden. Before the conquest and for many years afterwards, human bearers had been the principal means of carrying goods. The first great wagon road had been constructed in 1530 and 1531 between Mexico City and Veracruz. Other new roads had opened western Mexico to easy access from the east. Like the streets, bridges, and aqueducts of the cities, and the churches and living quarters of the conventos, the roads were built by Indians under the system of tribute labor. The Camino Real de la Tierra Adentro from Mexico City to Zacatecas was constructed between 1550 and 1555 for use at first by Indian bearers and then by pack mules and wagon trains. Heavy

3.2 Zempoala area, aqueduct.

equipment, minerals such as lead, mercury, and the raw and coined silver, as well as wines and food in barrels all required wagon transport. At regular intervals inns were established for overnight stops. Run by Indians or Spanish ranchers, the inns provided provisions at fixed prices so that travelers would not be tempted to raid the Indian villages or ranches along the way. Inns in unpopulated country frequently were designed as fortified presidios to provide military protection against the Chichimec Indians who were a persistent threat to the safety of travelers. Towns such as Querétaro and San Miguel (now designated San Miguel de Allende) grew in importance as way stations on the highway.

The need for a good and regular supply of water was clear in a country marked in its temperate central area by a half-year-long dry season. After the capture of the city of Mexico, Cortés had ordered the restoration of the Aztec aqueduct from Chapultepec.

Concern for an adequate supply of water for the city continued throughout much of the colonial period. Water was brought in from Santa Fe in the hills southwest of the city and from Azacapotzalco on the western shore of the lake as well as from Chapultepec. The original aqueduct was raised to flow over an extensive arcade before the middle of the sixteenth century. Its reconstruction in the 1590s took four years, three hundred Indian workers, and at least thirty thousand pesos. The most ambitious of the city's aqueducts was completed in 1620 to bring water from Santa Fe around the edge of Chapultepec hill and over nine hundred arches into the city from the west to a terminus near the northeast corner of the Alameda. A comparable number of arches was required to raise another aqueduct which ran into the city from the southwest, directly from Chapultepec. Innumerable other aqueducts were built by the Spaniards for conventos, towns, and haciendas. The normal form was the Roman arcade. Lengthy eighteenth-century aqueducts survive in Querétaro, Morelia, and Zacatecas. A very modest one still functions near the Mission Espada in San Antonio, Texas. The most noted of Mexican aqueducts is located on the northeastern border of the state of Mexico between Zempoala and Otumba over three series of arches. The longest,

incorporating sixty-seven arches, some reaching 120 feet in height and 8 feet in thickness, took five years to complete. The entire work, under construction by Indians for seventeen years in the mid-sixteenth century, was designed and supervised by a single Franciscan friar, Francisco de Templeque. A starkly handsome aqueduct, flanked by towers reminiscent of the minaret of the great mosque of Sammara, is at Los Remedios on the western edge of Mexico City. Another very impressive one is the many-tiered Arcos del Sitio near Tepotzotlán.

Distribution of water within the cities was by ducts to important buildings, by fountains at street corners, and by human water carriers. Thomas Gage wrote of "water-men" in 1625 selling water "from street to street, some in little boats, others in earthen tankards upon mules' or asses' backs." Large ornamental fountains were prominent features of the cities and towns of New Spain throughout the colonial period and served as gathering places for their people. An early document records the payment of fifty pesos to a mason, Juan de Entrambes Aguas, for erecting a fountain, basin, and column in the central plaza of Mexico City. Three notable fountains were constructed in the eighteenth century to disperse wa-

3.3 *Chiapa de Corzo, fountain, interior.*

3.4 Chiapa de Corzo, fountain.

ter from the aqueducts running into the capital, two on the one from Chapultepec. A fountain stood near the Chapultepec gate, and the famous *Salto del Agua* stood at the terminus. The latter has been reconstructed at Tepotzotlán and replicated on its original site. The even more impressive Fountain of the Musicians at Tlaxpana at an intermediate point on the other aqueduct was demolished needlessly in 1879. Important sixteenth-century fountains included one in Texcoco, which was demolished in 1942. Its quadrilateral basin had bastionlike projections at its corners connected with outwardly curving sections in the middle of each side. The superstructure radiated from a powerful round central pier in flattened arches to columns placed at the edges of the convex projections. These four columns were sustained from their outer sides by graceful flying buttresses. A simpler but related fountain with eight round peripheral piers circling a giant pier at its center, which supported an escutcheon carrying the town's coat of arms and an inscription in Nahuatl, survives in Tochimilco east of Puebla.

The most remarkable of Mexican fountains was erected about 1560 in the far south in Chiapa de Corzo, a modest community of Indians located on the north slope of the Central American highlands as they rise from the Isthmus of Tehuantepec. The structure, designed by the Dominican Fray Rodrigo de León and completed under the supervision of another Spaniard, combines Renaissance, Gothic, and Islamic features in a unified whole that has no direct precedent in

Spanish architecture in Europe or in America. The plan combines an inner and an outer octagon. The inner, housing the fountain (Fig. 3.3), is covered by a dome that appears smoothly uniform from the exterior as in the Renaissance fashion but is constructed as an eight-sectioned vault in the medieval manner. The vault is sustained by eight wedge-shaped piers that are supported by the eight semicircular flying buttresses of the outer octagon. The material is brick, common in Andalusian architecture since Moorish times and convenient in Chiapas where building stone is not easily available. The decorative brickwork, produced by both molding and cutting, is Moorish in derivation. The arches opening into the interior octagon in each of the eight bays and the eight semicircular arches of the sturdy flying buttresses are strongly marked with shadow that is produced by an alternation of flat bricks, projecting and recessed. Bricks projecting in diamond shape create forceful panels of ornamentation above the arches and on the inner surfaces of the wedge-shaped piers beneath them. The parapets at the top of each of the eight bays are marked by superposed pairs of diamond forms set in recessed panels. Special forms of brick create pinnacles above the piers and buttresses and above the merlons at the top of the circular stair tower attached to one of the buttresses.

The most ambitious of Mexican water engineering works was the *Desagüe* of Huehuetoca, a combination of drainage canals and tunnels north of the capital. The flooding, which had been endemic during the rainy season in preconquest Tenochtitlán, worsened because of new Spanish methods of agriculture and the deforestation of the slopes and valley of Mexico caused by relentless cutting of timber. Major floods in 1604 and 1607 convinced the civil authorities that the traditional Aztec methods of relying upon dikes at critical points in the chain of connected lakes would no longer suffice. Approval was given to a plan proposed by a German-born printer, interpreter for the Inquisition, cartographer, and mathematician whose name was hispanicized as Enrico Martínez. Martínez proposed to drain the northernmost lake, Zumpango, and Río Cuautitlán, the largest in the valley, to prevent their water from flowing into Lake Texcoco and ultimately pouring into the city's streets. In addition he proposed to draw water north from Lake Texcoco to the lower end of Lake Zumpango. Full implementation of Martínez's proposal was long delayed. But work progressed rapidly on the first phase after ground was broken on November 28, 1607. Roughly 1,500 Indians were employed at one time, over 60,000 in all. They worked with pick axes and shovels digging over four miles of drainage canal and the necessary dikes and bridges for roads. Perpendicular shafts were also dug at intervals through the range of hills forming the northern rim of the valley in order to excavate the four-mile-long tunnel, which was approximately thirteen feet high and ten feet wide and which led ultimately to the Gulf of Mexico. On September 17, 1608, the viceroy and the archbishop attended the ceremonial opening of the system as water first flowed out of the valley toward the gulf. Enrico Martínez later reported that only twenty-one Indians and two Spaniards had lost their lives in completing the great project and for the first thirteen years of its maintenance. Its cost was substantial, almost a fifth of the annual royal revenue from silver mining, and there was resistance to the effort needed to maintain it. The crumbling roof of the tunnel was shored up at critical points at first with planks supported by pillars and later with masonry arches, but the tunnel deteriorated so much that it was of little use in the great floods of 1629–34. Although approximately eighty years old, Martínez was briefly jailed as a scapegoat, then freed and asked for advice on the *Desagüe* until his final illness. Subsequent efforts to restore the system continued periodically throughout the seventeenth and most of the eighteenth century. Its expansion to Martínez's complete scheme was initiated in 1856 and inaugurated by Porfirio Díaz in 1900.

The Major Cathedrals

Mérida, Cathedral of San Ildefonso

Although post-Maya Yucatán was the first of Mexico sighted by Spaniards, it was not pacified until twenty years after the conquest of Tenochtitlán. Mérida, capital of Spanish Yucatán,

was founded by Francisco Montejo, son of Francisco Montejo, comrade of Cortés, and cousin of Francisco Montejo, founder of Valladolid in Yucatán. Mérida was located on the Maya site of Tiho. So much stone was reclaimed from the flattening of four of the five pyramids of the ceremonial center that there was a ready supply for construction as late as the 1580s. Few houses were of stone. Indian dwellings in the seven outlying barrios were thatched huts of wood, such as are omnipresent in rural Yucatán today. A secular parish was established in 1542, the year Mérida was founded. The Franciscans arrived four years later, adapting the fifth pyramid as a platform for their convento and occupying, for 270 years, buildings that had been part of the pagan religious complex.

In 1563 construction was initiated by Bishop Toral on an audaciously ambitious cathedral for an aspiring capital whose population had not yet reached one hundred Spanish settlers. The designer is not known, but he must have been a European who had been in the Caribbean and was familiar with the earliest of American cathedrals, Santo Domingo, constructed between 1512 and 1541. Two architects who directed construction of the cathedral are known to have worked on the fortifications of Havana: Pedro de Aulestia, who is recorded as being in charge in 1571

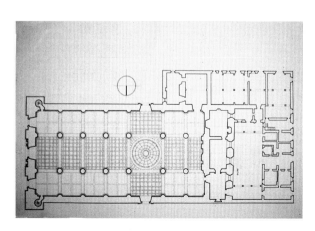

3.5 *Cathedral of Mérida, plan, from* Cuarenta Siglos de plastica mexicana: Arte Colonial.

and 1572; and Juan Miguel de Agüero, who completed the dome in 1598. Among the other masters of works were Francisco de Alarcón, Francisco Claros, who was responsible for some defective work, and Gregorio de la Torre.

In plan the cathedral of Mérida (Fig. 3.5) is rectangular, consisting of two joined squares and ordered by simple mathematical relationships like the plans of the Cathedral of Santo Domingo and several Spanish cathedrals beginning with Toledo in the thirteenth century. The interior is subdivided into a nave and flanking aisles and into seven bays that are constructed in accord with the ideal dimensions of the Italian architectural theorists of the Renaissance. In six of the seven bays, the four of the nave and the two in the sanctuary beyond the crossing, the aisle bays are square and those of the nave rectangular, examples of the ideal form whose long side equals a diagonal line drawn across a square formed from the short side.

3.6 Cathedral of Mérida, interior, diagonal view.

3.8 Cathedral of Mérida, central section of the facade. See also Plate III.

3.7 Cathedral of Mérida, longitudinal section, from Cuarenta Siglos.

The seventh bay, located between the nave and the sanctuary and under the dome, is deepened into a square in the nave and into rectangles in the aisles.

In type the cathedral is a hall church, its aisles equaling its nave in height. Cylindrical piers support domed vaults, which are decorated in the nave, and simulated transepts with a network of ribs resembling classical coffers. The interior of the semicircular dome, the earliest surviving in Mexico, is also covered by a coffered network, as are the pendentives. The dome supports a lantern that on the exterior is linked to finials by delicate flying buttresses which resemble ribbons. An inscription on the dome reads, "The master of this was Juan Miguel de Agüero, the year 1598."

The tall austere front of the cathedral is dominated by narrow flanking towers and a blind arch in its central element. It is dated 1599. The towers have plain two-stage belfreys of unequal size, the earlier constructed between 1597 and 1600, and the later not until 1773. The great blind arch encloses the main portal, the unadorned opening to provide light for the choir, and above it the patch of graceful strapwork ornamentation which is the decorative highlight of the facade. Between the towers and the arched central element are recessed strips of bare wall into which are cut the side portals. The whole clifflike facade rises high above the vaults in a false front and is crowned at differing levels by balustrades. The portals are relatively small in scale, dwarfed by the towers and the great central arch. Their ornamentation is of a restrained, purist Renaissance style. The central portal is framed by pairs of filleted Corinthian pilasters enclosing statues in niches. The side portals are framed by austere arches and pediments.

GUADALAJARA: CATHEDRAL OF THE ASSUMPTION

Guadalajara was founded in the early 1530s, shortly after Nuño de Guzmán passed through the area in his campaign to create a fiefdom in western Mexico. Franciscans began activities in a nearby Indian community, Tetlan, as early as 1531. A royal governor arrived in 1537

3.9 Cathedral of Guadalajara, interior, from Manuel Toussaint, Colonial Art in Mexico, *p. 114, photograph by Gabriel Ibarra.*

when the Spanish villa was located northeast of the Río Grande de Santiago. The settlement was relocated to its present site southwest of the river in 1541. Seven years later the first bishop arrived with secular clergy to establish the cathedral parish. At that time the city had approximately three hundred Spanish citizens, a roughly equivalent number of blacks and mulattoes, and about three thousand Indians, living primarily in the suburban barrios.

The first cathedral was small and of makeshift thatched and adobe construction. A larger more architecturally pretentious structure was erected of similarly perishable materials in 1565 by Indian workers under the direction of Alonso de Robalcava. It was destroyed by fire nine years later, but as early as 1568 planning was underway for the present cathedral. Royal acknowledgment of the project came in a cédula of 1576. The designer is unknown. Martín Casillas was in charge of construction in 1599. At that time the walls and piers were virtually finished and the question of the vaulting became critical. Diego de Aguilera, maestro mayor of the Cathedral of Mexico, was asked for advice and he recommended the most Gothic design followed in any Mexican Cathe-

3.10 Cathedral of Guadalajara, facade.

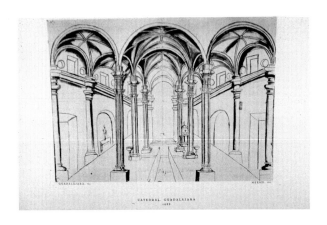

3.11 Cathedral of Guadalajara, interior, drawing of 1689 in the Archive of the Indies. Diego Angulo Íñiguez Planos de monumentos arquitectonicos de América y Filipinas existentes en al Archivo de Indias, Laminas I, Lamina 14.

dral. Ribs rise from clusters above the piers and spread across the shallow-domed vaults, joining other, supplementary, ribs in decorative patterns. The structure was ready for dedication in 1618.

Like Mérida and most Spanish cathedrals—from Seville, whose construction was initiated in 1401, to Jaen, in mid-sixteenth century—the Cathedral of Guadalajara is of the hall church type. In plan it is rectangular, with square towers placed outside the corners of the rectangle and projecting slightly beyond the central portion of the facade. A square-domed sanctuary bay projects from the center of the rectangle at the rear. Six square nave bays, covered with the patterned domed rib vaults, lead to the sanctuary. The aisle bays, covered with simpler domed rib vaults, are rectangular, slightly narrower than those of the nave. The interior elevations are influenced by those of the Cathedral of Málaga, built between 1550 and 1564. The springing of the bundled shafts of the vault ribs is supported by composite piers, consisting of square cores faced on the four sides with Doric half-columns, and full curved entablature blocks. Lunettes at the top of the exterior walls of the aisle bays are pierced with fenestration recalling Málaga; central rectangular windows are flanked by smaller round ones.

The facade is severe, broader than it is high and punctuated with plain buttresses. The three arched portals are framed with severe classical orders, more vigorous than those at Mérida and in a happier relationship to the facade as a whole. The present upper towers—consisting of a square stage with a pilaster order and two arched openings on each face, a quasi-Baroque octagonal stage alternating paired oval openings and scroll buttresses, and a quasi-Gothic spire—were constructed in the nineteenth century after an 1818 earthquake. The low-arched parapet with bristling pinnacles, which now rises above the central facade, was also a later addition. The interior was redecorated in Neo-Classical white and gold.

Three drawings, dated 1689, in the Archive of the Indies in Seville suggest the cathedral's appearance at that time. The towers were then topped with simple domes resting on octagonal stages, with their eight-arched openings ornamented by an applied order of half-columns. Below the octagon was a squat square stage containing two arched openings on each face but without the present pilasters. A drawing of the interior represents the principal present forms bare of their overlay of white and gold Neo-Classical decoration. No retablos are represented and few church furnishings of any sort. The walls are notably austere, without any ornamentation about the round and rectangular forms of the modest windows of the upper lunettes, marked below by ponderous unfluted half-columns, and topped by bulbous rounded entablature blocks and by large unadorned arches enclosing inset altars.

MEXICO CITY AND PUEBLA: THE CATHEDRALS OF THE ASSUMPTION AND OF THE IMMACULATE CONCEPTION OF MARY

By the middle of the sixteenth century the first cathedrals of Mexico and Puebla seemed unworthy of their aspiring cities, as the imaginary speakers in Dr. Cervantes de Salazar's *Dialogues* of 1554 demonstrate. Years earlier royal decrees of 1536 and 1544 had commanded the erection of a new cathedral for the capital. A plan had been sent to Spain in 1546 by Viceroy Mendoza but it seemed unsatisfactory to the court, and a new decree, specifying that the costs of the new structure be shared by the crown, the Indians, and the Spanish settlers, was issued on August 28, 1552. Archbishop Montúfar wrote in 1554 that he and Viceroy Velasco wished to initiate construction of a cathedral on the scale of the Cathedral of Seville, the largest in area of all European medieval churches. If a village of a hundred or so Spaniards undertook as ambitious a structure as the Cathedral of Mérida, only a structure as grand as Seville seemed adequate to the aspirations of the largest city in the Spanish empire. Overly ambitious foundations were laid for a church running from west to east, but four years later the archbishop suggested that the city should be satisfied with a cathedral of the size of Segovia or Salamanca, the last of the major Gothic cathedrals still under construction in Spain. Some preliminary work on construction of the present structure may have begun as early as 1563. The minutes of a meeting of clerical officials held on February 15, 1570, read:

> It was agreed that it be located and built on the site where the arcade called Lerma stands using part of the small plaza which is in front

of the houses of the Marqués de Valle . . . oriented north-south, with the Puerto del Perdon toward the Plaza Mayor and the bell tower at the front of the said church, and that it should be built with three well-lighted naves, and lateral chapels all roofed in wood.[12]

Puebla's original cathedral, constructed a decade after Mexico City's, was for some time the most admired religious structure in New Spain, but its condition deteriorated so that the architect Claudio Arciniega was sent from the capital to inspect it in 1564. Some repairs had been made in 1555 and partial reconstruction was made in 1587. Meanwhile a new cathedral was planned. Material was collected and some preliminary work was probably initiated as early as 1555, or a few years later, but little was actually built until the arrival of the architect Francisco Becerra in 1575. Before he left for Peru five years later, Becerra developed a plan for the new cathedral and initiated construction. Like the design approved in Mexico in 1570, Becerra's plan called for a rectangular structure including a nave and side aisles with flanking rows of chapels. Towers were conceived for the four corners of the structure but there was no provision for a central dome.

Both Becerra's design and the initial conception of the new Cathedral of Mexico, which was to face toward the great plaza and the site of the generally scorned old cathedral, were, despite Archbishop Montúfar's references to the late Gothic cathedrals of Salamanca and Segovia, based on a more up-to-date model—Vandelvira's design for the new Cathedral of Jaen begun in 1543. Rectangular hall churches were intended, resembling in plan the double-square layout of the Cathedral of Mérida. Towers at all four corners may have been planned in Mexico, as well as in Puebla, and in the capital a wide flat chevet for the sanctuary was designed to push through the northern wall of the rectangle. Construction work proceeded with some speed there on the walls and the vaults of the chapels on the northern periphery. Masonry vaulting was adopted instead of the wooden roofing mentioned in the minutes of February 15, 1570. The square piers were faced on four sides with Doric half-columns. Had con-

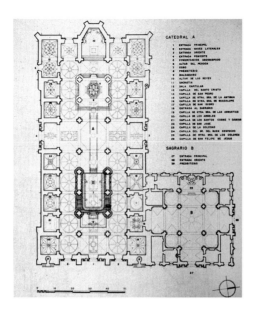

3.12 *Cathedral of Mexico and the Sagrario, plan, from* Cuarenta Siglos.

struction followed the original scheme, the "three naves" within the outer tiers of chapels were unlikely to have been as "well lighted"[13] as the minutes hopefully anticipated.

In 1584 Claudio de Arciniega was named Maestro Mayor of the Cathedral of Mexico and began an extensive revision of the plans. Arciniega had come to New Spain as a young man in the middle of the century and had designed the celebrated Tumulo Imperial, the most classical structure yet erected in New Spain. It was built in 1559 in Pedro de Gante's chapel of San José for the commemoration of the death of the Emperor Charles V. Arciniega's modifications were suggested by Juan de Herrera's design for a new cathedral for Valladolid. Herrera, the most severe of Spanish designers, had completed Philip II's Escorial. His austere style would continue to influence much of Spanish architecture during the seventeenth century as well as the cathedrals of Mexico and Puebla and other Mexican buildings. For the Cathedral of Valladolid, which was never fully constructed, he conceived a double clerestory structure with a rigorously centralized double-square plan.

Arciniega's changes, which set the pattern followed during the very extended period of construction, called for raising the vaults of the nave above those of the aisles, for raising the aisle vaults above those covering the flanking tiers of chapels and, probably, for changing the decora-

3.13 *Cathedral of Mexico, interior, diagonal view at crossing toward sacristy.*

3.14 *Cathedral of Mexico, diagonal view from the southwest. See also Plate IV.*

tion of the aisle vaults from the ribbed Gothic designs used for the northern peripheral chapels to saucer domes with spokelike ribs, more in keeping with advanced contemporary taste. But two ribbed vaults of Gothic type would be constructed as late as 1623 to cover the special area of the sacristy. Arciniega pierced the lunettes of the wall rising above entrances to the chapels by three arched windows, the central one much larger and higher than those that flanked it. These windows provided ample light for the aisles. The nave, towering above the aisles, was covered by a barrel vault intersected in each bay by transverse vaulting in order to provide light through similar triple windows piercing the lunettes of the upper walls. As a result of Arciniega's modifications, the completed cathedral has the three "well lighted naves"[14] called for in 1570. The principal architectural features of the interior—the barrel-vaulted nave, the saucer-domed aisles, and the tall piers decorated by fluted Doric half-columns which continue up across the barrel vault as transverse arches—are drawn from the Renaissance vocabulary of classical forms, but the whole has the tall, airy lightness characteristic of a Gothic cathedral.

The exterior, in contrast, is severe and massive. Although broken by the powerful towers and dome with its steep lantern, the dominant effect is horizontal, marked by the extended balustrades over chapels, aisles, and nave. Although softened by the warmth of the buff stone, the whole is stern, shaped by a Herrerean sensibility. The interior was completed by the closing of the central dome and the last of the vaults in the 1660s under the direction of Maestro Mayor Luis Gómez de Trasmonte. During the 1650s intensified activity in construction had been ordered by Viceroy Don Francisco Fernández de la Cueva y Enríquez de Cabera, 8th Duque de Alburquerque, who may have felt embarrassed by the near completion of the Cathedral of Puebla in the 1640s. Alburquerque's interest in the progress of the work was shown by almost daily visits of inspection. In 1654 he oversaw the week-long hoisting into place of the great bell, Doña María, which weighed fifteen thousand pounds. He also presided over a dedication in 1656. Yet at the sec-

ond and final dedication in 1667 the facade, the towers, and the side portals remained uncompleted. (The construction of these elements will be described later.)

By that time the interior of the Cathedral of Puebla had been virtually finished for eighteen years. The author of the transformation of that structure from hall church to double-leveled basilica is not known. Claudio de Arciniega may have been influential. His brother Luis had been

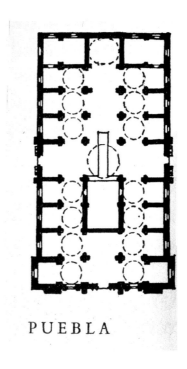

PUEBLA

3.15 Cathedral of Puebla, plan, from George Kubler, Art and Architecture in Spain and Portugal and their American Dominions, fig. 31.

in charge of construction between 1589 and his death in 1601. Because work in Puebla had progressed less rapidly on the hall church design than in Mexico City, conversion to the double basilican type was easier than in the capital where the walls were advanced too far to be completely modified. The logical order of the Herrerean centralized double-square plan is evident in the total structure in Puebla from the foundations up.

In 1626 construction had been interrupted, and eight years later Juan Gómez de Trasmonte, Maestro Mayor of the Cathedral of Mexico and father of Luis Gómez de Trasmonte, had been directed by the viceroy, the Marqués de Cerralvo, to visit Puebla in order to examine the condition of the structure. Gómez de Trasmonte arrived early in 1635 and remained until 1637. He formulated plans for completing the cathedral, suggesting new methods of vaulting and concerning himself particularly with the problem of constructing and supporting the dome over the crossing.

Rapid progress in finishing the main fabric of the Cathedral of Puebla followed the arrival in New Spain in 1640 of Juan de Palafox y Mendoza. Palafox was the illegitimate son of an Aragonese marqués and protege of the Conde de Olivares, principal minister of King Philip IV. He arrived with dual powers as visitador general responsible for assessing the administration of the previous viceroy, and as bishop of Puebla. A man of severe rectitude, Bishop Palafox moved energetically to reform the ecclesiastical practices of his diocese and to purify the moral conduct of the country as a whole. For a brief period he acted as viceroy and he was offered the archbishopric of Mexico but he refused it, believing that a bishop should remain faithful to his diocese. Palafox became the central figure in the colony, admired, and even loved by his secular clergy and by the natives of New Spain generally, but distrusted and resisted by the viceroy, the archbishop of Mexico, the mendicant orders, and the Jesuits, who later blocked the efforts of King Charles III to secure his canonization.

During his nine years as bishop, Palafox constructed a well-endowed seminary, 2 colleges, 50 new churches, and 140 Baroque altarpieces. He was determined to oversee the completion of his cathedral as an emblem of the reformation of Christian Mexico. Puebla, because of its agricultural supremacy, was the richest diocese in New Spain, possessing double the resources of the archbishopric of Mexico. Palafox was able to dedicate to the construction of the cathedral twelve thousand pesos annually from his nearly fifty-thousand-peso income as bishop, three thousand from the income of the cathedral chapter, and another three thousand annually from the crown.

Yet these funds fell far short of the three hundred seventy thousand pesos expended in the eight years of his building campaign. In his final years, after he had been relegated to the obscure and impoverished bishopric of Osma in Castile, Juan de Palafox was struggling to repay the massive debt he had assumed in Puebla.

The concentration of much of the cath-

3.16 Cathedral of Puebla, interior, diagonal view of crossing and transept.

edral's construction within eight years make the building considerably more unified than its counterpart in the capital. The dedication took place on April 18, 1649, after Palafox had been recalled to Spain but before he sailed with the annual fleet in June. The festivities began at dawn and lasted all day with twelve hundred clergymen participating in services. Indians and blacks put on performances and choral music was conducted by the leading composer of New Spain, Juan Gutiérrez

Padilla. In his sermon the bishop evoked Jacob's visionary ladder to heaven as the prototype of all Christian churches. Recalling the words of the patriarch, he declared, "surely the Lord is in this place. . . . How full of religious awe is this place. . . . The House of God is the gate of heaven."

Bishop Palafox's adviser on artistic matters was Mosén Pedro García Ferrer, a priest from Aragon or Valencia, who had supervised the construction. The interior is generally similar to the Cathedral of Mexico save for decorative features and a few details of construction. The transverse arches of the bays of the nave do not reach as close to the top of the barrel vault, and, as a result, form lunettes in the wall rising above the aisle which are smaller than those in Mexico City. These lunettes are pierced by a single round window instead of the three arched rectangular windows which are used in the nave lunettes in Mexico. These triple windows are used in the aisles of both cathedrals in the lunettes in the walls above the flanking chapels. Fluted Doric half-columns and transverse arches are also common features.

In Puebla the saucer-domed roofing of the aisles was originally plain, marked only by transverse ribs separating the bays, and the vaulting of the nave was decorated only by a simple

3.18 Cathedral of Puebla, general view.

geometric pattern which can still be detected. The overall impression of the interior was even more sober than in Mexico City where there was a different sort of geometric ornamentation in the nave and a spoke rib pattern decorating the saucer domes of the aisles.

The severely rectangular interior measures 325 by 100 feet, appreciably less than Mexico's 375 by 180. Both cathedrals have choirs providing for the religious ceremonies of the clergy and occupying much of the entrance end of the nave (Figs. 3.12 and 3.15). Both had baldachins farther along their naves and both had chapels with major altars and retablos at their ends; Puebla's is placed against the flat rear wall of its rectangle and Mexico's arches deeply into the polygonal sanctuary which pushes through its rear wall. In the early nineteenth century Puebla's interior was refurbished, covering the vaults of the nave and domes of the aisles with coffering and white paint and enlivening the coffers and the graystone supporting members with gilt trim, transforming the original Herrerean severity into a Neo-Classical sparkle of white and gold. At that time Manuel Tolsá designed an impressive, if a trifle ponderous, baldachin, which José Manzo and others constructed. Manzo also modernized the retablo major, the original design of which, with the earliest twisting Salomonic columns in

3.17 Cathedral of Puebla, interior, capilla real.

57

3.19 Cathedral of Puebla, dome.

covered by colored tiles. The dome over the crossing, supported by an octagonal drum and by flying buttresses of charmingly awkward design, is probably the second oldest surviving on the central plateau, preceded only by the modest dome of the Church of Santa Teresa in Puebla. Completed about 1640 during Bishop Palafox's building campaign, it was designed by García Ferrer and built by the master mason Jerónimo de la Cruz. Within the next forty years, thirty-six domed churches were constructed in Puebla alone. The north

3.20 Cathedral of Puebla, facade.

3.21 Cathedral of Mexico, western side facade.

Mexico, was attributed by Bishop Palafox to Juan Martínez Montañes, the great sculptor of Seville. It had originally been constructed under the direction of Mosén Pedro García Ferrer and Lucas Durán.

 The exterior of the Cathedral of Puebla (Fig. 3.18), soberly constructed of gray stones, still reflects the austerity of Juan de Palafox and exemplifies the continuing influence of Herrera's counter-Renaissance style. The stony mass is enlivened by a dome over the crossing, which is decorated with colored tiles, and by towers 200 feet high, which are topped by small domes also

tower was completed by Carlos García Durango in 1680 on the basis of a design by Luis Gómez de Trasmonte and Roderigo Díaz de Aguilera. Its identical counterpart on the south was finally constructed nearly ninety years later by Miguel Vallejo. The square towers are divided equally between their tall plain bases and two stories of belfries, with balustrades and small domes at the top. The belfries, decorated with severe Herrerean pilasters and entablatures, have on each face two tall arched openings in the lower stories and four shorter ones in the upper ones. Small towerlike structures project forward from the inner sides of the bases of the flanking towers, separating them from the central portion of the facade. The central facade, containing two stories at the sides in front of the aisles and rising to three stories in front of the nave, is restrained in its ornamentation of orders of paired half-columns but enlivened by scenes in low relief, statues, and other decoration carved from light stone which contrasts with the dark masonry of the main fabric. The last of its three portals was completed by Francisco Gutiérrez in 1664. The north portal,

3.22 *Cathedral of Mexico, facade.*

somewhat richer and more lively in ornamentation, was begun by Carlos García Durango in 1684 and completed by Diego de la Sierra in 1689.

Considerable progress was made during the 1670s and 1680s toward finishing the exterior of the Cathedral of Mexico, which remained incomplete when the interior was dedicated in 1667. The rear entrances to the north had been completed in Herrerean severity as early as 1615. The transept portals were completed under the direction of Cristóbal de Medina Vargas Machuca in 1688 and 1689. They demonstrate the thawing

of severity during the intervening three-quarters of a century, as they rise from a sober lower-story through a more ornamental middle-story to an upper-story where the growing Baroque taste clearly appears in twisted columns and a fragmentary double pediment.

The facade of the Cathedral of Mexico has a strong horizontality below the belfry stages of the towers. The plain bases of the towers, which in Puebla are separated visually from the central facade by projecting vertical elements, here join in the massive horizontality. Pilasters at their corners are placed on the same plane as severe rectangular buttresses flanking the central portal. All of these elements are welded to the plane of the main wall behind them by pairs of inverted ornamental consoles. The belfry stages of the towers are set back from the tower bases and rise from the same plane of the main wall. At this juncture a strong horizontal accent is provided for the whole facade by moldings linked to the line of the balustrades placed above the neighboring side portals. Only the facing of the nave, later embellished with a low arch and a cubic housing for a clock, interrupts this horizontal line, and it is marked by a horizontal molding at the base of its balustrades.

The three portals of the facade were conservatively designed in 1672 by Luis Gómez de Trasmonte and Rodrigo Díaz de Aguilera with simple semicircular arched doorways flanked by pairs of restrained Doric columns which enclose niches with statues at the wider central portal. Above the doorways are religious scenes carved in low relief, also flanked by pairs of columns and figures in niches. Windows above the reliefs, which provided vertical emphasis in Puebla, have been eliminated. The upper columns of the central portal are Ionic with zigzag ornamentation reflecting changes of the design made by Cristóbal de Medina. Those of the side portals, constructed between 1684 and 1689 under the direction of Medina, are Corinthian and are dramatically twisted, expressing a taste for Baroque animation which would soon sweep Mexico. The relief over the taller central doorway represents the Assumption of Mary, reflecting the dedication of the cathedral.

The lower of the two belfry stages of the east tower (Fig. 3.22) is also from the seventeenth century, and its eighteenth-century counterpart in the west tower follows the same design. Unlike the simple severity of treatment of paired openings at this level in Puebla, a complex pattern of arched openings for bells was cut into the surface of the tower. Five openings were cut into each face with two superposed openings at the sides placed so as to occupy the full height of the entablature. In the center the large opening leaves a significant portion of bare wall above it.

During the first half of the eighteenth century the interior of the cathedral was modernized by three structures designed in the new *estípite* style by Jerónimo de Balbás, an immigrant from Spain. Immediately after entering the nave, worshippers were confronted by the Retablo del Perdón; after rounding the choir they saw the tall tabernacle and behind it, against the rear wall, the glittering height of the magnificent Retablo de los Reyes (Fig. 7.2).

On the exterior the towers remained as stumps until almost the end of the viceregal period. A competition for designs for completion of the cathedral was won by the brilliant, short-lived architect, José Damián Ortiz de Castro, in the middle 1780s, and both towers were finished in the spring of 1791. The selection of Ortiz de Castro's Neo-Classical design over Baroque competitors, led to the completion of the structure in a style harmonious with its sober sixteenth-century beginnings. Despite the wide diversity of its parts—patterned late Gothic vaults, sober interior piers and exterior ornamentation, sparkling retablos and paintings from three of its four centuries of construction—the cathedral forms a remarkably coherent whole.

In planning for the completion of the towers, Ortiz de Castro sought the appearance of sturdy solidity and the actuality of relative lightness to prevent tilting on the softness of the former lake bed and to minimize the threat from earthquakes (Fig. 8.2). The upper belfry stage appears at first glance square, scarcely less massive than the solid stage below. More careful study discloses a relatively light, hollow, inner octagon faced with piers at the four corners. The striking bell-shaped tops of the towers seem of solid stone but are constructed of thin, light *tezontle*, faced with a thinner veneer of cut stone and held in place by iron hoops.

Some time after Ortiz de Castro's death in 1793, the Spanish sculptor-architect from Valencia, Manuel Tolsá, took over the finishing of the structure (Fig. 8.3). He completed the top of the facade with the bare, hard-edged arch and a cubic clock stage, softened with statuary, as was the upper belfrey stage of the towers. Tolsá faced the octagonal drum of the cathedral's dome with a palisade of pilasters and segmentally arched pedimented windows and added a very tall lantern to bring the height of the dome closer to that of the towers. In an effort to soften the awkward transition between low dome and steep lantern, Tolsá designed a wide balustraded ring around the base of the lantern and created looping curves in the ribs, which run up over the surface of the dome dividing it into segments forming eye-catching scrolls. This final work of construction on the exterior was completed in 1813, three years after Father Hidalgo sounded his "grito" of Dolores, "Long live Our Lady of Guadalupe! Long live Independence," and eight years before Agustín de Iturbide captured the city of Mexico from the remaining forces loyal to the king. New Spain endured for nearly three hundred years. Its principal cathedral was under construction for two hundred and fifty of those years.

MORELIA: CATHEDRAL OF THE TRANSFIGURATION OF CHRIST

Morelia was the third capital city of Michoacán, after Tzintzuntzan, the ancient capital of the Tarascan Indians, and Pátzcuaro, where Bishop Quiroga planned an incredible cathedral with five converging naves intended to hold all thirty thousand Indians congregated from along the shores of Pátzcuaro. In 1541 Viceroy Mendoza, annoyed at the bishop's failure to consult him about placing the capital in Pátzcuaro, declared that the city of Michoacán should be located on the site of the future Morelia, an obscure place named Guayanangareo, which was called

3.23 *Cathedral of Morelia, east side.*

3.24 *Cathedral of Morelia, upper facade.*

Valladolid by the Spaniards. In 1826 Valladolid was rechristened Morelia in honor of a native son, the parish priest José María Morelos, who became the ablest of the leaders of the first struggle for independence. Despite the viceroy's designation of Valladolid as capital, governmental administration was not moved from Pátzcuaro until 1576 and the bishopric not until four years later.

A cathedral of adobe and wood was soon built by three hundred Indians. It was partially burned in 1584 and was reconstructed. Repairs were made at various times. As early as 1583 the chapter of the cathedral petitioned the Audiencia to initiate construction for Michoacán of an enduring cathedral of stone, as had been authorized by royal cédula of 1576. Plans were approved by Viceroy Martín Enríquez, but little was done. In 1614 two architects were brought from the capital to inspect foundations which had been constructed, and another royal cédula authorized a modest-sized cathedral. Over the next few years a dispute regarding its size and grandeur developed between the crown and the local authorities and their architects, who included the maestro mayor of the Cathedral of Mexico, Alonso Martínez López. A plan was presented in 1621 to Viceroy Guadalcazar for a church of three aisles with a dome over the crossing, like the cathedrals of

Mexico and Puebla. Not until 1660, approximately a century after construction was initiated on those cathedrals, were the plans approved that led to the present Cathedral of Morelia.

The designer was an Italian, Vicente Barroso de la Escayola, who had worked on the structure in Puebla. Substantial construction was under way between 1672 and 1674 and after 1683. Several of the subsequent architects had worked in Mexico City. The cathedral was dedicated in 1705 but the facade was not complete twelve years later, and the towers were not finished until 1744. Despite its extension over roughly three-quarters of a century, construction seems to have followed the original design. Unobtrusive eighteenth-century decorative details appear on the towers and the facade, but the whole is even more consistent than the Cathedral of Puebla, Morelia's closest relative among Mexican cathedrals. Like Puebla, Morelia is severe and vertical, lifted by tapering 200-foot-high towers and a ribbed dome covered by blue, yellow, and white tiles. The dome, its octagonal drum, and its lantern are simpler in outline than their Puebla counterparts and, because of the prominent ribs of the dome and prominent finials of the drum, seem considerably more vertical. The towers rise above sturdy, plain bases similar to those of Puebla and Mexico, through square belfry stages to smaller octagonal second belfry stages and still smaller octagonal upper stages, which are capped by tiled domes. Clear indications of their mid-eighteenth-century construction appear only in the half-octagonal belfry openings of the square stage and the roll of the cornice line above them.

Like the towers, the facade (Fig. 3.24) preserves an overall appearance of restrained severity softened, as in Puebla and Mexico, by panels of relief sculpture carved in a light stone which contrasts with the pinkish brown trachyte of the general fabric. Severe buttresses separate the portals, and the framing pilasters seem quite restrained. Closer observation reveals touches of playful eighteenth-century decorativeness within the sober linearity of the whole. The pilasters, bases, niches, and reliefs are decorated or framed by sunken panels and by flat apronlike shapes called *pinjantes* or lambrequins. The sculptured relief over the central portal is framed above by a many-faceted arch, and the whole top of the facade is broken up and down into a dancing profile of finials, interrupted pediments, and stepped moldings.

In plan the Cathedral of Morelia is a three-aisled basilica without the flanking tiers of the chapels of Puebla and Mexico. Its narrower width contributes to the general sense of verti-cality. The soaring interior once contained tall retablos designed by Isidro Vicente de Balbás, adopted son of Gerónimo, and was wholly redecorated in the mid-nineteenth century. At that time the flanking plazas were cleared and a handsome cast metal fence was constructed. The nave is lit by circular windows in lunettes like those of Puebla. Horizontal moldings and capitals are less vigorous than those of the two older cathedrals; as a result the interior is dominated by tall narrow arches and tall delicate moldings rising from floor to top of vault with only a single insignificant interruption.

Completed in the decade when the final phase of the Mexican Baroque was initiated in the *Sagrario* constructed beside the Cathedral of Mexico City, the Cathedral of Morelia is an essentially conservative structure, sister to the older cathedrals of Puebla and Mexico, and illustrative of the continuing restrained classicism, dominant in Mexican building during the seventeenth and early eighteenth centuries and reemerging after a few decades of Baroque exuberance. Only in the sparkling polychromy of its tiled domes and the delicate decorative play of some of its details does the cathedral suggest the spirit that would liberate Mexican architecture from the protracted dominance of the Herrerean taste.

IV
Baroque Religious Life and Architecture I

In the judgment of French historian Fernand Braudel, the cultural waves of the Baroque, emanating from the Mediterranean culture and centered in papal Rome and Hapsburg Spain, "were possibly more deep, full, and uninterrupted than those even of the Renaissance."[1] In architecture the international diffusion of the Baroque style was much more rapid than that of the Renaissance. The beginning of fully Baroque architecture can be plausibly located in Rome in 1624 with Gianlorenzo Bernini's designs for the baldacchino of St. Peter's and the Church of Santa Bibiena. Important structures informed by the Baroque were designed in Venice within less than a decade, in Paris within less than thirty years, and in Protestant London within half a century. Although distinctly Baroque structures were not constructed in Spain and in Mexico until nearly the end of the seventeenth century, Baroque qualities are apparent before mid-century in Spain and in the 1680s in the great screen facade placed in front of the Church of the Soledad in Oaxaca in southern Mexico.

The Baroque is a popular, emotional style that was developing as the austere Catholic response to Protestantism—represented in architecture by Philip II's Escorial—was waning. Many of the religious practices identified for censure by the Protestants were retained and emphasized. Religious life centered on public rather than private devotional exercises. Ritualistic ceremonies, processions, performances of religious dramas, and splendid painted and sculpted images were used to arouse the feelings of the people. The reformers had attacked devotions dedicated to the saints and the Virgin, calling them idolatrous. Baroque Catholicism exalted the traditional saints and sanctified on a single day in 1622 four important new ones, Teresa of Avila, Philip Neri, Ignatius of Loyola, and Francis Xavier. Mary, Mother of Christ and Queen of Heaven, was perceived and presented as the affectionate mother of everyone, even of the most humble, a person easily approachable and exceedingly compassionate.

In architecture the creators of the Catholic Baroque constructed churches wholly unlike the "meeting houses" of the Protestants that were soberly restrained lest they distract the congregation from the preached word of God. Baroque churches are grand churches, increasingly ornamented and increasingly brilliant. They are houses of God glittering with gold and filled with dramatic light, designed to obliterate the miseries of the mundane and sordid life the congregation has left outside. The intention is to provide a foretaste of paradise, to transport the congregation to another world by means of lively images of saints and angels, Virgin Mother, and all three persons of the Christian Trinity set against shimmering surfaces of luminous gold.

Lavish provision was made for retablos, the gilded altarpieces which had ornamented churches in New Spain since the sixteenth century, and which survive notably in the Franciscan churches of Huejotzingo and Xochimilco. Installed along the side walls and in the side chapels as well as in the sanctuaries above the high altars, they were produced in workshops and required the skills of many craftsmen in addition to the designers—usually the major creators of images—painters, or sculptors. Essential specialists were the *esambladores*, experts in joinery and structural sculpture, and those who finished a work after it had been built, carved, and given a coat of white gesso: the *doradores*, who applied gold leaf; and the *estofadores*, who painted the structural elements, the narrative panels in relief, and the flesh and the costumes of the statues in the round.

The arrival in the 1570s and 1580s of the Jesuits and several other religious orders and the rapid opening in the cities of conventos for both men and women marked a decisive shift in the religious life of New Spain. Much of the earlier vision of a pure church for the Indians persisted throughout the colonial period in areas remote from central Mexico, especially in the missionary activities of the Franciscans in the Sierra Gorda, New Mexico, and California, and of the Jesuits in Tarahumara, Sinaloa, Sonora, and Baja California. But in the principal centers of the colony religious activities increasingly focused upon the European population. The bishops, their diocesan clergy, and their usual allies, the Jesuits, gradually replaced the mendicant orders as the molders of religious life.

Although Spaniards continued to be appointed to the principal positions in the hierarchy of the church, creoles, those born in America, gradually became predominant in the priesthood; and the diocesan clergy almost invariably supported the interests of the creole population against the viceregal bureaucracy and the mendicant orders. *Capellanias*, endowments created by prosperous creole families to support sons who became priests, linked the fiscal interests of the

community with the secular church and assisted in increasing the influence of the secular clergy. The families retained control of the principal sums, using them to purchase property, to increase an investment, to float a mortgage, or, in some cases, for venture capital. The clerical sons lived off the interest.

As the diocesan clergy grew in numbers and prestige, the mendicant orders became defensive of their traditional privileges and too frequently became more concerned with their personal lives than with their mission of bringing Christianity to the Indians. The soft lives of the friars, their fondness for good food, pleasant music, and charming women, is a dominant theme in the admittedly biased memoirs of the "English American" Thomas Gage, a former Dominican author whose celebrated account of life in Mexico and Guatemala was published after he renounced Catholicism for Cromwellian Protestantism. Some of the clergy exemplified extreme Counter-Reformation piety. Fray Antonio de Roa, an Augustinian stationed in the 1570s on the northern fringe of the area of the sedentary Indians, was sufficiently notable to be described at length a half-century later in Juan de Grijalva's history of the Augustinian order in New Spain. "When he said mass his tears were so abundant that his sacristans had to give him three successive handkerchiefs."[2] In traveling to *visitas* in the mountains near Molango, he would have two Indians lead him by a halter and lash him fifty times at each of the numerous roadside crosses they passed. He customarily intensified the effect of his preaching on a congregation by first walking over hot coals. On one occasion at a shrine in the Molango area which was decorated with a picture of Christ's feet being washed by Mary Magdalene, he kissed the feet of an Indian judge and had himself stripped and lashed until he bled copiously. He then had pitch poured over him and lit.

Religious orders for women were coming into increasing prominence in the cities of New Spain by the final decades of the sixteenth century. In the 1540s Bishop Zumárraga had objected to the freedom of the uncloistered tertiary Franciscan sisters, or beatas, who had come from

Spain to teach the daughters of European settlers and of the Indian nobility. The nuns sent subsequently were not allowed to move freely through the secular society but were enclosed in convent walls. Unlike the friars of the mendicant orders and the Jesuits, they withdrew from the world instead of working to make the world more Christian. Societies such as the Capuchin branch of the Franciscans and the Discalced, or Barefoot, Carmelites, St. Teresa's order, established modest-sized convents of fifty or fewer nuns and were known for austere living. Normally these nuns slept on wooden boards, wore coarse robes, maintained silence, ate simply, and fasted frequently. Some wore hair shirts; others cilices, circlets of bristle gripping their limbs; still others wore ropes tied around their necks and crowns of thorns beneath their veils. There were some extraordinary instances of extreme penitential piety in the many convents ordinarily characterized by an easy way of life. In times of epidemics nuns attempted to propitiate divine displeasure by praying, singing, and drawing their own blood. In nocturnal processions described by an eighteenth-century priest, Cayetano de Cabrera y Quintero, nuns marched along the cloisters and corridors of their convents resembling "souls in pain from another world . . . their cries rising to the heavens . . . their blows drawing blood," clad in "harsh hair shirts, until then kept out of sight" and "wondering at finding themselves uncovered and in the open air."[3] In other processions they dragged huge wooden crosses until their shoulders bled, and they sometimes drew crosses on the ground with their tongues, sweeping it clean but leaving traces of blood and saliva as the hard surface abraded the soft tongues.

Normally, life in most Mexican convents was not demanding and the less austere orders attracted by far the greater number of applicants. By the mid-seventeenth century, convents enrolled a significant portion of the female population. Their rapid growth was due more to the customs of a society inhospitable to unmarried women than to powerful religious feelings. Convents served as refuges from marriage, as female communities of support for those reluctant to marry, and as places offering a pleasant alternative

manner of living to those faced with the prospect of an uninviting marriage or those who were unable to produce a sufficient dowry. They provided substantial opportunity for women to act independently of male authority as was demonstrated by the vigorous resistance the convents made against bishops who attempted to reform their comfortable way of living. The importance the general society placed upon the nunneries was reflected in the careful scrutiny given proposals for their establishment. Women wishing to found a convent had not only to find a wealthy patron and to gain support of the other orders and the bishop; approval of the cabildo, or city council, was required as well as that of leading private citizens and, in some cases, of the viceroy himself. Disclosure of sufficient assured funding was necessary lest the convent become a burden upon the society. Dowries were essential for women who wished to join a convent, increasing gradually from an average of two thousand pesos in the sixteenth century to an average of five thousand in the nineteenth. Charitable foundations provided dowries for orphans and daughters of families that lacked money, but aspirants greatly outnumbered the dowries available. In 1798 the strict Discalced Carmelite convent of Santa Teresa Nueva in Mexico City had a waiting list of thirty-nine young women for its fourteen endowed places. Only one of these places had become vacant in the 1790s.

The fiscal resources of the larger convents gradually increased through dowries; through *reservas*, funds contributed for the support of particular nuns during their lives and that frequently were left to the community after their deaths; through donations of pious individuals; and through bequests. Convent funds were invested in haciendas and, increasingly, in urban real estate. By the eighteenth century convents were serving on a large scale as substitutes for banks, extending liens to those wishing to mortgage their property and extending loans to leading citizens at 5 percent interest. In 1744 La Concepción Convent of Mexico City had investments of 857,720 pesos with over 500,000 in real estate and the rest fairly evenly divided between loans and liens. La Encarnación invested 872,050 pesos:

over 550,000 in real estate, over 200,000 in liens, and the rest in loans.

Sor Juana, Octavio Paz's remarkable study of the life and works of the great Mexican poet of the late seventeenth century, Sor Juana Inés de la Cruz, and of her social, intellectual, and religious milieu, provides much interesting information about the convents of Mexico City, especially in regard to San Jerónimo, her residence for twenty-six years. According to a surviving document, *Rules and Constitutions Which by Apostolic Authority Must Be Observed by the Nuns of the Supreme Doctor San Jerónimo, in This City of Mexico* (1702), life in the convent was ordered and largely communal. The nuns' sleep was broken before three in the morning for the prayers of "matins" and "lauds," and the day proper began at six with "prime," the first of the canonical hours. Then mass was heard in the choir of the church, and breakfast was served at eight. The prayers of the "tierce" at nine were followed, according to the regulations, by communal labor in the convent's sewing room. At noon came the prayers of the "sext," followed by the midday meal. "Nones" were observed at three and then there was probably a siesta. Fruit was served at dusk. Vespers were held in the choir at six and then came dinner and time for recreation. At nine the prayers of "complin" concluded the day's activities.

Despite the prescription in the *Rules and Regulations* of communal praying, working, and eating, the nuns of San Jerónimo and of most other convents of New Spain lived what were primarily private lives in their own quarters. There they lived and prayed—attended by slaves and servants, and accompanied by young female relatives and other protegés or students—and were visited by other nuns. Their meals were cooked and served in their own living quarters and their sewing was also done there, despite the provision for communal work in the general sewing room. The rules specified that the nuns should sleep on mattresses without sheets, clothed in a coarse woollen gown "and a little scapular, girded and veiled."[4] Paz doubts that these relatively austere regulations were observed.

The Conceptionist nuns of the Convent of Jesús María wore rings and bracelets of jet and

4.1 Portrait of Sor Juana Inés de la Cruz by Juan de Miranda.

had modish pleats in the coifs over their heads and in the scapulars worn over their tunics. The Jeronimite sisters were similarly dressed. Their tunics were white with elegantly tapering sleeves and were draped front and back with black scapulars. Their white coif was covered by a black veil and over the scapular, reaching almost to their chins, was a sizeable oval ornament decorated by a religious painting. Draped around their shoulders was a very long string of rosary beads which extended to their knees.

The officers of the convent were elected by secret ballot every three years. The prioress was assisted by a vicaress. In addition there were a gatekeeper, one or more instructors of novices, two or more disciplinarians, a manager, and a bursar. The bursar also served as treasurer and kept the convent's books. Sor Juana was twice reelected to this last office, which also involved supervision of construction work within the convent. In addition there was an archivist and, in some convents, a librarian.

San Jerónimo is a large unadorned convent, the earliest surviving in Mexico City. It was organized around a sizeable cloister and, although in Sor Juana's time it contained only about fifty nuns, it extended to an area of almost five football fields. Its original geometric clarity was transformed over the years into heterogeneous architectural confusion by the building activities of the individual nuns who constructed "cells" in what had been open spaces. Despite their name, the cells were normally of two stories and several rooms. They included a sitting room, a small kitchen, a room for sleeping, and space for one to five servants and for the girls often entrusted by their families to nuns for care and education. Most cells included a bathroom with a tub and a bowl for the coals used in heating the water. Outside were a patio and a small garden. The cells were built with little concern for the original architectural design of the convent or for their relationship to other cells. Passageways were obstructed, cubicles built on the flat roof, and small fountains erected where they were not expected.

Thomas Gage's account of the active social life of the nuns of Mexico City emphasized their entertaining friars in the *locutorios*, rooms where the nuns were separated from their visitors by wooden bars. Male and female visitors were regaled by secular songs and delicacies from the kitchen. Many of the Mexican national dishes are reputed to have been created in the convents of Puebla and Querétaro. Paz portrays Sor Juana as holding a virtual salon in the *locutorio* of San Jerónimo and quotes the account of one of her visitors; Juan Ignacio de Castorera y Ursúa, editor of the third, posthumous volume of her works and subsequently bishop of Yucatán, describes her as "arguing the most difficult [theological] questions with Scholastic rigor, advancing with the greatest delicacy her comments on various sermons, or spontaneously composing verses in divers meters, astounding us all and winning the acclaim of the severest critics among the listening courtiers." Those drinking Sor Juana's chocolate and listening to her discourse included intelligent clergymen, viceroys and vicereines, distinguished foreign visitors, and men of learning, the American-born professor of astronomy and mathematics in the University of Mexico, Carlos de Sigüenza y Góngora, and his guest, the German-educated Father Eusebio Kino, who would soon publish a book reaffirming, against his host's printed opinion, the traditional argument that comets are omens of evil events.

Sor Juana collected paintings, gems, scientific apparatus, and musical instruments, converting her cell into a sort of museum. According to her contemporary biographer, Father Diego Calleja, she had four thousand books. She may have painted her own portrait and written music. Whether she played any of the instruments she collected is uncertain. She studied musical theory and contributed to the programs of musical education and musical performance for which San Jerónimo was noted. She wrote lyrics for songs performed during entertainments in the viceregal palace and for villancicos performed in spectacles celebrating the beginning of the great liturgical holidays at matins in the cathedrals of Mexico, Oaxaca, and Puebla. Fiscal support for the matins festivals was provided by wealthy citizens. In 1730 there were foundations supporting eleven different holiday festivals. Funding ranged from slightly over four thousand pesos up to twenty thousand.

Plays were also a specialty of the convents and of Sor Juana. On some occasions the normal rules were suspended and lay people were admitted to the nuns' performances. Somewhat more than a third of Sor Juana's total literary production was for the stage. A charming, precocious, illegitimate child without an identifiable father, she had lived in the viceregal palace for four years of adolescence as a favorite of the vicereine, Leonor Carrito, wife of the Marqués de Mancera. After entering San Jerónimo she established a relationship, perhaps even closer, with María Luisa Manrique de Lara y Gonzaga, wife of a later viceroy, the Marqués de Laguna. She and Carlos Sigüenza y Góngora had created allegorical programs to decorate the triumphal arches erected at the west portal of the cathedral and in the Plaza of Santo

Domingo for the ceremonial entry to the city of the Lagunas in 1680. Sor Juana's plays included comedies written for performance before the viceregal court, complete with introductory allegorical dialogues; supplementary festive skits and songs; and for the *fin de fiesta*, playlets as epilogues. She was a great master of the *auto sacramental*, a one-act allegorical religious play which was a Baroque version of medieval religious drama written for the festival of Corpus Christi.

Life in Mexican convents changed little over the centuries. Twenty years after independence, Frances Calderón de la Barca, the Scottish-born wife of the Spanish Minister to Mexico, visited the convent of *La Encarnación* in the capital in the spring of 1842 and found within a conventual life virtually unchanged since Sor Juana's time or, probably, since the sixteenth century. The convent seemed to her a palace with a number of "galleries and courts" and a high-walled garden "kept in good order, with its stone walks, stone benches, and an ever playing and sparkling fountain." She was struck by the picturesque sight of nuns wandering singly or standing in groups in the garden "while the sun was setting behind the hills, and the noise of the city was completely excluded, everything breathing repose and contentment." Particularly impressive was the cleanliness of everything from the refectory to the dispensary of medicines and "especially of the immense kitchen, which seems hallowed from the approach of even a particle of dust." After her tour of the convent Señora de la Barca was entertained in a large hall hung with paintings, seated in an old-fashioned high-backed armchair, and fed "cakes, chocolates, ices, creams, custards, tarts, jellies, blancmanges, orange and lemonade, and other profane dainties, ornamented with gilt paper cut into little flags." Before leaving at nine in the evening, she was shown the nun's choir in the church and asked to play a Mozart sonata on an old organ, "the servants blowing the bellows."[5]

Most Mexican nuns were modestly educated and had little of Sor Juana's insatiable desire to learn. The instruction they imparted to the young women who lived in convents under their tutelage was limited, for the most part, to feminine accomplishments desirable in proper married women—cooking, needlework, and music. Devotional training was stressed, not abstruse learning. No female order devoted itself particularly to teaching until 1753 when the Company of Mary, or *La Enseñanza*, opened the first of a series of prestigious schools. *La Enseñanza* was sponsored in Mexico by Sister María Ignacia Azlor y Echeverz, heiress of the greatest of northern landholders, the marquieses of San Miguel de Aguayo.

The ordeal of the final years of Sor Juana's life began in late 1690, four and a half years before she died as a result of nursing her sisters during an epidemic, when she was tempted by her friend Bishop Fernández de Santa Cruz of Puebla into writing a letter criticizing a sermon. The sermon had been delivered forty years earlier by a noted Portuguese Jesuit, Antonio de Vieyra, who was greatly esteemed by the bishop's rival, the woman-hating, self-scourging Archbishop of Mexico, Francisco Aguiar y Seijas. As a result of this indiscretion, Juana was forced to succumb to the dominating influence of her powerful Jesuit confessor Antonio Núñez de Miranda, the censor of the Inquisition, and persuaded to abjure her former life as having lived "in religion without religion." Her precious library and collection were turned over to the archbishop who sold them to procure funds for his impulsive campaign of charity to the poor.

In 1691 Sor Juana wrote a remarkable autobiographical letter, a *Response* to Manuel Fernández de Santa Cruz, bishop of Puebla, who under the pseudonym of a nun had published her letter criticizing the Jesuit's sermon and in the prologue had admonished her for devoting herself to secular rather than religious writing. In the *Response to Sor Filotea de la Cruz*, Sor Juana tells of her eagerness to learn as a child, of her refusal to eat cheese because she'd been told that it made one slow-witted, of her lopping off chunks of her hair when she failed to meet the deadlines she'd set for herself in mastering grammar, and of her urging her mother, who would later successfully manage the family hacienda, to dress her as a man when she was old enough to enter the university.

She goes on to explain her choice of the

life of a nun, conceding that the religious life involved conditions, incidental but not essential, that were repugnant to her intellectual nature. She stresses her "total disinclination" to marriage and explains that learned advisers had dissuaded her from attempting a solitary life devoted to study. Such impulses, they had convinced her, were a temptation she had to resist if she was to ensure her salvation. Self-centeredness was not tolerated in women in seventeenth-century Mexico. But, with concern for the effect of her words on the admonishing bishop, she wrote, "Wretch that I am, I brought into the convent with me my own self and also my worst enemy, my love of writing which, I am uncertain whether, was sent from Heaven as a gift or a punishment. For instead of dying down or going out amidst all my religious devotions, it blew up like gunpowder, proving that privation stimulates the appetite."

Sor Juana's explanation of her feelings, as a woman and a nun trying to educate herself, is gripping. She writes of the difficulties she had,

not only in lacking a teacher but in lacking fellow students with whom to discuss and work on the subject matter. My only teacher was a mute book, my only fellow students an inkwell which had no feelings; and instead of explanations and exercises I had many interruptions. . . . I would be reading and in the next cell they would decide to play and sing; I would be studying and two maids would have a squabble and come to me to settle their argument. . . . Only those who have known community life know how true this is and only the strength of my vocation could keep me good-natured, that and the great love that exists between me and my beloved sisters, for love is union.

Sor Juana centered much of her response to the bishop on the notorious remark attributed to St. Paul, "Let women keep silence in church . . . for it is shameful for women to speak." She argued that the pronouncement should be limited to the physical church of the male hierarchy, a matter of "pulpits and bishop's thrones."[6] In the church of the spirit, the community of the faithful, she wrote, women should be allowed to study

privately following the examples set by Saints Gertrude, Bridget, and Teresa.

Sor Juana was an extraordinary woman in Baroque Mexico, dazzlingly exceptional in a confining colonial setting, anomalous in her intellectual life in a provincial nunnery, and ultimately a victim of the rivalries and jealousies of the male clerical hierarchy. Religious life for ordinary Mexicans of the seventeenth and eighteenth centuries was communal and ceremonial, reflecting the responses of Catholic Rome to the attacks of Luther and the other Protestant reformers.

The Catholic church had regained lost territory in Europe and pushed with immense enthusiasm and energy into vast new areas of America and Asia. In Christianity's numerically most successful campaign of evangelism, millions more were brought into the church than had been lost to Protestantism in northern Europe. In contrast to the Protestant emphasis upon the individual reading the Bible and upon worship within the family, reformed Catholicism reasserted the importance of the bishop and public communal worship in the parish. Primacy was given to the traditional channels to God's grace, the eucharist and the other sacraments. The saying of mass was established as daily practice for priests, and penance became a frequent rather than an annual practice for the laity. Receiving communion became much more frequent and devotions distinct from the mass, such as benediction and the exposition of the eucharist for forty hours, were fostered.

The spectacular nature of public religion is suggested by the memorial funeral procession for Philip IV in 1665. The entire clergy of the capital marched en masse through its streets. There were 1,325 secular priests and, in the ranks of the regular clergy, 340 Franciscans, 180 Augustinians, 160 Dominicans, 130 Jesuits, 120 Mercedarians, 80 Carmelites, and 70 members of the hospital orders, San Hipólito and San Juan de Dios. The multiethnic makeup of the lay population was expressed by the religious confraternities and related organizations—eighty-two of them for Indians, sixteen for blacks and mulattos, and nineteen for Europeans, either native-born or immigrant. For great singular occasions and for regular liturgical events such as Holy Week and the feast of Corpus Christi, such groups paraded, bearing aloft banners, images, and crosses demonstrating the public power of Baroque Catholicism.

Emphasis was placed on the exemplary lives of the saints and of the Virgin, and in Mexico ceremonies and festivals related to the patron saints of the villages and of the barrios of the cities became of great importance in the communal life. The Virgin and Santiago, Lord St. James, patron saint of Spain who was reputed to have appeared thrice to lead the conquistadors in battle, were so revered in Mexico that the Indians at first supposed that "Santiago y María" were the dual deities of Christianity. As early as the 1520s with the dedication of San José de los Naturales—Pedro de Gante's famous mosque-shaped open chapel for the Indians of Mexico City—the cult of St. Joseph, Mary's husband, became significant. Other saints particularly venerated in Mexico included St. Peter, St. Jerome, St. Francis, and the new Jesuit saints, Ignatius of Loyola and Francis Xavier. Representations of Christ usually placed a theatrical emphasis upon suffering, portraying the Man of Sorrows with His gory back lashed at the pillar, His twisted, tortured body sacrificed on the cross. Characteristic of eighteenth-century Mexican religious feeling was the powerful cult of the Christ of Ixmiquilpan. A devotional tract, *The Self-Renovation of the Sovereign Image of Our Crucified Lord Jesus of Itzmiquilpan* reached a fifth edition in 1729. Notable pilgrimages were devoted to the image of the Black Christ at Chalma and to Our Lord of Sacramonte above Amecameca.

Devotion to Mary was universal. Communities fostered particular local images and at least 1,756 different towns were named in the Virgin's honor. The European cults of Our Lady of Carmen, Our Lady of Light, Our Lady of Solitude, Our Lady of Sorrows, Our Lady of Refuge, Our Lady of Loreto, the Immaculate Conception, and the Rosary had massive followings. Mexican centers of pilgrimage and Marian devotion grew increasingly in importance in the seventeenth and eighteenth centuries. In western Mexico, in the area of Guadalajara, Zapopan and San Juan de Lagos became noted places of pilgrimage. The principal site in the Puebla area was Ocotlán, a place above Tlaxcala where an Indian christened Juan Diego was reputed to have seen an apparition of the Virgin in 1541. The two important centers near Mexico City were the hilltop shrine of Nuestra Señora de los Remedios and Guadalupe, the most visited of all the places sacred to Mary in the world. The cult of the Virgin of Remedios is related to the retreat from Mexico on the *noche triste* of July 1, 1520. The battered remnant of Cortés's Spanish and Indian forces, after flight from the city over the western causeway, took temporary refuge at an Aztec temple on a hill. At this site an image was later discovered by an Indian nobleman, Juan Tovar, who had been guided by a vision of the Virgin. The small statue of Mary and her Child was a "saddle image" like those carried from Spain by the conquistadors and was believed to be the image that Cortés had placed within the terrifying temple of the Aztec god Huizilopochtli to Christianize it and that had been lost during the flight from the city.

According to pious tradition the miraculous episodes at Guadalupe began ten years earlier than the vision of Ocotlán, when a poor Indian, also christened Juan Diego, passed the hill of Tepeyac, sacred to the Aztec mother-goddess Tonantzin, on his way to mass on December 9, 1531. Suddenly he heard birds singing and, at the crest of the hill, he saw a golden light and a young woman calling to him "Juan, Juanito." The woman identified herself as "Holy Mary ever virgin, mother of the true God" and sent him to Bishop Zumárraga with the direction to build a temple at Tepeyac. The bishop seemed unimpressed. The Virgin appeared a second time and sent Juan back again but the bishop asked for some proof of his story. Informed of this the Virgin promised to provide a sign the next morning. Juan did not appear then because of the dire illness of his uncle, but on the day following he was accosted by the Virgin who descended the hill, assured him of his uncle's welfare, and directed him to the cold, desertlike summit to pick some roses for her. He found several types of Castilian roses blooming in the frosty morning dew and carried them to her in his tilma, a cape of roughly woven cactus cloth. She arranged the Spanish roses, tied the cloak around his neck so that they would not fall out, and ordered Juan to show them as proof and sign to the bishop. When Juan untied his cloak in the bishop's presence, the roses dropped on the floor, and on the cactus fabric of his tilma appeared a brightly colored image of the vision of Mary which he had seen.

A chapel dedicated to Our Lady of Guadalupe—a principal Spanish image of Mary

4.2 The Image of the Virgin of Guadalupe.

centered in Guadalupe in Estremadura, home province of Cortés and other leading conquistadors—was erected of perishable materials at Tepeyac some time after 1531. A sturdier structure, probably the third, was erected at the order of Archbishop Montúfar in 1555 before he preached a sermon at the site on September 8, the following year. Yet a number of significant questions regarding the origins and development of the national cult have been raised by Jacques Lafaye in his important study, *Quetzalcoátl and Guadalupe: The Formation of Mexican National Consciousness 1531–1813.* Lafaye suggests that the cult may have been originally transplanted as a colonial extension of the Estremaduran cult. The naming of the site *Guadalupe* and the sixteenth-century practice of celebrating the feast of the Virgin on September 8, the date of the Spanish feast and the date observed on the calendar of the Catholic church, or two days later on September 10, support Lafaye's belief that the original chapel at Tepeyac was a daughter shrine of Guadalupe in Estremadura. Two important sixteenth-century accounts of the Virgin's image describe it as a statue, similar to the image of Estremadura, rather than as a painting.

In 1556 Archbishop Montúfar, a consistent supporter of the Mexican Guadalupe and the founder of the first adobe basilica, conducted an investigation into a sermon of a Franciscan Provincial, Fray Francisco de Bustamente, that had attacked the cult for fostering superstition and thereby undermining the whole Franciscan effort to create an ideal Church of the Indians. Nothing, Father Bustamente was reported as having said, is more likely to prevent the Indians from becoming good Christians. Ever since the work of conversion, we have told them not to believe in idols but only in God and the Virgin. "To tell them now that an image painted by an Indian could work miracles will utterly confuse them and tear up the vine which has been planted."[7] There was no mention in the investigation of 1556 of an apparition and there is no reference to miraculous happenings at Guadalupe in the surviving writings of Bishop Zumárraga.

Viceroy Martín Enríquez, who visited Guadalupe immediately after arriving in Mexico, wrote in a letter of 1575 that "the cult began to grow because a cattle dealer let it be known that he had regained his health by making a pilgrimage to . . . [the] chapel." All viceroys subsequent to Martín Enríquez and all archbishops subsequent to Montúfar professed devotion to the image of Guadalupe. The painting, together with the statue of Our Lady of Remedios, was carried to the cathedral in 1629 to invoke the protection of Mary from the great flood that shattered the city's dikes, washed away thousands of adobe houses, forced divine services to be held on church roofs, and drove a substantial portion of the Spanish population to take refuge in the lakeside communities of Coyoacán, Tacuba, and Tacubaya. In 1736 another of the series of devastating epidemics caused at least forty thousand deaths in the city's population of roughly one hundred fifty thousand. After the reputed failures of the images of the Virgin of Loreto and the Virgin of Remedios to alleviate the epidemic, the image of Guadalupe was invoked by solemn oath. Authorized by Juan Antonio Vizarrón y Eguiarreta, who was serving both as archbishop and as viceroy, the priest Cayetano Cabrera y Quintero in 1738 proclaimed the patronage of the Virgin over the capital in a work entitled *The Coat of Arms of Mexico: Celestial Protection of this very noble City, of New Spain, and almost all the New World, Holy Mary in Her Prodigious Image of Guadalupe of Mexico City, who Appeared Miraculously in the Archepiscopal Palace in 1531 and Was Sworn the Principal Patroness of Mexico City the Past Year, 1737, Amid the Anguish Inspired by the Epidemic Which, Having Especially Struck at Indians, Mitigated Its Fury Because of the Great Shade Cast by Mary.* Eight years later, old and ill, Archbishop Vizarrón led delegates from all the dioceses of New Spain in acclaiming Our Lady of Guadalupe as patron of the entire colony.

Jacques Lafaye believes that the cult of the Virgin of Tepeyac was strengthened by its gradual transformation from a branch of the Spanish cult of Guadalupe to an Indianized form more appropriate to the mestizo American nation Mexico would become. From the beginning the site was sacred to the Aztec goddess Tonantzin, and the traditional account placed the Virgin's appearance at the top of the hill close to the ruins of her temple. As early as 1556 Father Bustamante spoke of the image as one recently painted "by Marcos, an Indian Painter," probably the Marcos de Aquino mentioned as a master artist by Bernal Díaz del Castillo. By the end of the century the image was firmly established as a painting rather than the statue, probably of European origin, which had been seen in 1568 by the English prisoner Miles Philips and which Viceroy Martín Enríquez wrote was generally likened to "the image of the monastery of Guadalupe in Spain." In the late 1660s a delegation traveled to Rome to request permission to shift the date of the feast of the Virgin of Guadalupe from September to December 12, a date within the period of the Mexican celebration of the Immaculate Conception, and coincident with the season of the apparitions. A second basilica of vaulted masonry was erected between 1609 and 1622. A highway for pilgrims from the viceregal palace to Guadalupe was begun in 1675. Upon completion ten years later it had fifteen monumental wayside stations to commemorate the fifteen mysteries of the rosary.

Lafaye identifies as central to the cult of the Virgin of Guadalupe and to the emerging national sense of the Mexicans as a unique American people a work written in 1648 by Miguel Sánchez, an influential preacher and theologian. The *Imagen de la Virgen Maria, Madre de Dios de Guadalupe, milagrosamente aparecida en México* contains the first undisputed published account of the miraculous happenings at Tepeyac, and a very important association of the apparition of Mary with the woman prophesied in the opening lines of chapter 12 of the Book of Revelations, "a woman clothed with the sun, and the moon under her feet, and upon her head a crown of twelve stars." The vision of the poor Indian Juan Diego is identified with the vision of St. John the Evangelist at Patmos. The appearance of Mary as a Mexican woman on Tepeyac hill is taken as a sign of God's intentions for the Mexican patria. "It follows . . . that God executed his admirable design in this Mexican land, conquered for such glorious ends, gained in order that a most divine image might appear here." As Luis Lasso de la Vega, the vicar of Guadalupe, wrote to Sánchez after reading his book, "all my predecessors and I have been slumbering Adams though all the while we possessed this new Eve in the Paradise of her Mexican Guadalupe." Mexican Adams could now believe themselves to belong to a people favored by God and regard their country as a new Western Paradise, as Miguel Sánchez wrote, "set aside, sure, and protected."

In the year after the appearance of Miguel Sánchez's book, Lasso de La Vega published in Nahuatl a brief account of Juan Diego and the divine apparitions. A few miraculous details were added and the grand figural theological exegesis—by which Sánchez found parallels between the events of December 1531 and the prophecies of the Biblical Apocalypse and the voice of God speaking to Moses out of Mount Sinai—was omitted. In a chapter of his important book, *The First America*, D. A. Brading has amplified the account of Lafaye. He stresses the speed with which the veneration of Our Lady of Guadalupe spread to other cities of New Spain in the second half of the seventeenth century. In Querétaro an image was first brought from Mexico City in 1659; a congregation of priests was organized under the patronage of the Virgin of Guadalupe ten years later; and a substantial church was consecrated with elaborate festivities in 1680. Chapels dedicated to the Virgin, and frequently located outside city limits and linked to the city by sacred roads, were constructed near Querétaro, in San Luis Potosí; in Tlaxcala, near Puebla; in the north in Zacatecas and Chihuahua; and in the distant south in Oaxaca.

Carlos de Sigüenza y Góngora, mathematician, epic poet, and historian of his native land, relative of the famous Andalusian poet Luis de Góngora and friend of Sor Juana Inés de la Cruz, wrote a pamphlet that described the spread of Guadalupan devotions in Querétaro. He also detected echoes of sixteenth-century native sources in Lasso de la Vega's Nahuatl narrative of the miraculous events believing that Indian narratives dating from the lifetime of Juan Diego preceded the books of 1648 and 1649. He sensed traces of the style of Antonio de Valeriano in the main account and of Fernando de Alva Ixtlilxochitl, the celebrator of Indian Texcoco, in the de-

scription of miracles at the end. Sigüenza y Góngora's pious wish to authenticate the Nahuatl account of the Virgin of Guadalupe—which D. A. Brading confirms may have had a basis in stylistic analysis as well as in the will to believe—and his scholarly study of the manuscripts and codices of Indian origin which had been collected by Ixtlilxochitl led to his publishing *Primavera Indiana. Poema sacro-histórico, idea de María Santíssima de Guadalupe*. Sigüenza y Góngora's poem celebrates the eternal Indian spring of the world in the Mexican valley of Anahuac sanctified by God and by Holy Mary of Guadalupe. Mexico is destined to become the "preeminent throne" of God and bring about human salvation because of Mary, "of omnipotent God the humble mother," "the splendid North Star of mankind's hope."

"From the day that the Mexicans began to regard themselves as a chosen people," writes Lafaye, "they were potentially liberated from Spanish tutelage." It was but a step from the seventeenth-century Mexican Guadalupan consciousness of Miguel Sánchez and Carlos de Sigüenza y Góngora to parish priest Father Miguel Hidalgo y Costilla's issuing his revolutionary "Cry of Dolores" in 1810, "Long live our very holy mother of Guadalupe! Long live America and down with the corrupt Spanish government!"

During the course of the seventeenth century Mexican religious architecture gradually took on some Baroque characteristics. Sixteenth-century churches had usually been simple in structure and restrained in ornamentation whatever their form. The vaulted, single-nave church became the norm for the friars but other types were used as well. Many of the earliest churches, erected during and just after the great initial campaign of conversion, had been large three-aisled structures, roofed with timber, and walled with adobe, reeds, wood, and other impermanent materials. Just after the middle of the century, a small number of carefully built masonry churches with restrained classical decorative features were designed on the three-aisled, timber-roofed pattern. Of twenty-nine Dominican churches listed in Robert H. Mullen's study, *Dominican Architecture in Sixteenth Century Oaxaca*, twelve had masonry-vaulted single naves and five were timber-roofed and three-aisled. Six others were cruciform, adding a transept and sanctuary to a single-vaulted nave. Five had chapels flanking the nave, a plan that transformed a structure wide enough to contain three aisles into one that gave the appearance of having a single unified interior volume. This scheme, called by George Kubler "cryptocollateral," provided very ample wall-to-wall width and also permitted the construction of internal buttresses between the lateral chapels to provide support for the wide vault over the nave.

Late in the century the single-nave church came to seem old-fashioned and architecturally limited. The admiration of early Christian simplicity and austerity, which had fostered simple unitary religious space, waned. Characteristic of the new thinking was Saint Carlo Borromeo, who made his archdiocese of Milan a model for reformed Catholicism but urged a return to traditional splendor in ecclesiastical architecture. Bishop Palafox, an admirer of Carlo Borromeo, had advised his pastors to dedicate their income to enhancing the ceremonies and ornamentation

4.3 Church of Santiago, Tlatelolco.

of their churches in order to increase their appeal to the Indians and because these structures were like wives to them, deserving to be loved because they gave them "position, sustenance, reputation and fortune, as the cathedral does me."[8] Domes began to appear in Mexico City in the first decade of the seventeenth century. The church built by Fray Juan de Torquemada for the Franciscan convento at Tlatelolco exemplified a pattern for church layouts that would replace the austere single-nave plan. The two-towered church of Santiago had a transept, a shallow rectangular apse, and a dome above pendentives covering its crossing area. In his prologue to *Monarquía Indiana* (1615, 1723), a three-volume chronicle of Mexico, its Indian greatness, its heroic conversion, and its Spanish and Indian present, Torquemada tells of his success in erecting a large vaulted church. Fray Juan enthusiastically describes Santiago Tlatelolco as "among the most distinguished in Christendom" despite his having been utterly alone, without mentors, and needing great knowledge of architectural matters. "The Lord," he wrote, "inspired me, even though I lacked previous knowledge or study [,] . . . to profit from the books which explain architectural construction."[9] Architectural books had not been available to the first generation of friar-designers but became plentiful in New Spain before 1600. Torquemada's inspired use of books led to an assured design of piers, pendentives, and a low hemispherical dome. Santiago Tlatelolco has undergone a rigorous recent restoration that has reduced the interior to surfaces of stark white stucco and rough gray stone and has darkened it with modern stained glass. In the pendentives huge stucco figures of the four evangelists holding quills and mounted on great winged figures—eagle, lion, ox, and man—survive from the seventeenth century to suggest the developing Baroque taste that would eventually envelop all Mexico.

Fray Juan de Torquemada had the benefit of architectural books unavailable to the friar-designers who preceded him, but he remained in the tradition of the self-trained amateur. Professionalism in architecture had begun with Claudio de Arciniega who had architectural training in

Spain. He had used Sebastián Serlio's book of architectural designs in designing the Túmulo Imperial, the funerary monument to Charles V erected in 1559 in San José de los Naturales, Pedro de Gante's open chapel for the Indians. Several architects, including Francisco Becerra and Juan Miguel Agüero, are known to have practiced in Mexico before Arciniega's death in 1593, but they were fewer in numbers than craftsmen, such as stonemasons, wood carvers, painters, and gilders, and they were later in establishing a guild. Although the Guild of Painters and Guilders was approved in 1557 and that of the Carpenters, Woodcutters, Joiners, and Violin Makers eleven years later, the Masons' Guild, which incorporated the architects, was not established until the final year of the sixteenth century. Ordinances regulating professional practice and attempting to establish a monopoly for master builders were approved but failed to control seventeenth- and early eighteenth-century building.

The establishment of the cruciform vaulted church with a dome over its crossing was gradual in seventeenth-century Mexico. In the earlier decades many important churches were still roofed in timber, continuing in the tradition of the still surviving first cathedrals of Mexico and Puebla. Frequently they were given an external protective coating of lead. Their interior decoration was spectacular and was celebrated by contemporary poets such as Bernardo de Balbuena, who wrote in his *Grandeza mexicana* (1604) about churches roofed with panels of gold. The designs were based on those of Moorish Spain and consisted of two principal types: the *artesonado* in which the ceiling was covered with decorative wooden coffers, usually square or polygonal, sunk between the beams; and the more complex *alfarje*, which contained panels decorated with repetitive interlacing patterns constructed of many small pieces of wood and which frequently incorporated gilded stars set off by blues and other brilliant colors.

Only a few of these ceilings remain. The *artesonado* covering the sacristy of the Church of the Hospital of Jesus is the only survivor in central Mexico City, and the *alfarje* covering the Franciscan church in Tlaxcala is the most notable surviv-

ing example in the country. A gifted carpenter-designer, Juan Pérez de Soto, created the ceiling erected over the second basilica at Guadalupe, which was dedicated in 1622. In the preceding decade he had designed the ceilings of the churches of the Colegio de Niñas, of the Casa de Profesa of

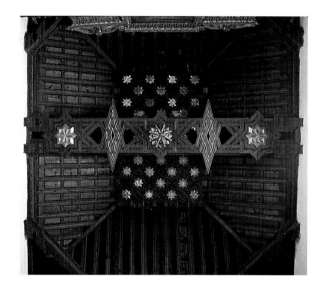

4.4 Ceiling of the Franciscan church in Tlaxcala.

the Jesuits (a small fragment of which survives), and of the Convent of Santa Inés. Other celebrated ceilings covered the metropolitan churches of the Dominicans and the Mercedarians. A series of remarkable designs for intricate *alfarje* ceilings is included in the architectural manuscript of Fray Andrés de San Miguel, a Carmelite friar and architect who was active between 1606 and the middle of the century, and who probably wrote his treatise while he was directing work on the *desagüe*, the city's drainage system, during the 1630s.

After a few decades a reaction set in against the elaborate Moorish ceilings, and the vaulted, domed types of church introduced at the opening of the century became standard. During the course of the century the layout of churches like Santiago Tlatelolco—of Latin cross plan with dome on pendentives over the crossing and towers flanking the facade—was given increasingly dramatic expressiveness. Towers were sometimes single rather than paired and octagonal as well as square. The dome, which at Tlatelolco is so low that it is scarcely perceptible on the exterior, was raised, often above an octagonal drum, frequently ornamented with ribs and lantern, and sometimes given an exterior sheathing of glazed tiles which, sparkling in the sun, made it the dominant exterior feature.

While the one- or two-towered, domed, cruciform plan was becoming normal for the Mexican parish churches, a related but different form was established for the churches of nuns. The type, which is probably based on Andalusian precedents, is exemplified by the Church of the Convent of La Concepción in Mexico City, completed in 1645. The single-naved structure is built parallel to the street with a series of pier buttresses providing a rhythm of verticals along the facade. Stronger vertical accents come from the single tower placed at one end and from the dome rising above the sanctuary at the other end. Twin doors, placed side by side and richly ornamented, provide generous access for the general populace to the central portion of the church. Decorated screens at one end of the nave on both floor and balcony levels permitted the nuns to witness the mass in their ample choirs unobserved by the lay communicants. Often a screened balcony placed near the sanctuary allowed the mother superior privacy in attending mass.

Throughout the seventeenth century and at least the earlier decades of the eighteenth, Baroque impulses met resistance because of the long-persisting fondness for sober severity, a legacy of the style of Juan de Herrera, architect of Philip II's Escorial. Austerity characterizes the exterior of the influential conventual church the Dominicans were building in Puebla contemporaneously with Fray Torquemada's Santiago Tlatelolco (Figs. 4.10, 4.11). Similar severity is still apparent in the interior in the underlying structure of the nave, despite the application, early

in the seventeenth century, of geometrically patterned decorative stucco to the vaults. Unadorned shafts and transverse ribs of gray stone define three large bays, each containing two arches of similar stone that support a wall that is undecorated below the level of the clerestory windows. Three prominent Jesuit churches of the eighteenth century still contain generally sober interiors: Pedro de Arrieta's La Profesa of 1714–20 in Mexico City; and two structures dedicated just before the order's expulsion from New Spain in 1767, La Compañía in Puebla and La Compañía in Guanajuato, then the richest of the century's mining centers. The decorative portions of most church exteriors continued in patterns established in sixteenth-century Spain. Retablo facades remained conservative with the classical orders applied in proper academic fashion. There was less disruption of the firm and clearly defined horizontals, of the entablatures, and verticals, of the supporting columns and pilasters, than in Spain.

Baroque decoration came to prevail in the design of church facades and side portals considerably later than in church interiors. Sober single-naved sixteenth-century interiors, such as Huejotzingo, Xochimilco, and Yanhuitlán, had been decorated by tall gilded many-staged retablos covering the end walls of their sanctuaries. Additional retablos were subsequently placed along the side walls or in decorated chapels. Ultimately, plain and simply painted surfaces came to seem too mean for the house of God, and polychromatic decoration spread over both walls and vaults. In *Art and Time in Mexico*, Elizabeth Wilder Weismann provides an eloquent description of the developed Baroque church interior that encloses the visitor in a mysterious gilded cave, a sort of paradise on earth, wholly distinct from the ordinary world outside. The chancel has become all gold and color, the vaults brightly adorned, and

> the nave lined with retablos until you cannot see the wall. . . . The ideal is saturation, with every flat area converted into lively form, and nothing too static or solid. . . . The work of art is the whole church, the cumulative effect of

everything in it. . . . The Mexicans call this ensemble the *conjunto* and . . . a rich Baroque *conjunto* will absorb almost everything. Starting with a hand-me-down Renaissance retablo over the high altar, the congregation may have added a pair of fashionable altarpieces every half-century for two hundred years, and moved them about, and reassembled them, and installed old forgotten saints from the lumber room, and introduced new cults . . .— without impairing the Baroque ensemble.[10]

The cumulative emotional impact of Baroque religious experience can be more fully recaptured by imagining splendid liturgical ceremonies set between banks of massed candles casting flickering lights upon the soaring retablos and punctuated by bursts of choral and orchestral sound echoing off the stone vaults.

The most dramatic addition to the church interior in the seventeenth century was stucco ornamentation on the walls and vaults of several Dominican churches located in the mountains to the southeast between the city of Puebla and the city and valley of Oaxaca. The Dominicans had employed professional architectural craftsmen more frequently than the other orders in the sixteenth century, and some time early in the seventeenth century imported the first of the stucco workers from Spain who would be employed ornamenting their churches for over a century. Work probably began at Santo Domingo in Puebla. The earliest decoration, restrained and laid flat on the surfaces, was of the vaults of the nave and under the choir (Fig. 4.11). It was based upon northern European Renaissance cartouche and strapwork designs. As these workers and their successors continued to decorate churches in the regions of Puebla and Oaxaca, ornamentation gradually became freer and more complex, developing into elaborate interwoven nets of strapwork scrolls, and ultimately swinging clear of the surfaces in three-dimensional swirls. Notable examples include the rhythmically swinging strapwork of the vault over the crossing of Santo Domingo in Oaxaca (Figs. 4.14 and 4.16); the sweeping vine supporting brightly colored human busts decorating the vault under the choir of the same church; the magnificent ornamentation of

the arch framing the chancel at Yanhuitlán; and the entire Chapel of El Santo Cristo in Tlacolula, near Oaxaca. The masterwork of the school is the Rosario Chapel added to the Church of Santo Domingo in Puebla about 1630, dedicated in 1690, and probably not finished until after 1725 (Figs. 4.18 and 4.19).

In the second half of the seventeenth century, exteriors gradually began to reflect the decorative impulses demonstrated earlier in many interiors. Retablo facades and side portals increasingly began to break away from Renaissance formality and take on a new animation. Although the construction of the Cathedral of Mexico remained generally faithful to its Herrerean origins, important suggestions of movement were added in the seemingly twisting columns of the upper stages of four of its five principal portals, and in the double curves of the six great pairs of volutes that tie the tower bases and buttresses to the facade wall (Figs. 3.21 and 3.22). Apparent movement was given to the columns decorating Mexican church facades by carving the fluting in ripples and by carving deep spiral grooves. These columns were called Salomonic, from their supposed origin in the temple of Solomon. But true twisted columns like those of Bernini's baldacchino in St. Peter's, or of great Spanish retablos like Bernardo Simon de Pineda's in the Caridad Hospital in Seville or José Benito de Churriguera's in San Esteban in Salamanca, were rare.

About 1730 several churches in Mexico City were decorated with waving pilasters, derived ultimately from a design in Guarino Guarini's *Dissegni d'architettura*. The interior portal leading to the chapel in the convent church of Regina Coeli had a waving entablature and a waving broken pediment with a double break as well (Fig. 4.28). The clearly defined rectangles, of the windows and sculptural reliefs of the second stage of facades directly over the portals, were broken by the use of decorative frames which had projecting "ears" at the corners. The firm semicircular arches of the portals were frequently replaced with polygonal ones, most often segments of octagons. Later, as the taste for Moorish designs revived, double-curved, three-lobed, and more complex arches, consisting of alternating angular and curved segments, were used. Pyramidal forms derived from the architecture of Herrera, which were used on the upper stages of facades, became complex and fluttering, suggesting the forms of vegetation and flowers. Human, geometric, and, especially, vegetative ornament was used to fill the areas above and to the sides of portal arches. Vegetation, especially grapevines, was used to decorate the Salomonic columns and, in some examples, to cover the whole portal area in a tapestry in low relief which sparkled in the strong Mexican sun. In the Puebla area, vegetative ornament was applied in stucco and brightly colored glazed tiles were set against dull red ones in diverse patterns. Facades lost their firm classical upper terminations with horizontal cornice or triangular pediment, and in some cases rose and fell as they followed the curve of the vaults behind them. Some skylines, such as that of the Cathedral of Morelia, were punctuated by an alternation of pinnacles and broken and multi-curved and -angled pedimental forms (Fig. 3.24). The most remarkable pirouetted against the sky, caterwauling down from the pinnacle at the center in swooping arcs (Fig. 7.24).

Most Mexican Baroque church facades were flat, infrequently punctuated, like the front of the Cathedral of Mexico, with simple vertical buttresses. The flanking towers, which had one to three square or octagonal belfry stages softened in profile by complex patterns of ornamentation, sometimes were placed slightly in front of the plane of the facade. In other instances the central facade formed a screen in front of the plane of the towers. The central section of the facade of the Cathedral of Oaxaca projects forward from the sections over the side portals so that it reaches the plane of the slightly projecting flanking towers. The whole facade creates a wavelike rhythm of alternating advanced and recessed segments.

Strongly projecting or recessing facades were constructed between the 1680s and the middle of the eighteenth century, but they were infrequent. In Mexico City the upper story of the portals of the Church of San Bernardo and the lower story of the facade of the Church of San Fernando move out from the plane of the wall. The entire central portal sections of the Basilica of Guadalupe, the Cathedral of San Luis Potosí, and the Church of the Compañía in Oaxaca project forward, as though a segment of a hexagon had eased itself out from the mass of the structure.

The most notable Baroque projecting facade was the folded green stone screen that was erected in front of the Sanctuary of Nuestra Señora de la Soledad in Oaxaca sometime before 1690. Designed by an Indian, Tomás de Sigüenza, it is related in arrangement to retablos such as those above the high altars of the Dominican churches of Puebla and Yanhuitlán. The giant screen curves out from a four-storied central section and straightens at its edges so that its three-tiered wings parallel the walls of the towers behind them. The vertical arrangement of the central section consists of a rounded, complexly framed portal, a sculptured relief of the Virgin of Solitude, a deep-set half-octagonal-headed window, and, at the top in a blind arch, the Virgin of the Immaculate Conception. The lower three stories are ornamented by Doric, Ionic, and Salomonic orders and by figures set in niches. At the

4.5 Facade of Soledad church in Oaxaca. See also Plate V.

top, the blind arch is framed by stark pilasters and complexly flowing patterns of curved strapwork. A somewhat-related tiled screen facade was added to the church at Acatepec near Cholula (Fig. 5.9), and a very different type, consisting of a carved stone central section and flat sides and wings covered with tile panels, was added to the sixteenth-century Franciscan church in Puebla.

Mexican recessed facades consist of two principal types, those set in relatively shallow depth under large arches or shells, and those set

4.7 *Facade of Salud church in San Miguel Allende.*

4.6 *Facade of Church of San Juan de Dios in Mexico City.*

deep in great cavelike niches scooped out of the center of the structure and usually decorated with shell ornamentation. Examples of recessed facades set beneath arches or shell overhangs include San Francisco in Oaxaca, the parish church of Panotla, and the sanctuary at Ocotlán, nearby in the State of Tlaxcala. The fully recessed niche facades include the Churches of San Juan de Dios in Mexico City, of San Cristóbal in Mérida, of La Salud in San Miguel Allende, and of the Third Order of San Francisco in Cuernavaca.

THE CHURCHES OF SANTO DOMINGO IN PUEBLA AND OAXACA AND THEIR ROSARIO CHAPELS

In the 1530s, friars of the Dominican order moved south from the area around Mexico City into the territories of the Mixtec and Zapotec Indians, following the route their leader, Fray Domingo de Betanzos, had taken on his thousand-mile walk to Guatemala. Conventual houses were established in Oaxaca and in Antigua, Guatemala, earlier than in Puebla. During the middle years of the century, the southern territories of Chiapas and Guatemala were detached from the Mexican province of Santiago and priories, major conventos which included houses of studies, were established in Oaxaca and Puebla.

San Pablo, the original mud-brick convento in Oaxaca, had disintegrated so that it was no longer inhabitable by 1569. Eight years earlier the Dominican bishop of Oaxaca, Fray Bernardo de Albuquerque, had written for fiscal support to Philip II and had asked that two-ninths of the tithes of the city be made available for the support of the Dominican establishment. Construction of the new convento, Santo Domingo, began about 1569 and was far enough along so that an intermediate chapter meeting could be held in October 1574. The date on the entrance (1575) probably indicates the completion of at least the first floor of the residential building. Work on the church must have been under way in the 1570s, but it was not entirely completed in 1624 when Thomas Gage passed through Oaxaca on his way to Guatemala. Gage, who described the church as the "fairest and strongest in these parts," was particularly impressed by the thickness of the walls that "being upon finishing" supported carts carrying stone and other building materials.

The ground plan of Santo Domingo in Oaxaca, like Santo Domingo in Puebla, is related to that of the church of the motherhouse in Mexico City. In Oaxaca the enclosing shape is rectangular. As in many sixteenth-century friars' churches, the visitor reaches the nave after passing under a vault supporting the choir. The tall barrel-vaulted nave is confined between chapels, four to a side, which open onto it through relatively small arched portals. Unusual in Mexico are the passages running laterally from chapel to chapel, creating what might be considered a narrow internal aisle on each side. Beyond the end of the rows of chapels, a shallow-domed space expands to the limits of the exterior walls creating the impression of transepts within the rectangular shape of the exterior. Against the end wall, and framed by wall segments which create the impression of a structurally separate chancel, a tall and elaborate retablo was fastened. The retablo was altered

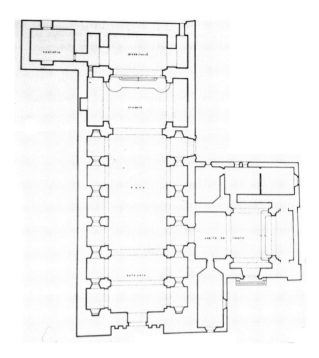

4.8 *Plan of Church of Santo Domingo and the Rosario Chapel, Oaxaca.* Oaxaca arquitectura religiosa, *p. 97.*

in the late seventeenth century, removed in the nineteenth century, and recently has been replaced by a modern structure suggestive of a seventeenth-century work.

The facade of Santo Domingo is set back between flanking towers, like the churches the Dominicans had built in the Indian communities of Coixtlahuaca, Teposcolula, and Yanhuitlán. The overall pattern of the lower three stories is related to the facade of Yanhuitlán around 1600, with niches set between classical columns flanking the arched portal, the sculptured panel, and the window, at the first, second, and third stories. At Oaxaca the towers are much more massive, and the columns and sculptural details of the inner facade more forcefully three-dimensional and placed closer together so that the design seems both more compressed and more powerfully resistant to compression. The broken pediment at the top of the third stage, and the nipped corners of the frame of the relief panel of the second stage suggest a late seventeenth-century date for the facade. It is possible that modifications were

4.9 Facade of Church of Santo Domingo, Oaxaca.

4.10 Facade of Church of Santo Domingo, Puebla.

made at that time to earlier construction. A fourth stage, which seems related to the upper stage of the late seventeenth-century Soledad facade in Oaxaca, culminates in a pediment-shaped gable and contains figures in relief set in a blind segmental arch. This stage is integrated with the broken pedimental forms that rise above the entablature at the top of the third stage.

In Puebla the church of the Dominicans replaces an earlier structure about which little is known. Work on the present structure began about 1571, roughly two years after construction was initiated on the residential building in Oaxaca and perhaps a few years before the church there was started. The church was probably completed in Puebla about 1611, except for the tower to the left that remained unfinished until the nineteenth century. The facade, which carries the date 1611, is one of the most severe in Mexico. At ground level two pairs of plain Tuscan columns on high bases flank a simple arched portal. At the second level the raised columns are replaced by plain

Ionic pilasters flanking a rectangular window that is surrounded by a thin, eared frame. At the third level the facade narrows. A pair of unornamented pilasters is placed on each side of a small relief of St. Dominic. Above the relief an entablature molding breaks, then rises slightly toward the level of the segmental arch of the parapet above. The stark grey of the facade is unbroken by any figures in niches and is relieved only by seven tiny decorative features in lighter stone, most strikingly by representations of four dogs, two above the spandrels of the portal, and two—placed above the upper entablature flanking a scrollwork Cross of Alcantara—with front feet on a globe and torches projecting from their mouths. The dogs represent the legendary dream of Juana de Aza de Guzmán, the mother of St. Dominic, who envisioned her son as a mastiff with a torch in its mouth rolling the world under its feet.

The plan of Santo Domingo, Puebla, is basically rectangular like Santo Domingo, Oaxaca, but it is more complex. A shallow rectangu-

4.12 *Retablo of Church of Santo Domingo, Puebla.*

4.11 *Interior of Church of Santo Domingo, Puebla.*

lar chancel projects from the rear wall of the rectangle, and the right front corner of the rectangle has been cut away. The visitor's sense of the spatial arrangement approximates that in Oaxaca. The nave is entered after passing under the choir vault, and a series of four chapels, as in Oaxaca, frames the nave on the sides. There are no interior passages linking the chapels, and each pair of chapels corresponds to one of two large, slightly domed, double bays of the nave. A third bay of similar size covers the central portion of the area of the crossing, where barrel-vaulted areas at the sides give the impression of constituting true transepts.

The principal retablo, which fills the whole end wall of the chancel and rises close to the vault above it, is more powerfully and dynamically shaped than sixteenth-century examples such as Huejotzingo. The linear horizontality of its entablatures is broken by projections, indentations, and by curving and gently arching and rising segments. The gilded columns form muscular groups of twos and threes. The present appearance of the retablo reflects changes made late in the seventeenth century and later. A 1688 contract provided that Pedro Maldonado, master of the most prominent workshop in Mexico City for the design and production of retablos, should modernize the altarpiece after the pattern of the one in the Church of San Pedro and San Pablo in the capital. The contract specified that new Baroque twisted and decorated columns, *salomónicas revestidas*, should be prepared for the lowest level, and the statues were to be recarved by Lucas from the barrio of Santa Ana in the City of Mexico.

Despite the remarkable character of the stucco ornamentation of the churches of Santo Domingo in Puebla and Oaxaca and their Rosario chapels, very little is known of the stucco workers or the chronology of their activity. We assume that a group of experienced Spanish stuccoists, probably from Andalusia, was brought to Puebla to decorate the vaults of Santo Domingo about the time of the completion of the facade in 1611.

These workers, or others with similar training, began the ornamentation of Santo Domingo, Oaxaca, somewhat later. It seems clear that the work in both churches and their Rosario chapels continued over an extended period, well into the eighteenth century in Oaxaca.

The decoration of the vaults and upper-nave walls of Santo Domingo, Puebla, may have been completed before the stuccoists moved on. The work there seems as early as any in Oaxaca or elsewhere. Perhaps the first decoration was applied to the vaults of the two large double bays of the nave (see Fig. 4.11). They are ornamented with firm, rather static, geometric patterns in white and gold. Cartouches are isolated against the plain wall surfaces that surround the clerestory windows in these bays. Ornamentation of the vault under the choir is more complex, combining modest-sized gilded elements, round and diamond-shaped, with cartouches and strapworks patterned in orderly swirls. The climax of the decorative scheme is the vault of the bay of the crossing, where cartouches and more freely composed strapwork ornamentation surround a gilded

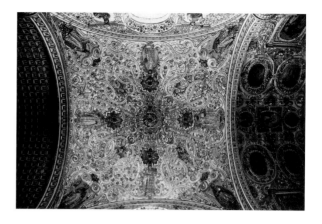

4.14 *Vault over crossing of Church of Santo Domingo, Oaxaca.*

circle set in an eared rectangular frame. At the edges of the design, pieces of strapwork rise from the surface of the vault to wrap around other elements of the ornamentation.

In Oaxaca, the ornamental stucco work of the church of Santo Domingo is freer and seems of later construction. The flaking decoration of the vault over the great staircase—which divides at the landing as it rises from the northwest corner of the cloister into the residential building— seems to have been finished before any work in the church. Cartouches, large strapwork scrolls— freer and cruder than those of the nave vaults in Puebla—and stiff stucco representations of Dominican friars are the principal features of the ornamentation. The domed vault over the simulated crossing of the church, which was probably the first vault completed in that structure, is more complex than any in the main church in Puebla. Full-length and bust-length representations of ecclesiastical figures are surrounded by a curving network of small-scale strapwork ornamentation. Above this strapwork is overlaid larger scale ornamentation, suggesting ribs, scrolls, and rhythmically swinging and interlacing ribbons. At the opposite end of the nave, the choir is also covered by a domed vault. Sixteen ribs, decorated with gilded, curving stems or fronds, enclose sixteen

4.13 *Vault over stair, convento building of Santo Domingo, Oaxaca.*

4.15 *Vault of the nave and of the choir of the Church of Santo Domingo, Oaxaca.*

4.16 *Vault under the choir of the Church of Santo Domingo, Oaxaca.*

ascending rows of diminishing stucco heads of Dominican prelates and friars framed in gilded cartouches. At the crown of the dome a gilded keystone is suspended, decorated by the dove of the Holy Spirit.

The barrel vault of the nave, divided by ribs into four sections to correspond with the arched portals of the chapels below, contains five rows of paintings which are framed by gilded stucco decoration set against a white ground. Some of the ornamentation is of strapwork, but there are also shells and other curving forms which suggest the rococo vocabulary of the eighteenth century. On the middle zones of the nave walls below elegant patterns of interlacing strapwork, fronds and cartouches decorate the areas between and above the arches of the portals. Somewhat related, but cruder and probably earlier, ornamentation occupies the sides of the vault under the choir, framing the most notable decorative ensemble of the church.

In a shallow oval at the top of this vault, a great curving and branching vine sustains, like flowers, thirty-three busts of kings, queens, soldiers, Dominicans, and other notables. At the top, in what seems to be a different and later style, is placed the Virgin and her Child surrounded by a corona of angels. The general design is derived from medieval representations of the family tree—descending from Jesse, the father of King David—that certified the royal human lineage of Jesus. Father Francisco de Burgoa, who lived at Santo Domingo from about 1618 during the probable period of the decoration of the choir vault, wrote later in life that the vine represents the descent and worldly nobility of the Dominicans' father St. Dominic, with a portrayal above the church's doorway of Don Félix de Guzmán from whose breast the celebrated vine springs. Elizabeth Wilder Weismann has questioned this interpretation and suggested that the representation is the old medieval Jesse tree with the kings of Judah transformed into folk versions of medieval royalty. Whatever the iconographic intentions of the friars who commissioned the work, the stuccoists created a work of great charm—a diverting melange of solemn-faced figures; stiff, small leaves; and heavy bunches of grapes supported by the wonderfully vigorous, swaying stem and the interweaving branches of the vine.

The Rosario chapels of the Dominican churches in Puebla and Oaxaca are entered at opposite ends of the churches, in Puebla on the left side just before the altar area and in Oaxaca on the right side just past the entrance. The devotion of the rosary developed among Dominicans in the late fifteenth century. To promote its development a legend was fostered of a miraculous appearance by Mary to St. Dominic during the bloody Albighensian struggle of the early thirteenth century. The cult was introduced to Mexico in the late 1530s, and a confraternity of Nuestra Señora del Rosario was organized in Puebla in 1553. Six years later, the first edition of a frequently reprinted pamphlet was published by a Puebla Dominican explaining the uses, festivals, and singing clubs of the Rosary. The intention to construct a separate chapel of the Rosary was first mentioned in 1596, fifteen years before the probable completion of the Church of Santo Domingo, but there is no written record of work being undertaken before 1632. Separate structures attached to churches for chapels were not known in sixteenth-century Mexico, but there are some Spanish examples.

Pedro García Durán and Juan Bautista de Alarcón are recorded as working on the decoration of the Rosary Chapel between 1632 and 1659 under the direction of the architect, Francisco Gutiérrez, who had contracted in 1596 to build the crossing, the sanctuary, two chapels, and the sacristy. The chapel was dedicated in 1690 and celebrated locally as the "Eighth Marvel of the New World." Completion of its decoration may have been delayed until about 1730. The central tabernacle was not consecrated until 1759.

The plan is cruciform, consisting of a nave of three rectangular bays (Figs. 4.18 and 4.19), a square bay at the crossing flanked by shallow rectangular transepts, and a rectangular bay at the rear similar in size to those of the nave. A dome rises above an octagonal drum, which is supported by the four arches of the crossing and intertervening squinches. The decoration of this straightforward structure creates a dazzling splendor. Seemingly the result of labor extended over almost an entire century, the Rosario Chapel reveals no apparent discordance. Details are subordinated to an overwhelming unity. The initial impression is of uniformity of style and of a quality of execution greatly superior to Santo Domingo, Oaxaca.

More careful observation reveals variations in style and workmanship. As is character-

4.17 *Presentation of the Virgin, Rosario Chapel, Church of Santo Domingo, Puebla.*

istic of Mexican Baroque decoration, the figurative sculpture is generally commonplace, executed with sufficient skill to provide accents and to fill gaps in the overall pattern but uninteresting if studied carefully. The large paintings of the Virgin and the Rosary by Joseph Rodríguez Cornero are of modest competence. Exceptional in the ensemble are two awkwardly but charmingly composed works of folk art; narrative panels of the life of the Virgin placed behind the tabernacle low on the rear wall of the chapel beneath the painting of the Propagation of the Rosary; and an arc of naked children, seen as angel musicians, surrounding God the Father, that decorates the area around a door in the wall of the elevated choir at the opposite end of the chapel. The nonfigurative ornamentation is of uniformly high quality. It consists primarily, in approximate order of execution, of flat strapwork, of three-dimensional strapwork, and of vegetative forms composed in fields or bands of swirls.

The area probably decorated earliest is that of the dome, drum, and squinches over the crossing, which was described in 1690 with breathless enthusiasm by Fray Díego de Gorózpe in his small book on parchment, *Octava maravilla del Nuevo Mundo en la Gran Capilla del Rosario.* The dome is almost wholly covered with strapwork laid flat on its surface and is divided into eight sections, which are defined by ribs in the

4.18 Crossing and dome of Rosario Chapel, Church of Santo Domingo, Puebla. See also Plate VI.

4.19 Nave of Rosario Chapel, Church of Santo Domingo, Puebla.

4.20 Ornamentation beneath a picture in the bay closest to the crossing, Rosario Chapel, Church of Santo Domingo, Puebla.

4.21 Detail of Hope and Faith vaults of Rosario Chapel, Church of Santo Domingo, Puebla.

form of stems growing from vases resting upon the cornice of the drum. At the center of each section, also resting on the cornice, is an arched window. Above the windows are six winged seraphs of Isaiah and above the seraphs are female figures representing gifts of the Holy Spirit, or, in one instance, Divine Grace. At the summit of the dome is a ring of jagged projections, the gilded rays of sun surrounding a band with an inscription from Isaiah, "Requiescat Super Eam Spiritus

Domini" (And the Spirit of the Lord shall rest upon her). At the center, projecting from a representation on the surface of the Dominican symbol, the Cross of Alcantara, is the white dove of the Holy Spirit.

Each of the eight sections of the drum contains a rectangular window, located below the arched window of the corresponding section of the dome. Each rectangular window is flanked by statues of virgin martyrs in niches. There are sixteen statues in all, two between each of the windows. The four squinches in the spandrels between the arches below the drum each contain a stocky angel, with stiffly spread wings, holding a ribbon inscribed with phrases praising and hailing the Virgin.

The nave seems to have been decorated after the upper areas of the crossing. The walls are ornamented with gilded three-dimensional strapwork framing three large paintings on each wall, and with elaborate brackets of strapwork, which are placed beneath the pictures and which increase in complexity as one approaches the area of the crossing. The brackets under the middle pictures on each wall are composed of rhythmically vigorous interlaces of strapwork and contain, at the top, the small head and shoulders of a knight of Calatrava clad in a helmet with three plumes, visor up. The brackets under the paintings nearest the crossing are more intricately overlaid and tangled. Their strapwork seems to be blown from the wide open mouth of a grotesque head with puffed out cheeks and furrowed brow, occupying the lower center of the complex composition. Overhead, the vaults are dedicated to the theological virtues: faith, hope, and charity. In the charity and hope vaults, intricate patterns of interlacing strapwork surround female figures in oval frames. In the charity dome, closest to the crossing and probably the first completed, elements of strapwork rise from the overall weave on the surface of the vault to swing over the edge of the frame of the central oval. In the hope dome, a section of tightly woven strapwork forms a perceptible oval around the central framed figure and provides a transition between it and the outer, more loosely composed strapwork. The faith vault, over the choir end of the nave and probably the last executed, has an outer frame of intricately curving rhythmic strapwork set against outer areas covered with swirls of vine.

These swirling patterns appear also in various places on the walls below, most notably in the borders framing the door to the main church and in various decorative bands in the area of the crossing and the bay behind it. They seem to constitute the latest of the ornamental patterns used to decorate the wall and vault surfaces of the chapel.

The tabernacle standing under the dome, which was added roughly thirty years after the completion of the decoration of the walls and vaults, fits its setting but is of only moderate interest in itself. The structure consists of two principal stages with a dome and lantern above them. Groups of three marble Corinthian columns are placed at the four corners of the large lower stage with great arched openings that break through the line of the entablature on each side, providing views of the centrally placed, pearl encrusted, doll-like representation of the Virgin of the Rosary, which is crowned in gold and holds a minute, gold-crowned child. The smaller upper story is set back and follows the same general design but has its arched openings contained within its entablature and substitutes, at its corners, triads of twisted, Salomonic columns for the tall marble ones below. Statues placed over the columns at both levels soften the transitions where the structure is reduced in scale as it rises. A winged angel is at the top perched upon the dome of the lantern.

In Oaxaca the rosary chapel was begun and probably completed within the decade of the 1720s, as the century-long decorative effort in Puebla was coming to an end. The chapel, which replaced an earlier one devoted to the Virgin of the Rosary located on one side of the main altar in the church, is cruciform in plan like the one in Puebla, but is more compact having a nave of only one bay and only a very shallow chancel beyond the crossing. Instead of a free-standing tabernacle under the dome, it has a retablo, recently rebuilt in the Baroque style, placed against the rear wall.

The ornamentation of the chapel (Figs. 4.22 and 4.23) creates a pleasant appearance although it seems, oddly, less uniform than that of the chapel in Puebla which took so long to complete. The upper areas—the vaults, the dome, and the lunettes of the walls above the cornice line—are profusely decorated. The white lower walls, perhaps the last to be finished, are treated with more restraint. Paintings in oval frames are carefully placed against the plain wall surfaces and decorated with shell and scroll forms and linked with a variety of ribbons, some suggestive of rosary beads. The vaults and lunettes are decorated with gilded and colored figures set in oval frames

4.22 *View toward choir and vault, Rosario Chapel, Church of Santo Domingo, Oaxaca.*

4.23 *Dome of the Rosario Chapel, Church of Santo Domingo, Oaxaca.*

and surrounded by pleasing patterns of tree and vine forms. The four Evangelists are placed in tri-lobed frames in the pendentives above the sober gilded pairs of half-columns and coffered arches of the crossing. Windows alternate with figures set in niches in the octagonal drum, and shells and fronds and other forms suggestive of the rococo merge with strapwork scrolls of the older style in the decoration of the dome.

The charming general impression the chapel makes on the visitor, especially by the decoration of the lower walls and the vault of the nave, is dissipated by careful study. The figurative reliefs are less interestingly executed than the best ones in Puebla, and the decorative ornamentation is loose and slack, wholly without the crispness of Puebla. As Joseph A. Baird wrote in *The Churches of Mexico*, the work is a slapdash representation of "adequate provincialism" with "passable execution"[11] but superficial.

THE JESUIT ESTABLISHMENT AT TEPOTZOTLÁN: THE *CAMARÍN* OF THE VIRGIN OF LORETO

The Jesuit province of New Spain, with that of Brazil the largest outside Europe, was late in being founded. In 1572 (thirty-eight years after St. Ignatius of Loyola founded his Society, or Company, of Jesus in Paris) fifteen Jesuits (eight priests and seven brothers) arrived in Mexico under the leadership of their provincial, Padre Dr. Pedro Sánchez, former rector of the University of Alcalá. For some time previously, Philip II had been urged by many in Mexico, including the viceroy, the inquisitor, Bishop Vasco de Quiroga, and the Audiencia, to procure Jesuits for the colony. None, however, were dispatched until after the order had been established for over twenty years in Brazil and had been forced to give up a blood-marked six-year struggle to convert the Indians of what is now the southeastern coast of the United States.

Before the death of Ignatius in 1556, the primary commitment of the society to education and to missionary work was established. In Mexico the Jesuits quickly secured the patronage of

Alonzo Villaseca, one of the colony's wealthiest entrepreneurs, and of Antonio Cortés, the Indian governor of Tacuba, and they founded in the city several educational institutions called colleges. These included Santa María de Todos Santos, for poor students of reputable families; San Gregorio, for Indian boys; and four other colleges constituting parts of the Colegio Máximo de San Pedro y San Pablo. Alonso Villaseca endowed the latter and named it for his patron saints. Outside the city, colleges were established during the sixteenth century in Oaxaca; Pátzcuaro, later shifted to Valladolid (Morelia); Puebla; Guadalajara; Zacatecas; and Veracruz. The Jesuit colleges and seminaries, which did not restrict their function to the training of priests, operated primarily on the secondary level, ranging at the extremes from instructing Indian boys in Christian piety, music, reading, and writing to instruction at the university level within the Colegio Máximo de San Pedro y San Pablo. These schools found ready applicants. The colleges of the Colegio Máximo had three hundred students in 1575, two years after its foundation, and doubled that number the following year.

In 1580 the Jesuits were given a benefice in the Indian community of Tepotzotlán, a few miles north of Mexico City, which had originally been occupied by the Franciscans. A residence was established for a few Jesuits to study the difficult Otomi language in preparation for missionary activities. Two years later a parish church was created for the Indian pueblo, and, in 1584, its governor, Martín Maldonado, gave the Jesuits several houses and valuable property to create the seminary of San Martín for the boys of the community. The earliest Jesuit novices in Mexico had been educated in the city in the complex of structures a few streets north of the cathedral, which had been given to the order by Alonzo Villaseca in 1572. A regular novitiate was established at Tepotzotlán in 1585 or 1586.

Substantial building at Tepotzotlán was made possible shortly after 1600 by the bequest of Pedro Ruiz de Ahumada, whose portrait statue remains in the domestic, or private, chapel of the Jesuits; he is kneeling in prayer clad in armor with handsome ruffs at the neck and wrists. The oldest surviving structures are the residential quarters surrounding the Patio de los Aljibes, the parish church for the Indians, and, in its original form, the domestic chapel. Father Andrés Pérez de Rivas, Jesuit missionary, provincial, and historian, praised the earlier seventeenth-century layout as cheerful and of sufficient capacity to keep the novices separate from the other Jesuits. He described the vaulted parish church which had been built by the Indians and restored by the Jesuits. The domestic chapel for assembly, prayer, and the exercises of both priests and novices seemed to him the most splendid element of the establishment. Father Pérez de Rivas particularly noted the altar shrine and gilded retablo containing a painting of the Virgin, which he informs us was copied, thanks to the personal intervention of the general of the order, St. Francisco Borgia, and Cardinal St. Carlo Borromeo, from the one in Santa Maria Maggiore in Rome believed to have been painted by St. Luke. In the mid-seventeenth century Tepotzotlán housed thirty-three Jesuits, ten priests, fifteen novices, and eight others.

Major additions were made possible by a large gift in 1670 from members of the Medina family: the Jesuit Pedro de Medina; his mother, Isabel Picazo; and his brother, Francisco Antonio de Medina, "Sargento Major Capitan," Knight of Santiago, and director of the mint. In his sermon at the dedication in 1682 of the great church of San Francisco Javier paid for by the Medinas, Father Francisco Florencia, S.J., compared the structure to a huge mint pouring out spiritual blessings to be credited to the "Noblissima Medinarum Gens."

The handsome facade, the tower, and the dazzling interior designed with retablos and paintings by Miguel Cabrera would not be completed until after the middle of the eighteenth century, a few years before the expulsion of the Jesuits from Mexico in 1767 (Fig. 7.30). Other important structures, however, were constructed in the decades after 1670. The residential quarters were greatly expanded to the rear, creating around the Patio of the Orange Trees a wholly distinct residential area for novices.

The Jesuits were leaders in the Counter-Reformation exaltation of Mary, the mother of Christ, and co-promoters with the Dominicans of the rosary. Another popular devotion centered on the house of the Virgin of Loreto. According to the legend, after the Turks captured Jerusalem in the late thirteenth century, Mary's house in Nazareth was flown miraculously by angels first to Dalmatia and then across the Adriatic to Loreto in the Italian coastal region near Ancora. A Jesuit of Lombard birth, Juan Bautista Zappa, arrived at Tepotzotlán in 1678 and initiated the building of a Santa Casa, a holy house of the Virgin, following the modest dimensions, thirty-one by thirteen feet, of the stone structure in Loreto. Miguel Venegas's life of Father Zappa provides an account of the communal participation in the work. "The whole town, and the inhabitants of the country nearby, inspired by Father Zappa's enthusiasm, came . . . and urged their friends to take part in so pious a task. Some worked at the actual building, some carried stone, others provided the needed materials, and all worked with such zeal that this angelic little chapel, with its sacristy and ambulatory, stood complete in less than a year."[12]

Father Zappa's Santa Casa was imitated almost immediately in one created by Father Juan María de Salvatierra adjoining San Gregorio, the Jesuit church for Indians in Mexico City. After a half-century Father Zappa's original structure was replaced by the present house of Loreto and its remarkable *camarín*, or ceremonial dressing room, for the Virgin. We know nothing of the location of Father Zappa's building and "sacristy," which was probably a *camarín*. It is possible that their foundations were used in the new structures that were described in the account, discovered by Pablo C. de Gante in the *Gaceta de México* of February 1734, of the enthusiastic ceremony of dedication held on the previous Christmas Day. The account attributes the direction of construction to two Jesuits, Juan de Ortega and Ignacio de Paredes.

The persons primarily responsible for financial support of the undertaking were Manuel Tomás de la Canal and his wife María de Hervas y Flores of San Miguel Allende, who are portrayed as kneeling figures in another of their philanthropic projects, the *camarín* of the House of Loreto attached to their home city's Oratory of San Felipe Neri. The construction of the Santa

4.24 Interior, intermediate level and vault, Camarín of the Virgin of Loreto, Jesuit Church, Tepotzotlán.

4.25 Interior, vault and lantern, Camarín of the Virgin of Loreto, Jesuit Church, Tepotzotlán.

Casa and *camarín* in San Miguel followed within a year the dedication of their counterparts at Tepotzotlán and shared some of their features.

The House of Loreto at Tepotzotlán is placed at right angles to the north side of the nave of the Church of San Francisco Javier in a domed structure with plain exterior walls. An imposing arched and broken-pedimented portal leads from the nave into a space from which the interior of the house proper can be viewed through a rectangular grilled opening. Passages, or aisles, at the sides lead back into the octagonal *camarín* at the rear. The left, or west, passage also provides access to the elaborately decorated reliquary chapel of San José, which was dedicated five years after the house and *camarín*, in 1738. These peripheral passages provided space for devotional processions.

The house itself is modest in dimensions and relatively modest in its decoration. Handsome benches and large and small paintings are now placed against the three outer walls. Above an altar on the rear wall, which is shared by the *camarín*, a gilded retablo frames in its center a glazed niche containing a doll-like representation of the Virgin of Loreto which Father Zappa is reputed to have brought from Italy in 1676.

The *camarín*, compact and tall, is overwhelming in the totality of its encrusted decoration, red and gilded, with accents of green, blue, and white. Wider and narrower segments of wall alternate around the octagon. The four wider sides contain sophisticated retablos framed with sharp-edged *estípite* columns, which were just beginning to become fashionable in Mexico in the 1730s. At the center of the retablos are glazed niches containing sculptured representations of St. Peter, St. Paul, the Immaculate Conception, and, visible through glass in the wall shared with her house, the back of the image of the Virgin of Loreto. The four narrower wall segments contain elaborate gilded areas framing paintings. Two of these narrow segments, which flank the wall shared with the Santa Casa, also contain doorways, with semioctagonal tops, which lead into the passages alongside the house. Marking the divisions between the eight sides of the octagon are pilasters decorated primarily with two superposed blackish busts of human figures with upraised arms supporting baskets of fruits.

The pilasters and the remarkable decorations of the dome and lantern are different in style from the retablos and the gilded frames, and are animated by the zestfulness of inspired folk art rather than the finish of metropolitan design. Ribs decorated with stylized floral patterns arch across the low dome from the tops of the pilasters, so that they constitute a continuous network of bands and divide the dome into an alternating pattern of triangular and larger, nearly rectangular, segments. Deep-set octagonal windows placed within arched frames ring the lowest sector of the dome, except on the side above the Virgin of Loreto where the retablo extends up into the zone of the dome. In the triangular segments the octagonal window frames are decorated with shells, and the narrowing apexes of the triangular areas above the windows are filled with large red segments of shells. The broader, approximately rectangular, sectors above the wider sides of the octagon are decorated so as to suggest heaven and are filled with innumerable stars, winged angel heads, circular forms containing monograms, and in one area, representations of the sun and the moon. Each of these sectors is dominated by a large winged archangel, standing with one leg placed upon a corbel and with the other booted leg thrust out from the vault toward the spectator below. The archangels' upthrust arms appear to support the banded rib of the vault above.

At the top of the dome, in the nearly square sector at the center of the pattern of intersecting rib bands, is an octagonal frame decorated at the corners by angels' wings and heads. Above the frame rises a multistage octagonal lantern, lit by concealed windows at two different levels, and providing at its apparent top a vision of the white dove of the Holy Spirit surrounded by aureoles of angel heads and wings.

The exterior of the lantern is relatively plain; it consists of two superposed domelike stages containing octagonal windows and a small windowless top stage, which resembles an ordinary lantern in form, above the level of the dove in the interior. Ornamentation is restricted to strikingly curved flying buttresses at the corners, scalloped fringes marking the upper edges of three of the stages, and triangular forms suggestive of small receding pediments which mark the top of the uppermost stage.

Both multistaged lanterns and banded vaults are extremely unusual in Mexico. The probable architects of the *camarín*, the Jesuit designers of the Chapel of San José, Juan de Ortega and Ignacio de Paredes, may have drawn inspiration from remembered Moorish designs in Spain or from the works of the great Baroque architects of seventeenth-century Italy. Banded vaults were a prominent feature of many Islamic structures in Spain, most notably of the great mosque in Cordova. An overall network of pilasters and banded ribs decorates the vault of Francesco Borromini's Chapel of the Congregation of the Propaganda Fide in Rome, completed in about 1650. Banded ribs and multiple stages are prominent features of the vaults and lanterns of several structures of the Theatine priest, Guarino Guarini, pictured in the plates of his posthumously published *Disegni di Architettura Civile ed Ecclesiastica* of 1686. Whatever the inspiration for the design, Islamic or Italian or both, the vault at Tepotzotlán is a simplified derivation, lacking the structural inventiveness of Guarini's designs and the full visual complexity of the Moorish ones. As in almost all works of the Mexican Baroque, the primary expressive means is an exuberant inventiveness of surface decoration. In the *camarín* at Tepotzotlán the banded ribs ornament the vault; they do not, as in Guarini's vaults, constitute it. The lantern has more structural complexity than the vault, but its forms are relatively traditional ones. Spatial and structural inventiveness are important qualities of much of the greatest Italian and German Baroque architecture; only rarely are they important constituents of the Spanish or the Mexican Baroque.

THE CONCEPTIONIST CONVENT OF REGINA COELI IN MEXICO CITY

The Community of Conceptionist Nuns of the Birth of Our Lady and Queen of Heaven, generally known as the Regina Coeli, was established in 1573. The second convent for nuns in Mexico City, it was established by nuns from the community of La Concepción, which had been in existence for thirty years. The Conceptionist order was the most prominent one in New Spain, and La Concepción was the source of much of the colony's female monasticism. Of twenty female convents in Mexico City identified late in the colonial period by Alexander von Humboldt, eight were Conceptionist and they contained well over half the total convent population. The order had been founded late in the fifteenth century by Beatriz de Silva, a Portuguese noblewoman resident in Spain. The order expressed particular devotion to the Immaculate Conception of Mary and was linked by Cardinal Cisneros with the Franciscan order of Santa Clara.

Regina Coeli, like its sister Conceptionist convents La Concepción and La Encarnación, and its nearby neighbor, San Jerónimo, the home of Sor Juana Inés de la Cruz, was a large establishment known for diverse, leisured patterns of living rather than for austere piety.

Nothing is known of the early structures of Regina Coeli erected in the years immediately following 1570. A church was dedicated in 1636 that had an intricately paneled Moorish *artesonado* ceiling. Another dedication took place in 1731, the year in which the handsome adjoining chapel donated by the Medina-Picazo family was begun. Miguel Custodio Durán, one of the city's leading architects, modernized the church before undertaking the design of the chapel. It is likely that the plan and general form of the church, which had been established in the building campaign of the mid-1630s, were retained.

The arrangement is similar to most of the churches of the convents for nuns in Mexico. A single nave is placed parallel to the street with a tower to the east and a dome over the area before the sanctuary to the west. At the eastern end of the interior are located the upper and lower screened choirs in which the nuns could attend mass unobserved by the general populace, who occupied the three bays of the nave and the larger bay under the dome. A large gilded retablo rises behind the altar, blocking off the polygonal extension of the sanctuary, and providing a dramatic termination of the vista to the west. The altarpiece was designed by a painter, Francisco Mar-

4.26 *Nuns' Church of Regina Coeli, Mexico City.*

4.27 *Interior of Church of Regina Coeli, Mexico City.*

tínez, who had collaborated with an architect, Felipe de Ureña, in designing another important retablo for the church shortly after Custodio Durán's modernization. At present virtually the entire surface of the side walls is covered with retablos, the most recent of them Neo-Classical. Light in the barrel-vaulted nave is subdued, but it increases dramatically in the area of the dome and the sanctuary because of the eight windows of the

drum and the four of the lantern of the dome. As a result the main retablo and the principal side one, the Altar de la Coronación, which fills the outer wall of the bay below the dome, catch ample light on the gilded edges of their faceted surfaces. The chapel endowed by the Medina-Picazos is placed at a right angle to the nave of the church, extending south from its middle bay. Retablos designed by Miguel Custodio Durán and the sculptor Juan José Nadal line its sides. The main retablo is set in a shallow rectangular bay that extends to the south beyond the domed principal bay. The side retablos are set off that bay in even shallower barrel-vaulted segments to the east and west. The side retablos are adorned with Salomónicas, and the main one is among the earliest in the city to display *estípites*. An elaborately decorated screened choir for the nuns occupies the fourth side, above the arched portal leading into the church.

The most prominent features of Durán's work at the Regina Coeli are the main portals on the street, the portal in the church leading to the chapel, the domes of both church and chapel, and the impressive tower. The portals exemplify characteristics of Custodio Durán's style evident in two other important structures attributed to him, the hospital churches of San Lázaro and San Juan de Dios. Both were endowed by the Medina-Picazo family which had made possible major additions to the Jesuit establishment at Tepotzotlán in 1670. The general arrangement of the portals was familiar in eighteenth-century Mexico. The principal exterior portal has an arched entrance below and a scene of sculptured relief above, both flanked with pilasters and capped with an entablature and a pediment. The interior portal (Fig. 4.28) consists of an arched entrance framed by pilasters, an entablature, and a pediment.

The most significant of Custodio Durán's modifications of these traditional decorative arrangements are the two layers in the pediments which break open at the center in the Baroque manner, and the ripples into the outer edges of the layered pilasters and their fluting. The interior portal, designed two or three years after the exterior ones, is more advanced in style. The rippling effect is extended into another dimension. In addition to the wavelike flow along the outer

4.28 *Interior portal to the Medina Picazo chapel, Church of Regina Coeli, Mexico City.*

ence of the major architect of later seventeenth-century Seville, Leonardo de Figueroa.

The tower placed at the northeast corner of the church is subtly proportioned (Fig. 4.26). The plain and square lower stage makes up just under two-thirds of the height of the whole. It is subdivided into a short base, a virtually cubic lower section, and a substantially taller upper section. The decorated upper stages of the tower are octagonal, diminishing in height as they ascend through two belfry stages to a dome and lantern. The lower stage contains alternating narrower- and wider-arched openings for bells, which are separated by Corinthian columns decorated with chevrons covering their lower thirds. The upper stage also alternates narrower segments and wider segments. The narrow ones have octagonal openings cut above figures set in shell-topped niches and the wider ones have openings for bells decorated by flowing double-curved Neo-Gothic arches. The Corinthian columns dividing the segments are set in front of a pilaster layer and have rippled fluting in their upper portions and floral patterns decorating their lower portions. The tower is capped by an octagonally segmented dome and a small lantern. Arched openings break up into the area of the dome. They are enclosed by alternating shorter and taller frames. The taller frames are placed above the double-curved Gothic arches of the upper belfry stage and terminate in scrolled pediments.

edges of the pilasters and along the outer edges of pyramidal projections—which rise like flaming daggers at both ends of the fragmented pediment—the pediment itself is made to undulate out toward the spectator and back toward the wall so that the whole portal is set into quivering motion.

Both the dome of the church and the dome of the chapel are set on octagonal drums that are designed in a restrained manner. They obtain their principal exterior esthetic effect from a cutting-back of plain wall surfaces in several layers around the windows so that the outer layer suggests a simplified pilaster at the margin of each octagonal segment. The domes themselves are divided into octagonal segments, which in the dome of the church are separated by ribs. The octagonal dome over the chapel, which was constructed later, is more complex. The surface is given a calmly undulating motion with each section curving in from its outer edges where it meets its neighbors, and curving out at its center to form a convex curve over the window in the drum stage below. The lanterns of both domes are octagonal, alternating arched windows and shell-topped niches. That of the chapel dome is supported by decorative buttresses terminating at their lower ends in scrolls. This feature, like some others in Custodio Durán's style, seems to reflect the influ-

GUADALUPE: THE BASILICA DEDICATED TO OUR LADY, 1695–1709

On March 25, 1695, Archbishop Doctor Francisco Aguiar y Seijas, zealous in charity, suspicious of women, and hostile to Sor Juana Inés de la Cruz, laid the first stone of a new basilica dedicated to Our Lady of Guadalupe. Most prominent in the distinguished gathering for the ceremony was Viceroy Gaspar de la Cerda Sandoval Silva y Mendoza, gentleman of the royal bedchamber and Conde de Galve. The viceroy's prudent exercise of his office had not been able to avert the frightening corn riot of 1692, which had left many dead and created general destruction totaling more than three million pesos. The 1690s, the final decade of Hapsburg rule, were discouraging to New Spain. The great floods of 1690 had filled the partially empty lake beds, covered the causeways, and flooded much of the isolated city. Insects destroyed what wheat had survived the floods, and, as a result, corn was in such short supply that it had to be rationed for years. Famine was nearly as threatening in 1695 as it had been in 1692, the year of the upheaval. Within a month of the ceremony of the cornerstone, Sor Juana Inés de la Cruz died after nursing her sisters struck down by an epidemic.

The new basilica was built as a replacement for one that had been completed in 1622. The earlier structure had been constructed of stone and covered with a mudéjar ceiling of patterned wood designed by Juan Pérez de Sota. After three-quarters of a century's use and severe damage from the flooding, it was beyond repair. That basilica was probably the fourth religious structure erected at the foot of Tepeyac Hill, once sacred to the Aztec mother-goddess, Tonantzin. The first, a chapel dedicated to the Spanish Virgin of Guadalupe, had been built by Cortés's Lieutenant Gonzalo de Sandoval at the end of the northern causeway to Tenochtitlán for his headquarters during the terrible siege. The third, a hermitage, had been built at the order of Archbishop Montúfar in 1555 or 1556 to help foster the growing worship of the Mexican Virgin of Guadalupe.

Little is known of the history of the design and construction of the 1695 basilica of Our Lady of Guadalupe apart from the date construction was begun and the date of the dedication, 1709. A huge sum, approaching 500,000 pesos, was raised from wealthy citizens and the diocesan treasury, and an edifice approaching cathedral size was proposed. The design is attributed to Pedro de Arrieta. A drawing of 1651 signed by José Durán provides an earlier conception of the structure.

Pedro de Arrieta's life before 1691, when he passed the examination of the Guild of Architects in Mexico City, is undocumented. He may have been born in Spain, perhaps in Levante or Aragon. He rapidly rose to prominence as an architect, being chosen architect of the Inquisition

and selected for his first term as Master of the Guild of Architects in the same year in which the basilica was begun. His application for the position of master architect of the cathedral and the viceregal palace, which he was awarded in 1720, listed as his works, in addition to the Basilica at Guadalupe, the important surviving Church of San Miguel Arcángel and the Church of the Casa Profesa of the Jesuits, several other churches and convents, the sacristy of the Dominican church, and a seminary building for the Cathedral. His listed secular works included two bridges, a structure for storing grain, and the principal slaughterhouse of the city. In addition to these works he was responsible for the design of the Palace of the Inquisition, constructed between 1732 and 1736.

The basilica is no longer open to the public because of structural weakness. A huge new circular sanctuary designed by Pedro Ramírez Vázquez now houses the miraculous mantle. Substantial changes were made during the 250 years of the basilica's use. At various times portions of the ornamentation were modernized, and substantial structural changes were made as well. The interior was redone in Neo-Classical style and virtually nothing remains suggestive of early eighteenth-century ornamentation. The exterior preserves much of its original appearance, although the building was substantially extended to the rear and was modified at the roof level where it now reveals metal and concrete reinforcements. In the 1940s the facade underwent significant renovation of its parapet and flanking upper windows.

The plan signed by José Durán called for a structure with nave and aisles but with entrance only to the nave. As in the Cathedral of Mexico, an octagonal drum and dome rose over a central bay equally distant from the entrance and rear walls. Octagonal towers were placed at the front corners, and a remarkable pattern of vaulting was suggested for the bays surrounding the dome that constituted a square area at the center of the structure. The four bays placed at the corners of the square were covered with ribless domes. The four intermediate bays, which abut the four sides of the central bay so as to constitute a Greek cross, were covered with Gothic-type ribbed vaults forming star patterns. No pattern in the vaulting is suggested for the tiers of three bays that flank the central area of the basilica at the front and rear ends of the plan.

Arrieta's structure incorporates some features suggested in Durán's plan, notably the octagonal towers and the octagonal central dome. In the interior the compound piers are faced on each of their four sides with half-columns, resembling those of the Cathedral of Mexico, and also corresponding with those of the plan. Ribless saucer domes have been retained at the corners of the central square but the star vaults have been replaced by groins. These vaults, like the other groin vaults of the nave, rise above the aisles to form cross arms. Rectangular windows set in lunettes placed above the tall arches of the nave admit a generous amount of light into the central area of the interior.

Arrieta's principal exterior additions to the scheme conceived by Durán were octagonal towers at the rear corners of the building matching those at the front, and doorways, providing direct access to the aisles, placed on either side of the principal portal. The combining of central dome with four-corner towers suggests the possible influence of Bramante's design for St. Peter's and two notable but only partially executed Spanish designs, that of Juan de Herrera of the late sixteenth century for the Cathedral of Valladolid and that of Francisco de Herrera, the younger, of a century later for the Pilar church in Saragossa. Such a scheme may have been intended for the Cathedral of Mexico by Claudio de Arciniega who admired the plan for Valladolid. At Guadalupe it provides a dramatic skyline as a visitor moves around the structure with towers forming shifting patterns as they are seen against the dome and, away from it, against the sky.

The facade is powerfully ordered, dominated by the strong vertical emphases of the flanking towers and the broad aspiring element at the center containing the main portal, but marked also by four clearly defined horizontal bands or moldings. All these horizontals are carried across to the outer edges of the facade where they are reinforced by setbacks or projections on the outer sides of the towers. Additional horizontal emphases mark the upper, belfry stages.

The section of the facade between the towers is organized within a square defined by the edges of the towers, the base of the structure, and a line drawn across the finial at the top of the parapet above the main portal. This central section is divided into two stories and the upper parapet, which at its tallest point equals each of the stories in height. The lower story contains

4.29 Facade of the Old Basilica, Guadalupe.

three semioctagonal-headed entrances, the central one set in a projecting section of wall and flanked by columns and niches. The second story has large windows placed above the side portals of the lower story, and, in its central projection, sculptured reliefs of the miracle of Tepeyac set between paired columns and niches. The present parapet, redesigned earlier in this century, contains in the central projecting section ornamented pyramidal forms that serve as terminations of the verticals rising through the columns of the stories below, and at the center an octagonally framed clock set within an outer frame of graceful complexity.

The facade is two-toned, strikingly patterned in dark and light materials, like Arrieta's earlier San Miguel Arcángel and many of the major structures which were constructed later in Mexico City. The convex central element, the parapet, and the two upper, belfry stages of the towers are light, constructed of *chiluca*, a gray volcanic stone resembling limestone. The rest of the structure—the bases of the towers, the walls, and the drum of the dome—are built of dark reddish brown bricks. Subsequently, the darker portions of many eighteenth-century buildings of Mexico City would be constructed with sizeable blocks of a soft volcanic stone, *tezontle*, of colors ranging from pink to dark reddish brown or purple. Color contrast in building materials was important in heightening the visual effect of the formal and decorative elements of the Mexican Baroque. The shift back to monochromatic materials would accompany the shift to Neo-Classical taste.

The strongly defined vertical and horizontal accents of the facade are less significant to the developing Mexican Baroque than the elements that suggest dynamic movement. Although the lower facade is constructed primarily of planes and angles rather than of the curving ovals of the developed Italian and German Baroque, the design is suggestive of curving movement. At their outer extremities the sides of the octagonal towers which slide back from the frontal plane are emphasized by prominent window frames and multiple setbacks, and the angles where the sections of the towers meet are softened by coins that minimize their angularity. The sections of wall between the towers and the projecting central element are planar, but a sense of curve and movement is conveyed by the semioctagonal heads of the doorways and the shallow arches over the windows. The central element is polygonal, suggesting a section of a hexagon, not a curve. Its ornamentation consists on the frontal plane of paired columns and niches, a delicate semioctagonal-headed opening, and softly sculpted relief panels; and on the receding planes of niche and column. It is visually suggestive, in its chiaroscuro-softened forms, of near curves rather than of sharply defined angles.

The handsome third stage of the facade was substantially modified several decades ago, and it may have been altered earlier. It now resembles designs of the second half of the eighteenth century, such as the Balvanera chapel of San Francisco. Old paintings, prints, and photographs portray a large octagonal window surmounted by moldings suggestive of a pediment at its center in place of the present small octagonal clock face with a charmingly intricate curved outer frame. The thin molding at the top of the parapet now descends from the center in a striking arabesque of sweeping curves. Older representations of the facade and the unaltered side portals suggest that the original silhouette was considerably less scintillating. Though less freely composed than the twentieth-century recreation, the original upper facade contained two innovations important in breaking from the restraints of seventeenth-century Classicism and in suggesting the future direction of Baroque design in Mexico City. The first innovation was the use of flamelike finials to surmount the paired columns of the two lower stages, and the second was the use of a thin molding to top the wall. Earlier designs such as the east and west portals of the Cathedral of Mexico carried the classical orders and their entablatures through three full stories and capped them with a pediment. The freely flowing upper facades of the mature Mexican Baroque followed from Arrieta's abandonment in his basilica of the traditional fully architectonic treatment of the third story. The fully Baroque Balvanera design was implicit in the design of Guadalupe, hence the temptation to redesign the original in the image of its descendant.

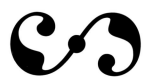

PLATE I. HUEJOTZINGO, POSA. SEE ALSO FIG. 2.3.

PLATE II. ACOLMAN, ATRIO CROSS. SEE ALSO FIG. 2.11

PLATE III. CATHEDRAL OF MÉRIDA, CENTRAL SECTION OF THE FACADE. SEE ALSO FIG. 3.8.

PLATE IV. CATHEDRAL OF MEXICO, DIAGONAL VIEW FROM THE SOUTH WEST. SEE ALSO FIG. 3.14.

PLATE V. FACADE OF SOLEDAD CHURCH IN OAXACA. SEE ALSO FIG. 4.5.

PLATE VI. CROSSING AND DOME OF ROSARIO CHAPEL, CHURCH OF SANTO DOMINGO, PUEBLA. SEE ALSO FIG. 4.18.

PLATE VII. CALPAN, SOUTHWEST POSA, LAST JUDGMENT RELIEF. SEE ALSO FIG. 5.6.

PLATE VIII. TEPALCINGO, FACADE. SEE ALSO FIG. 5.16.

Plate ix. House of the Conde de San Mateo de Valparaíso, portal. See also
Fig. 6.19.

PLATE X. HOUSE OF THE MARQUÉS DE JARAL DE BERRIO, FACADE, LOWER LEFT SIDE. SEE ALSO FIG. 6.31.

Plate XI. Sagrario, Mexico City, south facade, portal, middle and upper level.
See also Fig. 7.28.

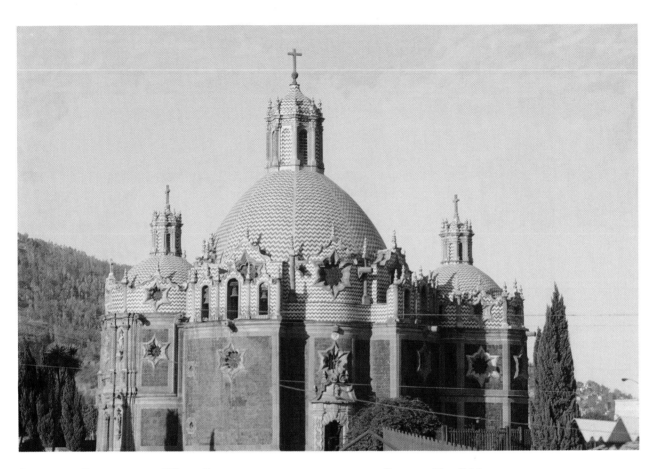

PLATE XII. CHAPEL OF THE WELL, GUADALUPE, VIEW FROM THE EAST. SEE ALSO FIG. 7.34.

PLATE XIII. CHAPEL OF THE WELL, GUADALUPE, SIDE PORTAL. SEE ALSO FIG. 7.35.

PLATE XIV. SANTA PRISCA, TAXCO, FACADE. SEE ALSO FIG. 7.13.

PLATE XV. HOUSE OF THE MARQUÉS DE PÉREZ GÁLVEZ, NOW THE MUSEUM OF SAN CARLOS, MEXICO CITY, PATIO. SEE ALSO FIG. 8.5.

Plate XVI. School of Mines, Mexico City, grand stair. See also Fig. 8.9.

V
POPULAR OR FOLK ARCHITECTURE

The energy of popular workmanship and the imaginative vitality of popular decorative taste have created much of the enduring appeal of Mexican viceregal architecture. Without the liveliness of popular creativity most of the buildings would simply be colonial replicas following at a distance the forms and styles of Europe. A few building types, such as the open chapels and *posas* of the sixteenth century, were developed beyond all European precedents because of the particular needs of the new country. Certain stylistic features of Baroque architecture were emphasized so much that they seem particularly Mexican. Among these expressive forms are tile-covered domes and towers sparkling in the sharp light, and shadowed concave facades and walls, articulated primarily by vertical rather than horizontal dividers rising to thin moldings set against the sky.

But most Mexican structures erected between the late sixteenth century and the middle decades of the eighteenth were patterned cautiously upon European models. Particularly pervasive and enduring was the influence of the sober style of Juan de Herrera, architect of Philip II's Escorial. A few Mexican examples capture something of the powerful spare sternness of Herrera's works, but most are only restrained. The outburst of decorative exuberance, which overthrew the Herrerean taste in Mexico and led to the magnificence of the mid-eighteenth-century Baroque, was substantially stimulated by the enduring popular love of ornamentation.

Throughout its history Mexican colonial architecture was influenced by the popular taste of its Indian and mestizo craftsmen. In the beginning the influence was apparent primarily in details of workmanship and decorative sense rather than in identifiable Indian features of form or style. The monumental architecture of the sixteenth century is distinctly European, following remembered medieval and Moslem forms as well as those of the new Renaissance classicism. Despite the modern Mexican eagerness to identify indigenous foundations for the nation, only a scattering of Indian motifs has been discovered in sixteenth-century architectural ornamentation. The friar and lay supervisors of architectural projects seem to have kept their Indian workmen under close control, providing drawings of European decorative features and, in some instances, instruction from trained European craftsmen. George Kubler has suggested that the generation of Indian architectural workers active during the great campaign of ecclesiastical construction between the early 1540s and the middle 1570s had been trained in church craft schools shortly after 1530. They had gradually mastered increasingly sophisticated building techniques, starting with barrel vaults constructed of coarse rubble and

5.1 Yuriria, facade.

tend the vertical accents of the engaged columns of the main order; and at the center, between the window above and the entablature below, three figures set in niches, the Christ child holding an orb and flanking child musicians.

But these features are difficult to recognize at Yuriria because the upper facade has been covered by an enveloping ornamental overlay that originated in a sensibility radically different from that of the Spanish designers of Acolman. On that facade the upper elements are delicately carved and placed with scrupulous care against a surface of ashlar masonry. The ornamentation is subtly contrasted with the plainness. At Yuriria decoration covers almost everything. Additional entablatures run across the facade above and below the arched window. A bishop is placed in a niche above the window to create an additional story. The principal change is the covering of what at Acolman were substantial areas of plain surface with coarsely cut bands of twisting ornamentation, which distract the eye's attention from the elements of architectural decoration derived from Acolman. Much of the ornamentation at Yuriria is suggestive of the spreading and curving tendrils

progressing to the careful stone-cutting necessary for decorative Gothic rib vaulting and the classical ornamental vocabulary of orders, entablatures, and arches.

A frequently noted sixteenth-century example of indigenous craftsmen's decorative sense is the modification of the design of the Renaissance plateresque facade of the Augustinian convento church of Acolman in the church of Yuriria (Fig. 2.20). The 1560 facade at Acolman, considered by Kubler to be the work of craftsmen from Spain, formed the model for simplified versions in Augustinian churches at Ixmiquilpan and Metztitlán. Roughly ten years later in Yuriria, an Augustinian town nearly two hundred miles to the west, the general pattern of the lower story of the Acolman facade was followed. On both sides of a double-arched portal, statues are set between pairs of plateresque engaged columns. In Yuriria the columns are divided into so many segments that they convey little sense of support, and the frieze of the entablature above them is decorated with winged angel heads instead of lion heads flanked by horses. Above the main entablature the Yuriria facade retains, with modifications, the principal features of Acolman: a centrally placed arched window framed by engaged columns and entablature and flanked by escutcheons; paired vertical elements rising on either side which ex-

5.2 Uruapan, hospital chapel, facade.

118

of plants. Some may be based upon the architectural orders. Most prominent are the four leaves or petals that expand broadly and crudely on both sides of the upper window from the central figure of a cupid-archer. Everything suggests the indigenous exuberance and love of overall ornamentation that in the future would repeatedly break free from the constraints of European taste.

A notably different example of Indian workmanship is the decoration created in the 1570s for the facade of the Franciscan chapel of Angahuan, a remote village in the state of Michoacán in west-central Mexico. It was recovered for art history by Manuel Toussaint in a newspaper picture relating to the bursting forth of a new volcano, Paricutín, in 1943. The chapel stands near a hospital, an arrangement normal in Michoacán, and seems related in its ornamentation to the remarkable hospital chapel of the largest community in the region, Uruapan. The chapels in both Angahuan and Uruapan both preserve ceiling elements that show the influence of the Mudéjar—the persistence in Christian Spain, and even in Spanish America, of Moorish ornamentation. The facades of both chapels also reveal Mudéjar influence, that of Angahuan more strongly than that of Uruapan. In Uruapan, the Moorish *alfiz*, a rectangular frame enclosing the

double-arched portal, seems checked by a Renaissance sense of propriety and is allowed to extend only slightly beyond the edges of the outer pilasters framing the portal.

The somewhat later scheme at Angahuan is bolder and far more visually striking. An *alfiz* extends broadly on either side of the portal arch. Another, smaller, framed rectangular panel of ornamentation, containing at its center a flattened statue of Santiago in pilgrim dress and along its upper margin four winged angel heads, is placed above the *alfiz*. The continuous pattern of ornamentation ascends to its narrowest and concluding element, the framing of a window with flanking vertical strips and a second *alfiz*. The design of the window enframement with its striking scroll-decorated arch seems derived from the frames of the windows of the hospital building in Uruapan.

The decorative detailing of the facades at both Angahuan and Uruapan is based upon the revival in Renaissance Europe of classical grotesque work representing human and animal forms amid swirling patterns of vegetation. In both the Mexican examples the carving is cruder, less suggestive of three dimensions, and less suggestive of living forms of vegetation than comparable work in Europe. The details at Angahuan are notably flatter, more abstract, and more decoratively powerful than those at Uruapan. The transformation of European motifs by popular indigenous taste is complete.

Work transformed by Indian sensibility was named *tequitqui* by José Moreno Villa and is memorably described by John McAndrew in his *Open-Air Churches of Sixteenth-Century Mexico*. McAndrew wrote that the lines in *tequitqui* carving are not weightless conductors of movement as they are in much European ornamentation but

5.3 *Angahuan, facade.*

visibly thickened in substance, they coil and shove their very corporeal forms with a restless serpentine force. . . . In the most successful examples of tequitqui . . . , the whole holds together chiefly by all-over surface tension, and not by the subordinating power of a few dominant forms or currents of movement. Coherence comes not from any organic or sequential interrelationship of parts, but from their insistent repetition in tight and seem-

5.4 *Huaquechula, north portal.*

5.5 *Tepoztlán, facade.*

ingly endless patterns, and from the incessant interaction of their outlines.

An important additional element in *tequitqui* design in McAndrew's description "is the abrupt pattern of sharp edges and abrupt bright-and-shade pattern which accompanies it, a step behind, like the second voice in a musical canon." This effect is heightened by the two-dimensional

quality of *tequitqui* work: "zones of flattened relief stand out in front of a neutral flat ground which has been cut back to an even depth behind them, so that everything lies strictly on the two levels as if the ornament had been neatly punched out with a cookie cutter and laid on a flat surface." [1]

The ornamentation of the facade at Angahuan may be the outstanding example of *tequitqui* in Mexico. Traces of the style are widespread, wherever Indian artisans' sensibility transformed the vocabulary of medieval, Renaissance, or Mudéjar forms which Europeans commissioned for Mexican buildings.

A different type of sixteenth-century popular decoration is evident in the north portal of the Franciscan convento church in Huaquechula, southwest of Puebla. *Tequitqui* is present in lesser elements, but the major features result from Indian adaptation of designs from European prints, probably devotional woodcuts or engravings but possibly illustrations from books. The portal is framed by a simplified, only partially understood, popular version of a Renaissance architectural order. The supporting elements on either side are divided awkwardly into bases covered with *tequitqui* ornamentation, undecorated piers, and plain engaged columns. The rounding of the columns is carried up into the entablature in larger swelling convexities.

The most interesting features of the scheme are decorative sculptures in low relief which were modeled after European prints. God in judgment, clothed in a wide-spreading tunic with arms upspread, sits over the flattened arch of the portal. The figure is carved into the three central voussoirs and the blocks above them. On either side, pairs of flying angels blow elongated horns of summons, and beneath them, awkwardly squeezed into the spandrels, crowned figures at prayer are supported by tightly packed cloud forms. Flanking the doorway, below the entablature marking the springing of the arch, are reliefs set in shallow niches representing Saint Peter holding a book and two keys and Saint Paul holding a book and a sword. Elizabeth Wilder Weismann has suggested that the saints reflect their origin in Flemish graphic art by their burgher costumes. She attributes peculiarities of the representation to the native artisan's attempt to render in low relief, images from flat prints that had created the illusion of roundness through perspective drawing. Through a misunderstanding of the conventions of perspective, the Indian carver has created stylized images of considerable decorative charm.

Popular renderings in relief sculpture of graphic originals are common in the sixteenth century. Other important examples in the general vicinity of Huaquechula include the portal of Tepoztlán, north of Cuernavaca, and the *posas* of

5.6 Calpan, southwest posa, Last Judgment relief. See also Plate VII.

Calpan. Huge, flat-winged angels appear to uphold the frame of the choir window at Tepoztlán; beneath them in a steep pediment are smaller figures, Mary standing on a crescent moon and holding a diminutive Christ child and the flanking saints, Dominic and Catherine of Siena.

The possible model for the crude representation of the judging Christ at Huaquechula is the powerful relief of the Last Judgment of the southwest *posa* at Calpan, for which a probable source, a woodcut in a book of saints, the *Flos*

Sanctorum, has been identified. In the Calpan relief the head of the stern judge is flanked by a stylized lily stalk on the left and by a sword on the right. His body is flanked by flying angels and by powerful interceding figures, Mary on the left and John the Baptist on the right. Below, in the spandrels of the arch, minute human figures are emerging from the rectangular openings of tombs, some with arms upraised, beseechingly, others in prayer. The linear, flattened decorative sculpture, which native craftsmen modeled after religious prints, frequently resembles the weightless sculpture prior to and during early Romanesque Europe rather than the tangible works of the late medieval and Renaissance periods.

The most impressive surviving example of sixteenth-century popular ornamentation of a secular structure is on the upper facade of the Francisco Montejo house in Mérida. The sculptors are believed to have been Indians from Maní. The lower story of the facade seems restrained in architectural ornamentation, tastefully European. Fluted Corinthian columns, placed in front of layered pilasters flank ornamented sunken panels, which surround the door frame and incorporate Latin inscriptions ("Amor Dei" and "Vencit"), and four portrait busts, two of them set in medallions. Over the center of the door is placed a figure suggestive of Atlas bent beneath the weight of a substantial corbel.

The balcony door of the upper story (Fig. 5.7) is framed by heads of putti alternating with paired scrolls, upright along the sides and slanting at the top. But the dominant features are two pilasters, each containing a towering bearded figure in armor grasping a sword and holding a halberd. Both feet of these men at arms press down on the wailing head of a demon or possibly of a vanquished Indian (Fig. 5.8). Outside the bases of the pilasters are smaller representations of wild men, creatures of the European imagination which were sometimes related to aboriginal Americans. The wild men hold knotted clubs and are clad in matted tufts of sheepskin. Above the door is a shield containing the Montejo arms and a helmet, both surrounded by panels decorated with symmetrically patterned vines which press against the borders, threatening to overflow. Under the strong horizontal cornice is a powerful

5.7 *Montejo House, Mérida, upper facade.*

5.8 *Montejo House, Mérida, upper facade, detail.*

frieze containing additional portrait busts alternating with symmetrical blocks of abstract ornamentation, which appear to be vegetative, loosely based upon the acanthus leaves of the Corinthian capital. Closer inspection discloses that the patterns are animal. Paired monsters sit opposite each other; from their backs curve long segmented necks leading to sharp-eared, agonized, bearded heads. At the top of the facade, above the horizontal cornice, is a pedimental shape, its sides formed by doglike lions; its center is occupied by a bearded bust leaning over a scroll inscribed with the name Adelantado D. Francisco de Montejo and the date 1549.

The seventeenth century was less rich than the sixteenth in works of popular architecture. Late in the seventeenth or early in the eighteenth century (dates are hard to establish), there appeared in village churches popular adaptations of the style of strapwork stucco ornamentation that the Dominicans had used in their establishments in Puebla and Oaxaca. The Church of Santa Isabel in Tepetzala, near Puebla, and the Chapel of El Santo Cristo, in Tlacolula in the Valley of Oaxaca, are notable examples. Two villages, less than a mile apart on the southern outskirts of Cholula near Puebla, Acatepec, and Tonantzintla, contain extraordinary folk baroque churches. The one at Acatepec has an interior that retains only a suggestion of its appearance before a fire in 1939, but its exterior is unaltered. There is an octagonal dome and lantern over the cross-

5.9 *Acatepec, facade.*

ing and, at the west front, unequal towers, the right supporting two substantial belfry stages, square below and octagonal above. The lesser tower on the left supports an open belfry set diagonally to its frontal plane. The outwardly curving screen facade, which recalls that of the Salud church in Oaxaca, contains on its central vertical axis a tri-lobed, double-angled portal enframement, a rectangular window, and a remarkable four-lobed and four-angled niche framed by an

122

eight-pointed star. All of these elements are covered with a dazzling array of glazed tiles, primarily yellow, blue, and green, set in a ground of unglazed blocks of brownish red.

The exterior of Tonantzintla, if visited after Acatepec, seems unexciting. The single tower lacks sparkle. The facade is flat and dominated in color by the brownish red background rather than the modest array of inset colored tiles. The most interesting features are an awkwardly designed tri-lobed frame for the doorway and the almost comic, stumpy folk statues set in niches on the periphery of the upper window.

The interior is overwhelming, the most extraordinary whole created by popular craftsmen in Mexico. Though repainted in the earlier part of this century in garish colors, primarily whites, blues, reds, yellows, and gold, it conveys much of the original Indian decorators' intentions. The profusion of ornamentation is so powerful in impression that extended and repeated study is needed if the visitor is to define the parts that contribute to the total impression.

The simpler surfaces reveal themselves first. The lower nave walls are plain, although covered by retablos of differing styles and periods and decorated by lavishly ornamental pilasters which culminate in human busts supporting, with their upraised arms, capitals consisting of baskets of fruit. The vaults of the choir, nave, and transepts are divided by greenish blue ribs into compartments containing varied patterns of stucco ornamentation, some primarily of stylized floral

5.11 Tonantzintla, vault of transept.

designs, some dominated by seminaked human forms, others combining complex floral strapwork and angel heads. The upper nave walls, the piers, arches, and pendentives of the crossing, and the interior surfaces of the dome are so thickly overlaid by heavy and complex ornamentation that the viewer is slow in comprehending the forms of the underlying structure. An arch, decorated by a strange array of brightly colored, wide-eyed heads, of plumes, fruit, and flowers, merges with an adjacent wall surface. The wall is covered with a thick swirling mass of white and gilded strapwork, small human figures, winged busts, and staring human faces, which fuses on either side with similarly decorated pendentives, and above with the dome. After some careful study the underside of the dome (Fig. 5.12) is perceived to be divided into eight sections by twisting stucco ribs. The surfaces present a stunning, confusing conglomeration of white strapwork, human heads, busts, arms, legs, and angel wings; all culminate in a darker yellowish aureole of heads and wings surrounding the dove of the Holy Spirit. The grottolike interior at Tonantzintla is an Indian version of the Rosario Chapel of Santo Domingo in Puebla (Fig. 4.18). That interior is dazzling in the profusion of its ornamentation. In this, the popular artisans have abandoned all restraint in their fantastic creation of an earthly paradise, overwhelming in its confusing richness, color, and light.

5.10 Acatepec, lower facade.

123

No popularly designed interior in Mexico rivals Tonantzintla and few share its lavishness. In many instances the interiors of village churches are simple, decorated by plaster, paint, and modest retablos. Decoration is most frequently concentrated on church facades and on features such as domes and *atrio* gates. Several striking popular facades were erected in small towns south and east of Cuernavaca, on both sides of the boundary between the present states of Puebla and Morelos. Jolapan in Puebla and Tepalcingo in Morelos are particularly remarkable. Jolapan is exceptional for its columns: some suggest the openness of basket work, others seem fantastic totem poles covered with human heads and busts and staring masks carved from forms of vegetation; still others sug-

5.12 *Tonantzintla, interior of dome.*

5.13 *Jolapan, facade, from Guillermo Tovar de Teresa,* México barroco, *p. 125, photograph by Augusto Zaldívar.*

5.14 *Jolapan, facade, detail.*

5.15 *Tepalcingo, upper facade.*

gest intertwined stalks of giant asparagus. As at Jolapan, the upper facade at Tepalcingo is dominated by a representation of God the Father and the Crucifixion. A compact, muscular Christ is stretched tautly on the cross. Beneath the cross, clutching at its base, is a kneeling, mourning figure and a grim skull with staring eye holes and a toothy upper jaw. Descending along the vertical axis are other images of Christ, one collapsing under the weight of the carried cross and another, most poignantly, sitting naked, hand bracing his thorn-crowned head as the man of sorrows. Outstanding among the widely diverse array of other figures are the semirecumbent images of naked Adam and Eve on the capitals at the springing of the portal arch. Unfortunately the facade of Jolapan has suffered in recent years from painting in bright primary colors: reds, blues, greens, and yellows. Some of the details benefit from the enlivening treatment, but the sense of a coherent whole has been obliterated. Tepalcingo, which had suffered from neglect and distracting painting, has been carefully restored and effectively repainted.

Five interesting folk Baroque churches were erected in the 1750s and 1760s after the belated pacification of the Sierra Gorda region of eastern Querétaro, not very far from the venerable Pan American Highway. The earliest, the church in Jalpan, was erected by craftsmen from Mexico City and local Indians under the direction of Junípero Serra, who spent eight years in the town before moving on to his missionary work in California. The most interesting interiors are in Conca and Landa. Conca also has a striking facade with three seated figures poised against the sky at the top, and flanking buttresses decorated by sprawling upside-down animals and topped by tapering cylindrical forms resembling chimney pots.

The area around Texcoco, east of Mexico City, contains several *atrio* gateways richly ornamented in popular taste. A common design includes three arched portals, the central one with three lobes. At Chiconcuac and Papalotla (Fig. 5.17) pinnacles and perforated forms are placed above the entablature and silhouetted against the sky.

The cathedral, formerly the parish church,

5.16 *Tepalcingo, facade. See also Plate VIII.*

in Zacatecas, the wealthy mining city of the north, is decorated by three outstanding examples of popular art, the two side portals and the tall screen facade. All are covered with a spreading overlay of shallow vegetative ornament. On the east side a crucifixion scene is placed at the upper level before a flowing theatrical curtain. The decoration surrounding the portal below the crucifixion seems earlier in style, possibly contemporaneous with that of the facade. The columns flanking the doorway (Fig. 5.18) are divided into two halves. The lower half is wrapped by diagonally spiraling vines, with large birds pecking at the grapes. The upper half consists of caryatid busts, their clothing incised with arabesques, and their heads and gracefully flowing upstretched arms supporting Corinthian capitals.

The facade of the church (Fig. 5.19) is marked by three superposed orders of columns set against a screen covered by decorative arabesques. The columns are encrusted by a remarkable variety of forms, among them vines, shells, busts, and child angels. The thirteen figures placed in niches between the columns represent Christ and his disciples, with Christ at the center of the upper order. The vertical axis descends from a figure of God the Father, in low relief set beneath a canopy crown at the top of the facade, down through the figure of Christ to a circular window and on to

5.17 *Papalotla, atrio gate.*

the portal at ground level. The central window, circled by a dense ring of coral-like ornamentation, suggests both a medieval rose and a huge sacred monstrance for display of the Eucharistic Host. The latter association is emphasized by a small figure holding a monstrance at the top of the circumambient ring. A broad arch, decorated similarly to the ring, enframes the delicate multilobed moulding surrounding the doorway below.

Outside and above the composition shaped by the columnar orders, the arabesque-covered screen curves in to the upper shoulders of the facade and then swings upward in a counter curve to terminate in large roundish finials. It provides a kind of frame for the canopy crown (restored in recent decades) that is placed over the incised representation of God the Father, yet also leaves the center of the upper facade open to the sky. The arabesques of the outer and upper screen surround the upper order of columns and the central image of God the Father. From ground level, they seem at first to constitute a confusing layer of swirling, rounded, floral shapes, ornamented by beadlike curving margins and punctured by irregularly located, jagged cuts of shadow. After careful examination with a sharp eye or a pair of binoculars, a remarkable array of celestial musicians emerges from the dense mass of floral forms on the surfaces surrounding the Heavenly Father. Some, broad-winged, blow horns or wind instruments; others play the violin or the guitar.

The outstanding example of Mexican popular architectural decoration in the United

States is the Church of San Xavier del Bac, one of the northernmost of twenty-four mission outposts founded by the Jesuit scientist, who had visited and been praised in a sonnet by Sor Juana Inés de la Cruz, Eusebio Kino. The church was begun in 1775, years after Father Kino's time, and constructed of well-plastered brick. It seems an apparition rising white from the grayness of the dry plain of the Tucson area. From the sides and rear, the whitewashed dome and sprightly parapet suggest Islamic forms as they curve up and down between scroll-flanked pinnacles. At the front, bulky square towers support smaller double belfry stages with the aid of scroll flying buttresses at their corners. The uppermost tower on the east is incomplete. Laid against the frontal plane of the towers is a tall, reddish sandstone retablo-type inner facade. A powerful horizontal string course which terminates at the outer edges of the building in large scrolls was designed to unite the ornamented central facade with the plain towers. Unfortunately the unifying effect of this string course is nullified by its present coat of white paint which obliterates its association with the

5.18 *Cathedral of Zacatecas, east portal, detail right side.*

5.19 *Cathedral of Zacatecas, facade.*

5.21 *Tucson, San Xavier del Bac, facade.*

5.20 *Tucson, San Xavier del Bac, west side.*

sandstone frontispiece. That central facade is decorated by three superposed orders of skinny *estípites* and folk statuary set in curtain-decorated niches. At the plain center of the elaborate ornamentation, a single shell is set above a balconied window.

The upper stage is of particular interest. Large scrolls, similar to those at the outer edges of the towers below, unroll from the outer moulding of the retablo to fill the lower corners of the zone. Above the scrolls the molding narrows and curves upward and inward until it dips into an inverted horseshoe arch at the center of the upper parapet. The arch is filled with a strange, diminishing cylindrical form, draped with what seem to be folds of cloth, which is now painted white. Other remarkable features of the upper zone are doglike lions in low relief holding branches of vegetation and fragments of entablature blocks, which are set diagonally across the *estípites* just as they are transformed into pinnacles.

127

VI
EIGHTEENTH-CENTURY PROSPERITY: DOMESTIC AND CIVIC ARCHITECTURE

In the late eighteenth century, Mexico was noted for its extremes in wealth and poverty, civilized living and coarse ignorance. Alexander von Humboldt would call it "the country of inequality."[1] The wealth of the most prominent inhabitants of New Spain was more substantial than in any other part of Spanish America. (It was also notably greater than in the United States where George Washington had to borrow money to travel to New York to his inauguration as president and Thomas Jefferson would, in 1812, be forced to sell his treasured collection of books to the new Library of Congress to ease financial difficulty.) At a time when the peso was more valuable than the dollar and the dollar had possibly one hundred times its present purchasing power, there were, in Mexico City alone, according to John E. Kicza, a recent student of colonial entrepreneurs, approximately a hundred families owning roughly a million pesos or more and a total of approximately four hundred families owning at least a hundred thousand.[2] Such wealth made possible the ambitious Mexican architectural construction in the years after mid-century.

The desire to accumulate wealth had been powerful in Spanish America from the beginning. Bernal Díaz del Castillo told his readers that he and his companions had come to America to serve "God and His Majesty, to give light to those in darkness, and also to gain riches which all of us usually sought."[3] Cortés had informed a messenger from Montezuma that he and his army suffered from an illness that could be cured only by gold. Later, deprived of authority by royal policy, he turned from conquest and exploration to business ventures. He initiated large-scale commercial agriculture in his personal domain, the Marquesado del Valle de Oaxaca, building the first sugarcane mills on the mainland and selling part of their produce in a store located on the ground floor of his palace in Mexico City.

The almost immediate breakdown of the traditional Spanish social order in America is revealed in a letter written to Charles V in 1525; the author is Rodrigo de Albornoz, a fiscal official left in authority in Mexico City when Cortés left on his unfortunate expedition to Honduras. Albornoz urged the emperor to prescribe proper styles of living for his subjects

> because the land is rich in food and in mines . . . and everyone becomes swollen with the desire to spend and possess, so that by the end of a year and a half, he who is a miner, or farmer, or swineherd, no longer will be so, but wishes to be given Indians, so he spends everything he has on ornaments and silks, and, if he has a wife, the same holds for her. In like fashion other mechanics cease the pursuit of

their trades . . . in the belief that they will be given Indians to serve them and support their families in gentility.[4]

Free from the constraints of hierarchical Spain, the members of the lower classes aspired to become aristocrats and initially sought affluence through grants of Indian labor under the encomienda system. By the end of the sixteenth century that path toward wealth was largely closed off by royal policies, and aspiring Spanish Americans increasingly followed the earlier example of Cortés in turning to large-scale agricultural and business enterprises in a manner alien to the generally anticommercial ethos of the Spanish aristocracy. By the middle of the seventeenth century the prominence in New Spain of those engaged in commerce seemed remarkable to those accustomed to the patterns of living of the homeland. The patron of Sor Juana Inés de la Cruz, the Marqués de Mancera, wrote in 1673 to his successor as viceroy that "the merchants and traders . . . approach the nobility, very much affecting their carriage and style. . . . It can be generally assumed that for the most part in these provinces the gentleman is a merchant and the merchant is a gentleman."[5]

In emulating the style of living of the nobility of Spain, wealthy Mexicans placed great value upon family ties and the advancement of collective family fortunes. Customarily a single patriarch, or in rare instances a matriarch, had power of attorney and directed family affairs. The Spanish legal device, the *mayorazgo*, or entail, was widely adopted to prevent the division of rural and urban property among many heirs and ensure it would be transmitted from generation to generation to the eldest son. The most striking institution of viceregal Mexico, the hacienda, or great landed estate, developed in the years around 1600, not, as formerly was believed, as a quasi-feudal, economically self-sufficient enterprise in response to the great diminishment of the Indian population and the consequent slowing of general economic activity. Instead, the great estates were integrated with other enterprises, located so as to supply, at a profit, the cities and the mining areas with grain, sugar, pulque, meat, and woollen and leather goods. They were supported by income which had been derived from the encomienda

system, from the holding of public office, and from mining and commerce. Like modern organizers of capitalistic enterprises, colonial entrepreneurs valued vertical integration, combined agriculture with the manufacturing and the marketing of produce, and created haciendas to supply the work forces of the mines they operated.

With the decline of Spanish power in the final years of Philip II and during the increasingly ineffective reigns of his Hapsburg successors throughout the entire seventeenth century, the trans-Atlantic trade diminished, the mining industry declined, and New Spain became less closely tied to economic direction from the mother country. Local industries, such as cloth manufacturing, developed. Trade grew with the other Spanish colonies, in part through smuggling practiced to circumvent royal efforts to regulate American commerce. Mexico City developed into a principal metropolis of the New World, a market and a distribution point for New Spain and for other parts of Spanish America, a supplier of goods to Peru and the Philippines, and a source of capital for domestic investment.

The city's population, drastically reduced during the great floods between 1629 and 1634, began a slow growth in the last half of the seventeenth century that increased perceptibly by the middle decades of the eighteenth. The effort to keep the Indians in their barrios separate from the Spaniards in the thirteen regularly laid-out blocks of the central *traza* failed because of the joined economic interests of Spanish employers and Indian seekers of employment. Black and Asian slaves were imported in substantial numbers and the ethnic mixture of the city became increasingly complex. In the eighteenth century, paintings of family groups of the *castas* became a popular genre, cataloguing ethnic diversity with extraordinary concern for the variety of types. There were mulattoes; *zambas*, those with Indian and black parents and names reflecting the many ethnic gradations in the groups, such as *moriscos*, offspring of a European and a mulatto; and *albinos*, offspring of a European and a morisco. The group that would ultimately inherit Mexico, the mestizos, were regarded as simply one of the many varieties of ethnic blending. Particularly prosperous families with part-Indian ancestry were admitted into Spanish society, and the recognition of the mestizos as the primary social group was long delayed.

The city was handsome in general appearance—with broad streets, uniform blocks of buildings, long arcaded aqueducts, eighty churches, most of them towered and domed, twenty large and substantially endowed conventos for nuns and another twenty for friars, frequently with an adjoining college. However, it impressed visitors with its poverty as well as its wealth. The streets were clogged with mud in the rainy season and were notable for the fragrance of garbage heaped at street corners and in front of many houses. The viceroy's palace, in addition to its official uses, contained a wine shop, a bakery, places to bowl and to play billiards, and a public room for card playing. Its upper corridors were populated by prostitutes who sometimes amused themselves by sketching lewd images on its walls. The central plaza, fronted by the palace on the east and on the north by the cathedral, contained stocks and a gibbet and was cluttered with the huts of market people, who often covered their roofs with sleeping mats, miscellaneous rags, hats, and even worn-out shoes. Pulque shops for both men and women were plentiful. Their drunken and frequently dangerous customers were everywhere. The city was widely known for *leperismo*, disorderly beggary.

The great riot of Sunday, June 8, 1692, began when two female tortilla sellers, outraged at the stoppage of free distribution of maize at the public granary in a time of shortage, created a disturbance and were lashed and beaten. Their companions, carrying one of the victims, rushed to the residence of the Archbishop Aguiar y Seijas. Barred at his door, through which no woman was ever allowed to pass, the frenzied women attracted sympathizers and other males ready for mischief. Subsequently the mob tried to capture both the viceroy, the Conde de Galve, and the chief official of the city, the corregidor. Frustrated, they set multiple fires in the viceregal palace and the municipal buildings, which were on the south side of the plaza. In the palace the damage included the chamber of the audiencia, the whole jail including the torture chamber, and so

much of the viceroy's residential suite that he was forced to move across to the east side of the plaza to the "new palace" of Cortés. Damage to the municipal buildings was even more extensive, and most of the public records were burned. The mob particularly enjoyed torching the coach of the corregidor and dragging it burning around the plaza. The total loss, including that from the looting and burning of nearly three hundred merchant shops and booths, came to more than three million pesos. An eyewitness, the scientist Carlos de Sigüenza y Góngora, who wrote the most detailed account of the uprising, blamed it on "an ungrateful, treacherous rabble of insolent Indian women" and the shiftless pulque-drinking Indian men and their companions and agitators, dissolute black and white vagabonds. At present, he wrote, more pulque is consumed in a single day than was drunk in Aztec times in an entire year. He denounced the behavior of the wild crowd that consisted, in addition to the Indians, of blacks from diverse African nations, of a wide variety of racially mixed types "mulattoes, *moriscos*, *mestizos*, *zambaigos*, *lobos*, and [of] Spaniards . . . who are the worst of them all,"[6] having willfully abandoned the restraints of civilized behavior. Four Indians caught setting fire to the palace confessed "without resort to any torture at all" and were sentenced to be shot. One avoided his fate by drinking poison. Subsequently, Sigüenza y Góngora wrote at the end of August, "five or six were hanged, one was burned, and many more whipped on different days."[7] A commission, which included Sigüenza y Góngora, recommended a return to strict segregation of Indians in their own barrios, curacies, and districts, where they should be organized and regulated and kept out of the central city where they are tempted to crime confident in impunity from authority because of their anonymity and seeming insignificance. Members of other races were accused of invading the barrios and corrupting the Indians with their gambling, thievery, and general dishonesty. Spaniards residing in the *traza* were blamed for protecting and profiting from renegade Indians, renting them rooms or shacks, and sheltering the insolent conduct that affronts public order. No major public disturbance marred the city between 1692 and 1767 when unruly mobs protested the expulsion of the Jesuits, but the ethnic mixing of the population, both in living and sexual arrangements, in the capital and other cities of New Spain had, despite the assessment and recommendations of the commission, progressed to a point where it could not be reversed.

At the other social extreme of Mexico City from the *léperos* and the sodden idlers of the pulquerías were a hundred or so extremely rich and influential families, at least half of whom had acquired titles of nobility by the early nineteenth century. The titles were in some cases awarded for services rendered to the viceregal government and in others virtually purchased by fiscal donations to the monarchy. Two Mexican titles had been granted in the sixteenth century. Cortés was named Marqués del Valle de Oaxaca, softening the royal actions depriving him of significant authority in the land which he had conquered. The second title was awarded to Miguel López de Legazpi, who had initiated the conquest of the Philippine Islands. In the early seventeenth century titles were bestowed on Francisco Pacheco de Córdoba y Bocanegra as Marqués de Villamayor and on Luis de Velasco II, the seventh viceroy and son of the second, as Marqués de Salinas. In addition, Velasco's daughter and her son were created Condesa and Conde de Santiago Calimaya in honor of his services to the crown. In 1627 titles were awarded to a great grandson of Montezuma and to Rodrigo de Vivero, a first cousin of Luis de Velasco who had distinguished himself as a government official, a soldier, and a diplomat. Vivero was named Conde del Valle de Orizaba. Late in the century, between 1682 and 1692, several more titles were given out, one of them, that of the Marqués de Aguayo, to the founder of the greatest landholding family of northern Mexico.

The descendants of the Cortés, Montezuma, and Pacheco de Córdoba families left Mexico to settle permanently in Europe. From those who were ennobled in 1627 or earlier and remained in America two families emerged that continued to be powerful throughout the remainder of the colonial period. The daughter of Viceroy Luis de Velasco II married her cousin, who had been made Conde de Santiago Calimaya, and her son married the daughter-in-law of Miguel López de Legazpi so that the family held the titles

of Marqués de Salinas and Adelanto de Filipinas as well as Conde de Santiago Calimaya. The family of the Condes del Valle de Orizaba, founded by Rodrigo de Vivero, frequently intermarried with the families of the Condes de Santiago and of the wealthy Mariscales de Castilla, and prospered primarily through sugar haciendas and other agricultural enterprises over many generations.

One result of the continued erosion of Spanish royal power and authority during the later Hapsburg reigns was a tacit compromise between the court and the colonial oligarchies, a looseness of control that permitted what J. H. Elliott has called self-rule at royal command. The system preserved nominal Spanish authority yet permitted the colonies to attain moderate prosperity despite the disasters that devastated the mother country in the seventeenth century.

A grandson of Louis XIV came to the Spanish throne in 1700 as Philip V and, despite protracted civil and European war over his succession, initiated a modernization of governmental, military, and fiscal practices following the centralized French model of his grandfather. The full effect of the reforms was not felt in New Spain until the reign of the third Bourbon monarch, Charles III, who appointed José de Gálvez as Visitor General in 1765 and subsequently as Minister of the Indies. The custom of selling positions on the royal administrative courts, the audiencias, to members of the wealthy American-born elite was stopped, and Creole representation was reduced from a majority to at most a third. A new type of salaried administrators, the intendants, were appointed to fill positions between the viceroy and the old district magistrates, the *alcaldes mayores* and the *corregidores*, and these posts were replaced by *subdelegados*. The earlier administrators had purchased their offices and customarily set up exploitive trade monopolies in Indian areas in order to prosper, after having borne the cost of their offices and of the taxes imposed on them and the cost of the merchandise extended to them by the import merchants of Mexico City. Gálvez also assisted efforts to reform the church to bring it into the enlightened eighteenth century. He oversaw the expulsion of the Jesuits and suppressed, with unprecedented harshness, the accompanying popular demonstrations of protest. Gálvez's efficiency in asserting royal authority and in disciplining governmental laxness and outright abuses did not please the Creole upper class that had grown accustomed to having its own way in New Spain. A well-placed contemporary critic acutely stated, "Gálvez has destroyed more than he has built . . . his destructive hand is going to prepare the greatest revolution in the American Empire."[8]

More to the liking of the prosperous Creoles than administrative reform was the expansion of trade and the revival of the mining industry that accompanied a rapid increase in population and led to a quadrupling of mining production in the eighteenth century. The greatest gain was in the 1770s after Gálvez reduced the price of mercury essential to the amalgamation of silver, reduced the royal tax on all production, and provided further special reductions and exemptions from taxation for operations involving particularly high risk or massive renovations of old mines. Institutions were established for the study of mining: the Academia y Escuela Teórica y Práctica de Metalurgia in 1779, and the Colegio de Minería in 1792. In 1778 the *comercio libre* decree opened trade between many American and Spanish ports. During the decades before the long delayed issuance of this decree, the Bourbon government had fostered the interests of the *consulados*, the guilds of international merchants of Cadiz and Mexico City. Then international trading took place at the great fair in Jalapa at the eastern edge of the Mexican plateau with the import merchants at an advantage in determining prices. Supplied often with more than 100,000 pesos for purchases, they could wait out the Spanish sellers who could proceed no further inland and had to pay storage charges if they did not arrange to sell promptly.

The great mining boom of the late eighteenth century depended substantially upon the sympathetic policies of José de Gálvez. Probably of even more critical importance were the innovations of the merchant capitalists of Mexico City in devising means of supplying credit. By this time many of the mines had been worked for well over a century and a half and had penetrated below the water level. Renewed productivity was profitable,

but it required constant drainage, massive investments of capital, and the patience to wait an extended period for profitability. It took a very long time before Pedro Romero de Terreros, later created Conde de Regla, got full return from his investment of more than a million and a half pesos in the mines on the Veta Vizcaína seam of silver ore at Real del Monte, north of Pachuca. A great deal of labor was involved in digging new shafts and in constructing a system of drainage tunnels which extended horizontally beneath the lode. When the final tunnel, 8,643 feet long, was completed, he enumerated the time it had taken, "twenty-three years, two months, and three days."[9]

The credit system had originated in the normal extension of loans by general merchants to miners for supplies. Before long, some merchants specialized in silver, extending credit to miners and receiving in return raw silver that they transported to Mexico City for minting. By the late eighteenth century two or three merchant creditors maintained practices resembling banking. The Fagoaga family extended credit to important miners and also received loans from others for which they paid 5 percent interest. They established a revolving fund of 400,000 pesos for purchasing ore and extending credit. Miners complained of the usurious rates of the silver financiers, but advancing money to an industry in which roughly three-quarters of the entrepreneurs, including some of the most able, failed, was an uncertain enterprise. There were many bad debts, and few silver merchants prospered for long.

The most remarkable mining venture of the late eighteenth century was initiated without credit from Mexico City. It was located above Guanajuato on the northern fringe of the Bajío, a grain growing basin two hundred miles northwest of the capital. The city's central lode, the Veta Madre, running a mile and a quarter long and in three parallel seams over a third of a mile across, had been discovered in 1550. Two centuries later Guanajuato was on the verge of becoming the greatest silver-producing center in the world and one of the two or three largest cities of New Spain. It produced a fourth to a fifth of all Mexican silver throughout the eighteenth century and served as the cornerstone of the increasingly important, relatively self-contained regional economy of the Bajio. The miners of Guanajuato, the textile workers of Querétaro, San Miguel, Celaya, and Salamanca, and the leather workers of Leon provided ample markets for the flourishing agricultural haciendas of the region.

In 1760 Antonio de Obregón, later entitled Conde de la Valenciana after his mine, began eight years of excavation to penetrate the central portion of the lode. He was joined in the enterprise by three local merchants. The steady expansion of the mine was financed primarily by weekly sales of ore to independent refiners, and much of the ore was refined by the owners of the mine. Between 1780 and 1810 the Valenciana produced two-thirds of the silver mined in Guanajuato. The total value of Valenciana production was thirty-one million pesos, with expenses of nineteen million, leaving a profit of twelve million. In good years the annual profit exceeded a million pesos. Substantially more than a million pesos were spent on three huge vertical shafts and a fourth was added later, reaching over six hundred yards down into the solid rock. This stone-faced octagonal shaft, the deepest in the world, was thirty-two feet in diameter. Over thirty-three hundred workers were employed in the maze of underground passages of the Valenciana.

Mines depended primarily on free labor, and miners were the most highly paid laborers in New Spain. Intermittent efforts of mine owners to reduce wages were resisted, as workers moved from mining center to mining center in search of better working arrangements. At Real del Monte, the Conde de Regla, a notoriously tight-fisted employer, provoked a strike and was unable to maintain an adequate force, despite buying a cadre of black slave miners and having been granted the right to draft labor from Indian communities in the area within ten leagues, roughly thirty miles, of his mines. Work was hard, disagreeable, and unhealthy. Many mines operated twenty-four hours a day, seven days a week with twelve-hour shifts. Later Alexander von Humboldt would report that miners seldom lived beyond thirty-five years. Tunnels were dark, filled with choking dust, and frequently uncomfortably

hot. Miners were often subject to shocking variations in temperature. Silicosis, pneumonia, and tuberculosis were prevalent. Falling rocks and cave-ins were a constant fear, as were fires. Smells emanated from rotting vegetation, animal and human excrement, and noxious gases.

Mining proper was done by skilled pickmen who pried chunks of ore from the seam and by peons who carried it to the surface, but other workers were needed to bail water, to construct platforms and timber supports, to brace the tunnels and drainage adits, and, in the refining mills, to pound the ore into pebbles for grinding, and to stir with their feet a muddy mixture of ore, pyrites and mercury. Horse and mule-driven whims, or capstans, were used to haul ore and water to the surface. The pikemen were organized in *barras*, teams of five or six, who worked in the same area of the mines. The standard daily wage was four reales, that is half a peso, but workers were also entitled to a *partido*, their share of the surplus pried out after the day's quota of ore had been secured. At Real del Monte, on a poor day, the *partido* roughly equaled the daily wage, and on a good day doubled it.

Work was particularly hard for the bailers and the peons who staggered in virtual darkness lit only by candles tied to their heads, under leather sacks of one hundred and fifty to two hundred or more pounds of ore, up notched-log ladders or twisting constricted passages which at unpredictable intervals dropped off at the side into deep pits. The threat of falling to crippling injury or death was constant. A French visitor questioned a ten-year-old worker in the Valenciana and learned that he had carried close to six hundred pounds of ore to the surface in four trips that morning.

Wages in Guanajuato were better than in Real del Monte. There are reports of miners sometimes making as much as three hundred pesos a week. A Spanish Capuchin, Francisco de Ajofrín, who visited Guanajuato in 1763, described in his diary the extravagance with which the wages were dissipated in weekend sprees. "They buy taffeta, fine cambric, delicate lace and other rich fabrics so that they dress like princes. By Monday they find themselves without a penny . . . and descend the mine nearly naked." Father Ajofrín was struck by the incongruity of the scene, the contrast between the actors and their costumes. "It makes one laugh to see these people of all shades of color, with faces like devils and huge hands, extremely black and ugly . . . , festively dressed in velvet breeches, gold tissue dress coats, [and] Dutch ruffled shirts."[10]

Weekends of drinking, gambling, and wild spending in costumes costly enough for princes or great noblemen brought diversion to the harsh lives of the mine laborers. They amazed visitors like Father Ajofrín with their masquerade. Their employers—the rich miners—and the rich merchants of Mexico City assumed the roles of noblemen every day in the week, not simply to masquerade in their costumes during riotous weekends.

The Bourbon dynasty expanded the program, initiated by the Hapsburgs, of awarding titles of nobility. Titles were bestowed on the rich as rewards and as incentives for support of projects of the crown. Nobles customarily paid substantial taxes on assuming or succeeding to a title and annually as a substitute for the feudal obligation of providing soldiers for the king. The most effective of the Bourbons, Charles III, was the most generous in granting titles, bestowing twenty-three in New Spain alone. Charles's government wished to stimulate technological progress and economic development. The king officially affirmed that mining was a "noble profession" and attempted to reverse the traditional Spanish aversion to manual labor by declaring that the work of craftsmen, such as carpenters, smiths, masons, and even tailors, was "noble" and could be rewarded with a title. He and his successors in the later colonial period awarded twenty-three titles to the miners of New Spain. Those engaged in mercantile enterprises were also rewarded, but less amply, receiving fifteen or so titles.

The Bourbons, like the first two Hapsburg monarchs, Charles V and Philip II, were intent on centralizing power in the crown and its officials and, conversely, reducing the influence of regional magnates. Consequently the nobles of New Spain were allowed no political power and

relatively few special prerogatives. Unlike the nobility of Spain they were not granted a *fuero* providing self-governing juridical privileges, although thirty corporate groups, such as the miners, were given *fueros* that allowed them to establish their own courts and to settle disputes among their members. Nobles were allowed fewer legal immunities than either the clergy or military officers. The privileges that were given to the possessors of noble titles were also granted to commoners who held office and to all lawyers and to all students and graduates of the University.

A substantial proportion of the wealthiest Mexicans—John E. Kicza suggests as many as half—did not choose to apply for titles. For those who received them there was the prestige conferred by royal confirmation of the family's purity of blood, religious piety, rectitude, and general importance. There was also an unrelenting demand for what Doris M. Ladd, a student of the Mexican nobility, has called "conspicuous consumption . . . by royal decree."[11] Noble families were expected to be rich, to maintain a manner of living suited to noble status, and to make sizeable contributions to the general welfare. Eight families who were unable to sustain a sufficiently grand style of life in the eighteenth or early nineteenth centuries had their titles recalled for penury. Several heirs to titles refused to accept them because they felt unable to assume the fiscal responsibility involved. In declining, one heir cited his "notorious poverty."[12]

Lavish display characterized noble weddings and funerals and other occasions for family ceremony. For the baptism of his first-born daughter, the Conde de Regla hired a hundred coaches, and a miner from Dolores is known to have spent thirty-six thousand pesos on the celebration of the ceremony for a godchild.

Support for military endeavors was sought by the Bourbons. Serving as a militia officer provided occasions for uniformed splendor and martial honors and conferred the privileges of the *fuero militar* on the entire family. Fifty-four noblemen are known to have served in the militia in the decades just before and after 1800. Some organized and outfitted units at their own expense. Others supported Spanish military campaigns through loans to the royal treasury. Within four days of being informed by the viceroy of the king's need, the Conde de Regla agreed to pay for a ship of the line to be named Nuestra Señora de Regla. He traveled to the capital to make an initial payment of 200,000 pesos. In addition to paying for the Nuestra Señora de Regla, and according to pervasive tradition, another ship of the line, the Conde de Regla loaned 400,000 pesos to Viceroy Croix, 800,000 to his successor Bucareli, and 150,000 to the royal tobacco industry during fiscal emergencies.

Nobles were expected to provide funding in such times. The Marqués de Villar del Aguila paid more than half the cost of the massive aqueduct that brought the water needed for the expanding city of Querétaro early in the eighteenth century. During the famine of 1786 the Conde de Pérez Gálvez fed the hungry in Guanajuato by opening his warehouse, as had the future Marqués de Jaral de Berrio in an earlier period of scarcity. In the 1790s, during the smallpox epidemic, the Conde de Regla and the Marqués de Vivanco set up emergency centers in Pachuca and Mexico City furnishing food and medical supplies and paying the doctors. In 1805 when the meat supply system in the capital broke down, a group of wealthy merchants, some soon to become nobles, lent 150,000 pesos to the city government to provide meat for the populace.

Cortés had founded the Hospital de Jesús in Mexico City and eighteenth-century nobles followed his example in church-related charity. The dowager Countess of Valenciana financed a seventy-two-bed Bethlemite hospital in Guanajuato. The building and support of colleges and convents and the creation of endowments to enable poor girls to become nuns were frequent acts of charity. Several noblemen supported missionary activity among the tribes of the north. The Conde de Regla, who was a member of the third order of San Francisco, spent at least a quarter million pesos in church work, mortgaging his lands to support missions among the Apaches in Texas. His cousin was martyred by Comanches at San Saba in west-central Texas. The most enduring of Regla's charitable enterprises was the creation of the Monte de Pieded, the national pawnshop, set up originally in the former Jesuit college

of San Pedro y San Pablo with an endowment of 300,000 pesos to provide interest-free loans to the poor.

The establishment of *capellanía*, or chantry, funds was a favorite way for the rich to make a pious contribution to the church. Created in wills, or by a bereft widow or widower, *capellanías* set up trust funds to provide for the saying of masses for the spiritual benefit of the soul of the deceased. Usually funded from liens on landed estates, the *capellanías* were frequently put at the disposal of relatives who were members of the clergy. *Capellanías* had the worldly advantage of constituting a fund of capital available for the making of interest-bearing loans useful in stimulating economic activity.

The most dramatic expression of piety was to pay for the construction of a splendid and costly church. Several of the most prominent miners commissioned churches. In Guanajuato miners supported the construction of a church at the Cata mine and the Marqués de San Juan de Rayas built a church, in honor of his patron saint, for his mine. The Conde de Valenciana and his

6.1 Guanajuato, Church of the Valenciana Mine.

6.2 *Guanajuato, Church of the Valenciana Mine, interior.*

partners and workers built one of the finest late eighteenth-century churches, San Cayetano, on the hillside beside his great mine, and contributed 30,720 pesos for the new facade of the Church of San Díego in the city. In Taxco, José de la Borda, who never sought a title of nobility, had earlier celebrated his second great mining bonanza by constructing, at a cost of nearly half a million pesos, the spectacular church of Santa Prisca y San Sebastián (see Fig. 7.11).

The affluence of eighteenth-century Mexico that made possible the construction of churches such as San Cayetano and Santa Prisca led also to a massive program of secular construction. So extensive was the building and rebuilding of houses in Mexico City that scarcely a civil or domestic structure survives unmodified from the period before the 1720s. The reconstruction of the viceregal palace, which had been badly damaged in the corn riot of 1692, was completed in

1697, but every other major public building in the capital was built or transformed after 1720.

The reconstruction of the ayuntamiento, or city hall, which in its location on the central plaza had also suffered in the corn riot, was begun in that year. The new *aduana*, or custom house, was completed in 1731, incorporating some portion of an old private structure on the Plaza of Santo Domingo. Plans for the *casa de moneda*, or mint, were first drafted in 1730 and the structure opened in 1734. The archbishop's palace, across the street from the viceroy's, was reconstructed between 1730 and 1747. A new building for the Inquisition was erected next to the *aduana* between 1732 and 1736. The Jesuit Colleges of San Ildefonso and of San Ignacio, better known as Las Vizcaínas, were constructed between 1712 and 1749 and between 1734 and 1767, respectively (see Figs. 6.16 and 6.17). A new home for the university was finished in 1757, and the Colegio de Cristo was completed about the same time. At least six major hospitals were built or extended in Mexico City during the middle quarters of the century.

Civic architecture rivaling that of the cap-

6.3 *The Aduana, Mexico City.*

6.4 *The Inquisition, Mexico City.*

137

ital was erected in other cities of New Spain. Puebla, which had become a great center of cotton textile manufacturing, rebuilt its Archbishop's Palace, covering the exterior with a diaper pattern of glazed blue square tiles set against a background of unglazed red rectangular ones. Rising above the broad roofs of the extensive palace, like the Christian cathedral emerging from the mass of the great mosque of Córdoba, is a library named for Bishop Palafox. Its handsome interior is groin-vaulted, floored with patterned tiles, and walled on each side above the principal level by two tiers of balustraded balconies for books. Several hospitals and colleges were also built in Puebla.

Notable structures in other cities include the seminary, now the governor's palace, and a Jesuit college in Morelia; the *alhóndiga*, or public granary, in Guanajuato, site of bloody slaughter during Father Hidalgo's uprising; and two notable buildings in Guadalajara, the Bethlemite Hospital and the palace constructed for the Audiencia of Nueva Galicia with its ponderously powerful Baroque portal.

Substantial private houses were conspicuous in the city-scapes of eighteenth-century New Spain and frequently praised by foreign visitors, but they were few in number. The poorest people, then as now, were fortunate if they had some sort of flimsy, impermanent shelter, offering shade from the sun, protection from summer downpours, and some lessening of the chill after dark. As late as 1813 fewer than 2 percent of families owned land on which structures were built within the city of Mexico. Most ordinary people, unlike their counterparts in the English colonies to the north, lived in multiple dwellings. Modest shopkeepers often lived in "cup and saucer apartments" located within large houses and other

6.6 *Casa de vecindad, Mexico City (from a mid-19th-century lithograph).*

structures. At street level a door opened into the shop, the saucer. Above the shop, frequently constructed of wood, was the cup, a mezzanine providing some limited space for private activities and sleeping and lit by a small window. Prosperous artisans and owners of small business enterprises such as bakeries usually lived in *casas de vecindad*, apartment structures of one or two stories and of varying size arranged so that several individual apartments opened off a central passageway or patio. Normally the apartments consisted of

6.5 *Governor's Palace (formerly Palace of the Audiencia) Guadalajara, center of facade.*

138

two rooms and a kitchen. More sumptuous *casas de vecindad* had four or more large apartments with several rooms each. An ornamental portal provided entry from the street, and at the opposite end of the central area was a common fountain and a niche containing a religious image. *Casas de vecindad* were usually owned by landlords living elsewhere and were frequently constructed with funds owned by religious establishments. Prosperous members of the professional and business classes, leading lawyers and physicians, local merchants and owners of food and pulque processing plants, and the like, were able to afford *casas solos*, single houses that, despite the name, were usually built as half of a pair of adjoining houses so that the families could each use a portion of the patio located at the center of the structures. A wall customarily divided each family's share of the patio from the other's.

The houses of the very rich, costing up to 100,000 pesos and sometimes sumptuous enough to be called palaces, were larger, wholly free-standing versions of the *casas solo*. The general arrangement followed Andalusian, and to some extent Aztec, precedent. Frequently the lower story contained shops opening off the street that were operated by merchant-owners or leased to others. The doors of the great portal opened to admit coaches to an entry hall and to the arcaded main patio beyond. Rooms opening off the patio at ground level contained offices, store rooms, and servants' quarters. A monumental stair led up to the principal living quarters opening off the upper arcade. On the front with a view over the street was the formal salon for receptions and its antechamber. Along the sides were bedrooms, a less formal living room, and, in the most elaborate houses, a chapel sometimes placed in a front corner. The dining room was opposite the salon at the rear near the kitchen and the servants' rooms, which were located on the rear patio above the coach house and stables. Sometimes a garden, providing a view of the city's churches and the surrounding mountains, was cultivated on the roof. The most extensive structures contained as many as eighty or more rooms and housed an extended family and ten to twenty or more servants. The largest household recorded in the 1811 census was that of Gabriel de Yermo, an important

merchant of Basque birth. Forty-two people lived in the house, including Yermo's wife, son and five daughters, twenty-five servants of diverse ethnicity—including Creoles, Mestizos, Indians—and one black slave. In addition there were a chaplain and eight Basque immigrants, among them three nephews who were associated with Yermo's business operations.

Living in these houses provided an ample sense of grandeur, considerable inconvenience, and even discomfort. As Elizabeth Wilder Weismann has written, "there were no cupboards, no clothes closets, few chairs, no water but in the courtyard fountain, and no heat at all."[13]

Roughly forty of these great houses survive in Mexico City, in varying states of restoration, alteration, and dilapidation. They are concentrated in the area near the Zocalo, the central plaza, notably along streets to the west, such as the Calle Madero, the Calle Isabel La Católica, and the Calle Carranza. Several important houses survive in each of the other cities that were

6.7 *House of Alfeñique, Puebla.*

prominent in the late eighteenth century. Of particular interest are the tawny stone houses of Morelia, the blue-and-red-tile-clad, stucco-fringed houses of Puebla (Fig. 6.7), and those of Querétaro with their remarkable patio arcades making bravura displays of curves, angles, and countercurves, striking examples of the enlivening of the eighteenth-century Mexican Baroque by Moorish reminiscences.

Two Houses of the Condes del Valle de Orizaba: The House of Tiles and the House of Masks

The Casa de los Azulejos, or House of Tiles (Fig. 6.8), is the most celebrated mansion in Mexico City and, since its transformation in 1919 into Sanborn's store and restaurant, the most visited. We know that it was rebuilt in approximately its present form in the eighteenth century but do not know with certainty the year of the construction, the designer, or the person who commissioned the work. The dates and designers of few houses of eighteenth-century Mexico are known.

The Houses of Tiles is located on the present Calle Madero. Formerly it stood opposite the very extensive Franciscan friary complex on the Plaza Guardiola close to what was the western edge of the city. The present structure and its predecessors on the site were occupied by one of the most prominent of Mexican noble families for nearly two and a half centuries. The earliest house was purchased by Diego Peredo Suárez, sometimes identified as Diego Suárez de Peredo, at public auction on December 2, 1596, for 6,500 pesos as a result of legal proceedings for debt against the builder, Damián Martínez. Diego Peredo Suárez included the house and 285 square miles of productive grain and pasture land in a *mayorazgo*, or entail, he created in 1610 for his daughter and his grandson Nicolás, the son of the second Conde of the Valle de Orizaba with whom he had quarreled. The value of the entail would increase two fold every twenty years for nearly a century and a quarter. Diego Peredo Suárez specified in his will that Nicolás "and all his successors in the *mayorazgo* shall carry my surnames

and titles, as well as whatever other surnames they may choose out of my ancestry."[14] As a result of the grandfather's insistence that his name be perpetuated, and a similar provision in the deed creating another *mayorazgo*, the last Conde had an official name that in its extension rivaled those of royalty, Andrés Diego Rodrigo Hurtado de Mendoza y de Gorréz Vivero Peredo Suárez y Jaso. By this time the head of the family had assimilated two additional titles, being the third Marqués of Ciria and the fourteenth Mariscal of Castilla as well as the eleventh Conde of the Valle de Orizaba.

The family's male founder, the first Rodrigo de Vivero, arrived in New Spain in 1560 ten years after his uncle, Luis de Velasco I, had assumed authority as the second viceroy. Like other well-connected immigrants, he prospered. Within three years he married the widow of Cortés's former secretary, who had been given encomienda rights over the Indians of Tecamachalco, an important town east of Puebla. The Viveros gradually acquired from Rodrigo's first cousin, Luis de Velasco II, a large sugar-growing estate which had been established by Antonio de Mendoza, the first viceroy, just east of Orizaba in a valley on the eastern slope of the Mexican plateau. An inventory taken in 1580 provides a detailed account of the estate. In addition to the sugarcane fields there was very extensive acreage of woods and Indian common fields, grain and cattle lands, and sheep pastures. There were 27,924 sheep and 15,200 cattle. The buildings included a substantial house and church. There were four structures for pressing, boiling, and refining sugar; some, according to the inventory, "spanned by two arches . . . and built of masonry with brick vaulting."[15] There were also modest adobe houses for Spanish administrators and black foremen and huts for the 147 slaves and the more numerous Indian workers. The livestock included scores of oxen and two sizeable herds of mules. This great complex provided the base of the family's wealth and the source of the title, Conde del Valle de Orizaba, taken in 1627 by Rodrigo de Vivero's son, also named Rodrigo, when he was ennobled. The second Rodrigo had served as Governor of Nueva Vizcaya, the Durango area of northwest New Spain, and as Captain General of both the

140

Philippines and Panama. The royal document, signed by Philip III, establishing the *condado* cited Rodrigo's personal expenditures in his campaign against the Chichimec Indians and his important services in Japan, where he secured Uragate as a port open, briefly, to Spanish galleons. The marriage of his son Luis, who became the second Conde, to an eleven-year-old heiress brought to the family's holdings the roughly 285 square miles of the Peredo Suárez *mayorazgo*, valued at over 100,000 pesos. Further substantial additions continued from time to time over the generations. The poorest marriage brought in only 300 horses. The final great acquisition came in 1823, shortly after Mexican independence from Spain, when half the property and the title of the Mariscales de Castilla came to the Conde del Valle de Orizaba. During the late eighteenth and early nineteenth centuries the lands of the family formed an extensive crescent, beginning in the east with the sugar fields near Orizaba, sweeping west and north through pastures for cattle and acres of grain which supplied the miners of Pachuca, stretching further west and south through fields of maguey cactus which produced pulque for the drinkers of Mexico City, and terminating in more sugar fields in the present state of Morelos. Very few families in Mexico sustained their prominence and wealth as long as the Condes of the Valle de Orizaba, who were dependent almost entirely upon agriculture. Their periodic financial difficulties occurred primarily because of erratic management and the costs of litigation over succession arising from the family's failure to produce a steady line of legitimate male heirs. On one occasion the Mexican family lost the title for several years to a Spanish relative, and subsequent fiscal litigation over an entail was protracted over a hundred and fifty years. In four different generations illegitimate children were recognized and provided for. Three who inherited the title were either illegitimate children or the children of illegitimate parents. Two condesas asserted themselves in ways that drew public attention. The third condesa continued to manage family affairs for four years after her husband's death, refusing to turn the official papers over to the court of the audiencia until litigation over the succession was completed. Graciana de Velasco y Saldívar de Castilla, who

inherited the title in her own right in 1702 because her only brother had died, persuaded her fiscally ineffective husband to turn over the management of family affairs to her. She devised a system of allocation of rental income that satisfied creditors who had been threatening to seize property for nonpayment of interest and made a significant increase in the revenue from the entail by providing funding for improvements on the estates. On one occasion she informed the judges of the audiencia that an account of revenue from her husband was in error because he failed to get information from the administrator who reported only to her.

Manuel Toussaint attributed the present House of Tiles to Graciana, citing her will of 1737 which records her rebuilding and enlarging of the family's city mansion. Toussaint suggests that her living in Puebla for some time until her husband's death in 1708 may have influenced her use of tiles although, as he states, no house in Puebla or anywhere else in Mexico is entirely covered with glazed tiles. We know that Graciana attempted to disinherit her son, José Hurtado de Mendoza y Velasco, whom she regarded as disreputable in part because he helped a convict escape from jail. The Peredo Suárez *mayorazgo* specified that the property should pass to the "most virtuous" child, not necessarily to the eldest son, and the countess argued that it should go to her upstanding daughter rather than to José. After some deliberation the audiencia drew a subtle distinction between mere mischief and real evil and supported the claim of the son.

A legend regarding the house represents a Conde father declaring to his disappointing son, "You'll never build a house of tiles." The meaning of this supposedly proverbial Spanish expression is that the son would never do anything worth remembering. According to the legend the son is transformed by his father's rebuke, becomes widely admired and rich, and actually builds the memorable House of Tiles.

There is some likelihood that the condesa's irresponsible son, José, is the source of the legend. Recovered from his early wildness and his mother's disapproval, he may have commissioned the final alteration of the house which created the unique tile-covered exterior. Documents in the archives of the Mexico City *ayuntamiento* confirm building activity on the site between 1755 and 1758. Floral details of the upper frame of the fountain in the patio and, less strongly, of the frames of some of the windows of the exterior suggest the probable influence of the rococo decorative style. This is more consistent with work done after mid-century rather than during the lifetime of Condesa Graciana who died about 1738. The fountain may, however, have been constructed after the major transformation of the house was completed. The date and the builder remain uncertain.

The house survived substantially unchanged into the twentieth century. Sylvester Baxter, the pioneer American student of Mexican colonial architecture, recalled its appearance at the turn of the century sparkling under the clear skies of the city looking "as if it had been built the year before, instead of standing in its present shape something like a century and a half." Baxter's impressions were contained in a piece he wrote for the *Architectural Record* in 1919 to express his apprehensiveness regarding the acquisition of the house by the Sanborn company for conversion into "a typical American drug store."[16] His apprehensiveness was not warranted. In the interior the low basement story and the story above it have been combined into a single tall story and ultimately the patio was covered over, but the exterior changes were minimal. More extensive modifications of the exterior had been made to the rear of the house fourteen years earlier while the building was occupied by the Jockey Club of Mexico. At that time a new front to the west was necessitated by the demolition of the old National Theater to permit the extension of the Calle Cinco de Mayo. The fenestration in the new section consists of two stories rather than three and the generally simplified articulation in stone resembles the older work only approximately. The new tiles applied to the walls, however, both on the Cinco de Mayo facade and along much of the south wall, closely resemble the original ones so that to the casual viewer the new section seems similar to the old one.

The initial impression of the building as a whole is created by its shimmering surface of tiles, blue with some accents of yellow set against white. Only after study does the observer notice the complex interplay of articulating elements constructed of what was originally a soft gray stone. The base of the building consists of unornamented blocks. The two lower stories are separated from the principal upper one by the shadowed horizontal created by a projecting cornice and by a line of balconies above it. A series of grills, pilasters, and stone frames, running from the base up toward the cornice around both the

6.8 *House of the Conde del Valle de Orizaba, Mexico City.*

6.9 *House of the Conde del Valle de Orizaba, Mexico City, detail of exterior, parapet and tile panel.*

142

superposed windows and the intervening slightly depressed panels of tiles, serve to unify the stories and create an intricate whole. Most of the ornamentation of the stone-framing members is placed within firm rectangular panels, but it is diverse in treatment and type. The more obviously striking decoration of the tile panels is also contained within rectangular framing and consists of patterns shaped by straight lines and right angles, resembling those of certain types of geometric oriental carpets.

The principal story above is composed less complexly of similar elements, with a window taller and more elaborately decorated than the others set above the powerful portal. At the top of the building is an attic parapet with niches for saints placed above the portal and at the corner. Ceramic finials and the moldings of the lower portion of the parapet, rippling up and down between them, provide a delicate topping for the walls.

Much of the interior has been lost in remodeling, and the present condition of the principal rooms of the upper story as sales rooms gives little sense of their original nature. The stair, with

6.10 House of the Conde del Valle de Orizaba, Mexico City, detail of the patio.

its Moorish ceiling and its tile dado, and with the addition of the recently restored fresco of José Clemente Orozco, is impressive. The restaurant-occupied patio remains virtually intact despite the distractions of the yellow glow from the plastic roofing above and the paintings of gardens and peacocks on the walls. It has a distinctly Moorish flavor with elaborate octagonal piers, instead of the usual stone arches, providing the support at both lower and upper levels on three of the sides. The piers support wooden impost blocks and lintels and stucco-ornamented, tile-decorated wooden friezes at the two levels. On the fourth side is a fountain set in a sort of grotto in the wall beneath a notched tri-lobed arch that is framed by powerfully swirling floral ornamentation and an outer margin of white tile flowers set in a blue tile ground.

In 1766 work was begun on a second house in the Mexico City area for the Condes of the Valle de Orizaba. This structure, known popularly as the Casa de los Mascarones (Fig. 6.11), the House of Masks, and located on the present Avenida Ribera de San Cosmé, was planned as a summer retreat and set in fields and gardens alongside the Santa Fe aqueduct well over two miles beyond the city's western limit. Conde José Hurtado de Mendoza was responsible for initiating construction. Despite the expenditure of over 100,000 pesos and several years work, the house was unfinished at the time of his death in 1771. The designer may have been Ildefonso Iniesta Bejarano y Durán, architect of San Felipe Neri Nuevo and the university. Only a fragment surrounding a patio survives in approximately its original form. The building has two stories, as its garden side reveals, but the facade has only one, of monumental scale. A blunt parapet now crowns the design with only the bases of the finials, visible in old photographs, that once softened the skyline and provided some continuity with the original construction below. The levels of the street and sidewalk have been raised, and trees planted along the sidewalk make impossible the comprehensive view necessary to convey the power of this architectural facade. The design of the House of Tiles expressed delicacy through compartmentalized complexity; the design of the House of Masks expresses simple forcefulness.

There are six very large windows, three on either side of the portal, which is crowned by a rippling baroque arch or lintel—the curious form suggests both. The windows are supported by layered, heavily ornamented brackets and crowned by powerfully layered entablatures. The wall surfaces surrounding the windows are covered by prominent blocks of rusticated masonry. The most prominent feature of the house, which gave it its name, is the order of life-size atlante figures

6.11 *Country House of the Conde del Valle de Orizaba, Mexico City, from Manuel Toussaint,* Colonial Art in Mexico, *p. 326. Photograph Instituto Nacional de Antropologia & Historia, Archivo Monumentos Coloniales y de la República.*

which stand on powerful *estípites* and support with their upbent arms capitals placed beneath the projecting waterspouts. The elements of the atlante-*estípite* order are placed diagonally at the corners and along the front between the windows, dividing it into massive bays. The full order is not used to flank the portal, but the powerful *estípite* forms which are used have a similar forcefulness. A curious feature of the house, recalling the original interior arrangement of the House of Tiles, is the low-ceilinged ground floor. In the House of Masks the existence of this floor is almost entirely disguised on the facade in order to secure greater monumentality. The only indications of its existence are modest vertical slits placed in the tall basement level on both sides of each window. The floor of the upper story is at the level of the

bottom of the windows, leaving sufficient room beneath it for the concealed story below. Both houses of the Condes of the Valle de Orizaba are unique. Commissioning two such remarkable and different houses within one or two generations would have been impossible without great wealth. Fortunately, the wealth of the Mexican upper class in the eighteenth century, which was unprecedented on this continent, was frequently accompanied by an interest in architecture and by remarkable architectural taste.

CIÉNEGA DE MATA, THE RURAL ESTATE OF THE RINCÓN GALLARDOS

The Ciénega de Mata estate originated in the activities of a remarkable man, Pedro Mateos, who began as an ordinary farmer. In the last years of the sixteenth century, probably with the assistance of influential friends on the audiencia in Guadalajara, he began to acquire lands for grazing in an area which was still vulnerable to attacks of Chichimec Indians. In 1605 he was granted the right to dam a stream in order to create what became a large artificial lake and a sizeable irrigation system for wheat fields, to erect flour mills, and also to install machinery for processing raw silver, in all likelihood from the mines of Tepezala in which his family had acquired a share. The *mayorazgo* created about this time by Pedro Mateos passed to his grandson Agustín Rincón, who shared his energy and drive for acquisition. Pedro had secured the assistance of influential friends. Agustín was active in public and military affairs as well as in agriculture and business. He was a captain and, ultimately, a general. He served in administrative posts in several towns and as corregidor of Zacatecas, a post that led to profitable contracts for supplying grain and mutton to feed the miners. He enlarged the family holdings by buying out small farmers pressed by drought, frost, and a depressed economy. By 1645 he held deeds to eighty-seven estancias—sizeable grants for sheep or cattle herding—and 180 caballerías—grants of about one hundred acres for farming. Intervening property was acquired by purchase from the royal government.

When Agustín's son, the sole heir, entered the Jesuit order, instead of giving all his property to the Jesuits he willed the hacienda to his niece, the wife of Captain Nicolás Gallardo. In 1697 her son, José Rincón Gallardo, had to settle title to his, by now, considerably larger landed estate. The governmental surveyor estimated its area at 202 estancias and 255 caballerías, only approximately half of which were properly recorded by title. In 1693 José had been commissioned captain of cuirassiers in the militia battalion of New Spain formalizing his offer made during the difficulties of the previous year's grain riot in Mexico City to aid the viceroy with five hundred men and a thousand horses from his domain. In appointing him captain, the viceroy specified that all military activities would be at José's expense with no drain on the royal treasury. Probably as a result of its dependence on Rincón Gallardo funding and voluntary cavalrymen, the viceregal government was obliging in legalizing the undocumented portion of Rincón Gallardo landholding. For what was to him a piddling 2,000 pesos José was able to secure official recognition of his control of the great estate which had taken a century to assemble, which would be increased for another hundred years, and which would endure little changed by Mexico's independence from Spain until it was broken up by the family in 1861.

The Rincón Gallardo's initial title of nobility was not awarded until the eighth generation, in 1810, the year of Father Hidalgo's uprising. In 1804 King Charles IV had asked the viceroy, audiencias, and city councils for nominations of those most worthy to be awarded four new titles of nobility he wished to create in celebration of the marriage of his son, Prince Ferdinand and María Antonia of Naples. Forty-four were nominated, and the four selected were appointed by royal decree in 1807, but only Colonel Manuel Rincón Gallardo of Aguascalientes and the Regiment of San Carlos, Dragoons of San Luis Potosí, completed the official forms, paid the fees, and was entitled Marqués de Guadalupe Gallardo.

Testimony in support of Colonel Rincón Gallardo's nomination identified his fortune as one of the largest in the Americas. Félix Ma-

ría Calleja, the formidable champion of Spanish authority who had successfully suppressed the revolutionary armies of Hidalgo and Allende and, later, those of Morelos, characterized him as a leader in making agricultural advances who constantly reinvested in his land, spending some 200,000 pesos in improvements, constructing new dams and workshops. The family has continued to be prominent in Mexican affairs, acquiring through marriage additional, now-honorary, titles of nobility. The current head of the family is Conde-Duque de Regla and Marqués de Villahermosa as well as Marqués de Guadalupe. Pedro Rincón Gallardo, the most prominent nineteenth-century member of the family was a brigadier general, a member of congress, Governor of Mexico D.F., ambassador to Russia, Germany, and England, and president of the Jockey Club of Mexico.

Modern Mexican land-distribution policies have greatly reduced the acreage of the haciendas, which only seventy-five years ago still dominated the countryside. Many haciendas stand desolate, abandoned to the elements. Some have been adapted to use as hotels or resorts. Some continue in greatly diminished use, a very few, such as the core hacienda of the Rincón Gallardo estate, remain under family control. In an issue of *Artes de Mexico* of 1966 devoted to the hacienda, Alfonso Rincón Gallardo recalled his childhood experiences on two different haciendas, one of which was no longer in operation, and told of his father Carlos's buying from his brothers their shares of the cattle ranch, the surviving fragment of Ciénega de Mata in 1939. In that year Carlos, an amateur charro, a distinguished horseman and roper, published the first edition of his *El Libro de Charro Mexicano*. Alberto describes his own pleasure in riding with the charros, "those extraordinary horsemen, pleasant companions, tanned by the sun, simple in tastes, frank, never tiring—the classic men of the great haciendas."[17]

During its prime, 2,500 or more people had lived within the Rincón Gallardo estate, distributed primarily between the headquarters hacienda at Ciénega de Mata, and fifteen other haciendas or major ranchos. By the late eighteenth century the cost of its work force absorbed about half the operating expense of an agricultural estate. Establishments like the Ciénega da Mata had managerial hierarchies consisting of general administrators, *mayordomos* for the satellite haciendas, foremen and subforemen, as well as cashiers and storekeepers. They also needed the services of skilled craftsmen such as millers, bricklayers, weavers, and, in some instances, distillers, tailors, and hatters. The general labor force included temporary employees who were paid wages as well as tenant farmers and debt peons. In the seventeenth century black and Indian slaves had been used. José Rincón Gallardo had owned 144 black slaves of all ages in 1683. The vaqueros, or cowboys, who constituted José's private cavalry brigade, already exemplified the skills with horse and rope that would later be celebrated in the western United States.

Hacienda owners were paternalistic despots, feeling responsible for their peoples' welfare, establishing parishes with resident priests for their spiritual behalf, and protecting them against injury from outsiders. They set up commissary stores to supply and, in some cases, to exploit their workers. The *hacendados* were granted substantial judicial powers, in some cases obtaining writs from the viceroy that excluded judicial officials from their territory except to investigate specific complaints or statutory offenses. Haciendas had their own jails, and *hacendados* had the power to conduct hearings and establish preliminary evidence just as the magistrates did in the towns. José Rincón Gallardo's commission as captain specified that he should "punish the disobedient." In 1692, the year before he was commissioned, he had been given the authority to track down and imprison or hand over to higher officials "thieves and brigands operating on the highways"[18] of the region and to apprehend violators of civil or criminal law.

The great estates provided few amenities of civilized living apart from the luxury of having many servants. Life was quiet and, in some regards, austere, if not primitive. Isolation was often extreme with days of slow and difficult travel needed to reach the capital or, even, the nearest city. José Rincón Gallardo maintained forty-four carriage mules to provide transportation at Ciénega de Mata. The discordant extremes of luxury and poverty in hacienda living in the nineteenth century were strikingly recorded in a book written in 1819 by an American merchant sympathetic to the revolutionists and critical of the old order. William Davis Robinson has left a sharp, if exaggerated, image of the "awkward grandeur" of the master of the Hacienda Jaral de Berrio out on the range with his rough, illiterate employees. He is wearing boots lovingly made on the estate and worth

> fifty to a hundred dollars; large spurs inlaid with gold and silver; a superb horse, with bridle and saddle which cost 150 to 300; a cloak, or mangas, richly embroidered, and full of gold and silver buttons, laces, and fringe. He lives in a spacious house, within whose walls every luxury is to be found which the country affords; but when he sallies forth, he is lost among a group of half-naked, badly fed wretches, whose only dress is sheepskins.[19]

Not surprisingly owners of large estates usually preferred to reside most of the year in cities offering a full calendar of social events, leaving day-to-day management of the estate to the administrator. A majority maintained substantial

6.12 House of the Rincón Gallardo family (now the Palacio Gobierno), Aguascalientes.

houses in Mexico City. Some preferred to live in the urban center nearest their latifundium. In the eighteenth century the Rincón Gallardos built a handsome Baroque structure which sets decorative moldings of light stone against plain walls of reddish purple *tezontle* and which contains two handsome arcaded patios and a powerful free-standing stair of double flights of steps. The house stands on the plaza in Aguascalientes diagonally across from the cathedral and now serves as the capitol of the state. The arduousness of transportation made family visits to the great estates few and extended rather than frequent and brief. Normally the family would arrive accompanied by guests, and the stay would be planned to coincide with local religious festivals or with important seasonal occasions which provided local color for the visitors. Alfonso Rincón Gallardo recalled visits in the early twentieth century to the Hacienda Santiago Ocotepec during the annual festival of Santiago, which was celebrated with cock fights, horse races, banquets, and fireworks. He also recalled the seasonal events of sheep and cattle haciendas like Ciénega de Mata, the brandings, the shearings, and the sport of roping calves and separating them from their mothers.

6.13 Hacienda Ciénega da Mata, church. Art and Time in Mexico, *photograph of Judith Hancock Sandoval (p. 220) (copyright Estudios de Historia de México Condumex).*

Religion was central to the life on the hacienda, and churches were the most prominent structures and the most lavishly decorated. In addition to seasonal festivals and Sunday masses there were daily services, normally prayers in the morning and, after the workday, evensong and the recitation of the rosary. The present substantial, domed, single-towered Baroque church of Ciénega de Mata was completed for Francisco Javier Rincón Gallardo in 1770. At about the same time Francisco Javier finished rebuilding the main house incorporating elements of earlier structures of the sixteenth and seventeenth centuries. The house, which faces the church across a small plaza, has nothing of the grandeur of the great house in Aguascalientes. Its principal external architectural features are a two-storied arcade running across its short side which faces the church, and a centrally placed stair with double flights on its long side. Hacienda houses of two stories were unusual. More frequently they were of one story with high vaulted ceilings. The principal house of the Marqués de Guardiola at the Hacienda of San José de Obra had twenty rooms with family living quarters of brick. The rooms were tall with beamed rather than vaulted ceilings, and the floors were of wood and adobe. The floors of the kitchen and work rooms were whitewashed dirt.

Patios served to provide some formal coherence and functional effectiveness in the placing of the heterogeneous structures of the hacienda. François Chevalier, the foremost student of the great landed estates, traces their architectural organization around two or more patios to that of the farm buildings of Andalusia and beyond them to the floor plan of the Roman villa.

The most common scheme was to organize the main house around a central patio and to place in close conjunction the church, coachhouse, stables, and pantry. Other patios might contain living quarters for the principal members of the hacienda staff, offices, work and store rooms, as well as the jail and storage buildings for the hacienda's produce. William Davis Robinson mentioned a great number of buildings for peons in his account of the great hacienda of Jaral de Berrio.[20] Probably they were flimsy structures set off by themselves like the slave quarters on a Vir-

6.14 *Hacienda Ciénega de Mata, principal patio.* Art and Time in Mexico, *photograph of Judith Hancock Sandoval (copyright Estudios de Historia de México Condumex).*

6.15 *Hacienda Ciénega de Mata, storage barn.* Art and Time in Mexico, *photograph of Judith Hancock Sandoval (copyright Estudios de Historia de México Condumex).*

ginia plantation. The most architecturally notable of the surviving structures at Ciénega de Mata, apart from the church, are handsome paired granaries, one of them now without a roof, and a patio with delicate arches of wonderfully intricate curving complexity.

Las Vizcaínas: The College of San Ignacio of Loyola in Mexico City

About 1733 the religious confraternity of Basques in Mexico City, the Cofradía de Nuestra Señora de Aránzasu, initiated the planning of a large secondary school for orphan girls of Basque origin which would be administered by the Jesuit order. Basque immigrants had been prominent in New Spain since the beginning. Three Basques, Juan de Tolosa, Cristóbal de Oñate, and Diego de Ibarra, had started the first great mining center, Zacatecas, and younger members of the Oñate and Ibarra families had pushed farther north to found Nueva Vizcaya, the region around Durango, and still farther north to found New Mexico. By 1742 the prominence of Basques in the *consulado*, the international merchant's guild of Mexico City, was so great that one of the two parties which elected a consul annually, and in alternate years elected the prior, was Basque.

Like the other dominant group in the *consulado*, the Montañes from the Santander region of northern Spain, the Basques had a strong sense of provincial identity. They considered themselves hidalgos, or nobles, despite their usual descent from ordinary peasant farmers and they looked down on those born in America and on other Spaniards, especially those from Andalusia. In 1764 they would form an economic society to support fellow Basques, the Amigos del Pais, and they were subsequently active in supporting, in their native province, a new college at Vergara that developed studies in mining and metallurgy.

Three names are carved above the great stair of Las Vizcaínas, officially known as the College of San Ignacio, in recognition of major roles in its founding, Francisco de Echeveste, Manuel de Aldaco, and Ambrosio de Maeve. All three had been consul, or prior, of the *consulado*. Aldaco was the principal silver banker of the city. A nephew of an earlier immigrant, Francisco Fagoaga, he had taken over the leadership of the Fagoaga family enterprises after his death. He advanced funds for José de la Borda's first great strike in silver at Tlalpujahua. The rules of government for the college were drafted by Francisco Javier de

Gamboa, the great Mexican foe of the Bourbon administrative reforms. Gamboa—who would write an important book on mining, serve for a decade as agent of the *consulado* in Madrid, and act as regent of the audiencias of both Santo Domingo and Mexico—was the son and grandson of Basque immigrants.

Land for the college was secured in late November 1733. Some initial plans had been prepared by Pedro Bueno Basori, but he died before the cornerstone was laid the following July. The person, or persons, responsible for the final design is not known although documents provide the names of two architects. Miguel José de Quiera is mentioned in a document concerning the grant of the land, and Miguel Rivera signed papers which indicate that he was in charge of overseeing construction on the site until his death in 1739. A plan of the complex, found in the Archive of the Indies and dated 1753, differs from the completed layout suggesting that modifications were made after construction was under way. A royal cédula of September 1, 1754, approving the foundation of the college suggests that after twenty years a substantial portion of the structure, at least, was finished. Two other cédulas of 1766 and of 1767 seem to mark the virtual completion of the complex. By 1767, 583,118 pesos had been expended. Five years later the leading architect of the city, Lorenzo Rodríguez, designed a portal for the chapel. Rodríguez, the Andalusian immigrant who had created the *sagrario*, or parish church of the cathedral, had married a niece of Miguel Rivera and had inherited his architectural books. Erection of Rodríguez's portal was delayed until 1786.

The design of Las Vizcaínas was influenced by that of the Jesuit College of San Ildefonso some blocks to the north. Construction there had been initiated between 1712 and 1718 and had been resumed about 1730, continuing until completion in 1749. San Ildefonso consolidated some earlier educational institutions and incorporated some earlier structures. The names of two Jesuit architects are known: P. Zorrella and Cristóbal de Escobar y Llamas. Zorrella was responsible for the first section built, the *Colegio Chico* at the eastern end; and Escobar, for the ex-

6.16 *College of San Ildefonso, Mexico City, Colegio Grande, portal.*

tensions to the west which contained the chapel and the great salon and which consolidated what were the two lower stories of the *Colegio Chico* into a single giant story. Both San Ildefonso and Las Vizcaínas are very large structures that have three interior patios and have red *tezontle* facades of immense length. The dimensions of Las Vizcaínas are approximately 420 feet across the main facade and approximately 460 feet along the sides. In both colleges the long horizontal of the facade is broken into vertical compartments by pilasters of light and contrasting *chiluca* stone, and is decorated by powerfully ornamented portals that push up through the top of the crowning parapet. Windows set deep in complex *chiluca* frames and placed dramatically against the plain, dark *tezontle* walls are major features of both facades. The frames are essentially rectangular but are enlivened by sharply cut moldings that incorporate curved elements as well as angular forms.

The design of Las Vizcaínas refines that of San Ildefonso to secure more verticality and more unity. A principal change is the elimination of the broad molding separating the floors,

6.17 *College of Las Vizcaínas, Mexico City.*

which provided a secondary horizontal accent at San Ildefonso. The pilasters between bays at Las Vizcaínas are giant, constituting an uninterrupted vertical pushing up through both stories from base to parapet. At the top of the facade the parapet has been simplified and strengthened. A two-stage setback has been eliminated and the parapet brought out to the plane of the lower wall. The horizontal mouldings have been minimized so that the eye is brought to focus on the silhouette against the sky as the parapet sweeps across each bay, curving up at either side to meet the finials. These have been halved in number and greatly increased in size so that their sharply cut, powerful forms extend the vertical thrust of the pilasters.

In accord with the more powerfully unified skyline is a softening of emphasis on the portals. At San Ildefonso the portals (Fig. 6.16) push forward from the plane of the wall and push several feet through the horizontal of the parapet in gables of cascading profile. At Las Vizcaínas the portals are barer, powerfully designed with sharply cut three-layered pilasters, and they are much more contained within the overall organization of the wall and its upper parapet. The handling of the windows is analogous. At San Ildefonso each window is placed high within its wall compartment of dark *tezontle*, close to its upper moulding, but with no clear relationship to the other windows or to the general pattern of architectural articulation of the total surface. The

light-colored stone frame makes an isolated, dramatic burst of decoration against the plain background of wall, but the overall scheme lacks coherence. At Las Vizcaínas the windows are brought together to form vertical pairs and are centered judiciously within the two-story compartments. The lower windows have rectangular frames with projecting "ears" at the corners and a low arch at the top. Those above have outer frames which are square with similar ears. Their inner frames are octagonal. Serving to relate the vertically paired windows to each other and to the overall articulation of the wall is a vertical molding, or series of moldings, beginning at the base of the structure and connecting it with the center of the lower window frame. The vertical line reappears above that window frame to link it to the frame above it and reappears again at the top of the upper frame to link it to the top of the parapet at the midpoint between finials. Thus a secondary vertical accent is created which ties the pairs of windows together and reinforces the more powerful vertical thrust of the pilasters.

Nothing of the interior of the college is as interesting as the facade. The three arcaded patios are competently proportioned but dull. Apart from Rodríguez's forceful portal the most striking feature of the chapel is its decorative dome which rises, without a drum stage, directly from its vaults. Ample light is supplied by a lantern and by dormer windows cut into the shell just above the level of the college's roof. Apparently the architect wished to keep the dome's profile relatively low so that from street level it would make only a minimal interruption of the powerful pinnacled horizontality of the top of the facade.

THREE HOUSES DESIGNED BY FRANCISCO ANTONIO GUERRERO Y TORRES

In 1769 Miguel de Berrio Zaldívar, an enormously wealthy resident of Mexico City and a knight of Santiago, decided to rebuild and modernize his family's mansion located at the corner of the present streets Isabel La Católica and Venustiano Carranza, two blocks southwest of the plaza, the Zócalo. The house had originally been erected in 1527 by a conquistador, Juan Cermeno. In early years it probably resembled a fortification like the structures facing the Zócalo portrayed in the plan in the Archive of the Indies of the 1560s. We have little detailed knowledge of the various modifications and repairs made in the house during the following half-century as it passed through the ownership of four different families. In 1683 it had been sold to Miguel de Berrio's grandfather, Captain Dámaso de Zaldívar, for 32,000 pesos and the assumption of liens on the property of Antonio de Medina y Picazo, who had acquired it at auction ten years earlier. Spanish-born Dámaso had come to Mexico to join his uncle José Retes, a silver merchant and operator of the government's apartado office which separated small amounts of gold from bars of silver. The Retes family owned cattle lands including the hacienda of San Diego de Jaral near the San Luis Potosí mines. Dámaso prospered and married a member of the Paz family of Zacatecas miners. He provided financial support for the reconquest of New Mexico and for the missionary efforts of the Jesuit Eusebio Kino in Sonora and present-day Arizona. An arrow wound received in a skirmish with marauding Indians on his hacienda led to his death. The house and a portion of his substantial holdings were inherited by his daughter Josefa who married a Basque immigrant, Andrés de Berrio y Diez Palacios. She and her husband bought lands that had been inherited by her brothers and consolidated the holdings in the great hacienda of Jaral which had eleven subordinate ranchos. They sold wool to the workshops of San Miguel and meat to mines in San Luis Potosí area and to the markets of the capital itself.

Miguel de Berrio succeeded to family leadership at the age of thirty-one when his father died in 1747. He had been a schoolmate of Francisco Javier de Gamboa at the College of San Ildefonso . Gamboa was the noted official and expert on mining who acted as Miguel's attorney. Miguel's marriage to Ana María de la Campa y Cos, who inherited the title of Condesa de San Mateo de Valparaíso in 1742, added to the family holdings vast areas of agricultural and grazing lands west of Zacatecas and farther north in the

area near Durango. The most important of the additions was the hacienda of San Mateo de Valparaíso, which had been created by one of the founders of Zacatecas, Diego de Ibarra, and which provided the condesa's title. Miguel held important offices in the royal treasury and drew public gratitude during the famine of 1750 by contributing supplies of meat and grain to the government warehouses in San Luis Potosí and Guanajuato. During the period the mansion was under construction, he formed a close relationship with Viceroy Antonio María de Bucareli who would support his application for a title in his own right. In 1774, King Charles III awarded him the title of Marqués de Jaral de Berrio, combining his family name with that of the hacienda of San Diego de Jaral.

The name of the architect chosen in 1769 by Miguel de Berrio to reconstruct the old mansion, first built 242 years earlier, is recorded in an inscription on one of the broad sweeping arches of the patio, Francisco Antonio Guerrero y Torres. The building is traditionally known from the title inscribed on another arch as the house of the Conde de San Mateo de Valparaíso. The structure is Guerrero y Torres's first recorded work. He had been born in 1727 into a family of prosperous landholders in Guadalupe not far from the shrine of the Virgin. A document records his supervising construction work in that town in 1752. Glenn Neil Patton, the discoverer of that document, also found one identifying him as superintendent of works of the College of San Ildefonso in the capital in 1761. He did not pass the examination of the Guild of Architects and become certified as a "maestro" of architecture until 1767. In the following year in his capacity as architect, he signed a report on damage to buildings in the city incurred by earthquake. When he was asked to redesign the Valparaíso house, Guerrero was forty-two years old and had had at least sixteen years of experience in supervising construction. Yet it was a remarkable commission for one so recently certified as maestro with no known accomplishments of independent architectural work.

Even more remarkable was Guerrero's achievement. Despite changes made in the exterior of the structure to suit the needs of the Banco Nacional after it purchased the house in 1882,

6.18 *House of the Conde de San Mateo de Valparaíso, Mexico City.*

much of the power of Guerrero's design remains. The initial impression is of a disciplined unity, powerfully articulated, strikingly different from the delicate multiplicity of the House of Tiles. Long, asymmetrically organized walls meet at the corner in a powerful tower that rises an additional story above the mass of the structure. The walls are of dark brown *tezontle*, and frames of the openings, of a contrasting cream-colored *chiluca*, unite the two stories, providing vertical accents which pass through the horizontal line of the intermediate cornice. Powerful finials are placed on the skyline above the intervening sections of *tezontle* wall in order to provide additional vertical accents.

The present verticality of the structure is greater than Guerrero intended. A mid-nineteenth-century print suggests something of its original appearance, showing the present very tall lower story divided into two stories of approximately equal height and separated by an additional cornice. The modern alterations have modified the balance of the structure, making it seem taller and barer below and lessening the importance of the upper story, which was originally taller than the others. Before the reconstruction of 1882-84, the openings for windows and doors of all three stories shared a type of enframement initiated in Mexico by the designers of the Ayuntamiento, completed in 1724, and the *Aduana*, completed in 1731 (Fig. 6.3). The sides of the

frames are continued vertically above the flattened arch crowning the openings until they reach the cornice so that they seem to constitute a pilaster order. This impression is enhanced by small scrolls placed at the junction with the cornice which suggest Ionic capitals. The uppermost story was given additional emphasis at its top by a frieze combining floral ornamentation, crowns, and shells; by a cornice moving forcefully in and out along the skyline to suggest the entablature blocks placed above the order of quasi-pilasters; and by out-jutting, gun-shaped waterspouts, which are supported by small atlantes sitting on lushly carved brackets.

The house's tower may reflect the fortified aspect of the original structure. Vertical emphasis is provided at its corner by facing the walls at their point of juncture with *chiluca* pilasters and uniting rippling ornamental mouldings in a climbing chainlike motif. On the upper story of the tower above the level of the main cornice, the ornamentation thickens and spreads to enclose the niche surrounding the statue of the Virgin traditional in Mexico City mansions. The niche is

6.19 *House of the Conde de San Mateo de Valparaíso, portal. See also Plate IX.*

crowned by a complex form incorporating two concave shells. At the sides are twisting columns that sustain, above their entablature blocks, huge layered scrolls.

The powerful thrust of the tower is set against the mass and ornamentation of the long walls. Although roughly equal in length and generally similar in the details of their ornamentation, the walls differ strikingly in formal composition. On the south side, the superposed openings in the two lower stories of the tower are framed by broad *chiluca* pilasters which extend up to the level of the main cornice. This strongly emphasized element is set against the other ten bays of the side with their more delicate *chiluca* enframements. An additional refinement is the complex spacing of the ten bays. Their separation from each other is emphasized by the placing of the ten finials above the cornice. Their combination into groupings of two bays each is suggested by the placing of the five powerful waterspouts. Their separation by varying widths of *tezontle* wall-surface between their *chiluca* enframements, possibly reflects the reuse of portions of the original structure and suggests another, more subtle pattern. The separations suggest a grouping of 2-1-3-2-2.

The west wall's eight bays are organized in two clearly defined elements. On the right, or tower, end is a composition of five bays centered on the portal, which is consequently placed well to the right of center of the wall. A second broad strip of *chiluca* pilaster like that at the corner of the building, and analogous to the strip which had been used on the south facade to isolate and emphasize the openings for windows in the tower, is used on the west to separate the major formal element of five widely spaced bays from three closely grouped bays at the left end of the wall. The closeness of their grouping creates a nearly solid mass of *chiluca* which provides an effective counterweight to the tower at the opposite end of the structure. Despite an inscription on an interior arch suggesting that this portion of the building was added by the Banco Nacional in the 1930s, these three bays were part of Guerrero's original design. We know this because of an eighteenth-century patio within this portion of the building;

also a mid-nineteenth-century print shows eight bays on the west side in a sharply foreshortened rendering.

Another concentration of light-colored *chiluca* is the ornamentation surrounding the portal and the French door placed directly above it. Both are enclosed by pilasters and surmounted by flattened arches with suggestions of dropped keystones at their center. The rather plain pilasters and the arches are framed by linear squiggles of curving ornamentation suggestive of the art of the pastry cook. Above the portal, seated winged cupids sustain the family arms placed in an oval frame pushed up into a range of triglyphs just below the gently undulating cornice.

Barely visible from street level on the south side are the octagonal lanterns of two small domes which break through the roof terrace and are covered with colored tiles arranged in shimmering patterns. The domes, the larger over the stair and the smaller over the chapel, nearly touch in a manner that anticipates the grouping of the three domes of the Chapel of the Well at Guadalupe, Guerrero's later masterwork.

6.20 *House of the Conde de San Mateo de Valparaíso, principal patio, with entrance to stair.*

153

6.21 House of the Conde de San Mateo de Valparaíso, stair. (Edificiones del Banco Nacional de México, photograph of Mark Mogliner).

The interior of the house has been altered for banking purposes, but several important features survive of this most remarkable domestic ensemble in Mexico (Fig. 6.20). The upper level of the principal patio is sustained, not by the usual arcade, but by one great arch per side. On the north is a conventional curved arch, slightly shallower than a semicircle. The other three arches are extraordinary, swinging across the patio's sides in great flattened arcs to intersect near the southeast and southwest corners before they drop downward and outward to the inner walls. Framing pilasters along these walls unite in tall ensembles, the doors below and, above, what were the windows of the mezzanine stage. Within the verticality of the pilasters, gently curving low arches frame both doors and the windows, and contribute to the pleasantly harmonious whole. A dominating decorative feature of the lower patio is the powerful layered Baroque portal set in the middle of the east wall, opposite the entrance to the building. Its forceful style is unlike the restrained handling of ensembles along the walls or the delicate decoration of the exterior portal. At the side, fluted Ionic pilasters, which are only slightly unconventional, support fragments of pediment and giant finials above. The intervening area surrounding the entrance opening is rusticated with surprisingly inventive patterning. The opening is surmounted by a tri-lobed arch springing powerfully out from the jambs and enclosing a strongly ribbed shell at its center. Directly above in the center of the broken pediment is a great swirling quasi-octagonal frame which discloses glimpses of the spiral stair beyond.

The upper level of the patio, with its flattened arches and decorative portal, is relatively tame, but the stair is unique in Mexico. It is a spiral of double flights reminiscent of several celebrated European stairs which were anticipated by studies of Francesco di Giorgio and began with Bramante's single spiral of the Vatican Belvedere. A famous double spiral at the center of the Chateau of Chambord may have reflected Leonardo's designs. Guerrero y Torres used Doric columns set on bases and crowned by diagonally sloping capitals to support the spiraling ramps which sustain the steps. There is an unobtrusive iron railing. The placing of the stair between the principal patio and the service area to the rear make possible a functional differentiation of traffic. The flight intended for use by the servants begins at the rear, and that intended for use by members of the family and their guests starts immediately behind the great baroque portal.

In 1775, three years after the completion of the Valparaíso house, Guerrero y Torres was asked by Colonel Juan Manuel Lorenzo Gutiérrez Altamirano de Velasco, eighth Conde de Santiago de Calimaya, to reconstruct substantially and to redecorate his family's house, two blocks southeast of Juan de Berrio's. The building, at the corner of the present streets of Piño Suárez and Salvador, now contains the Museum of Mexico City. The Altamirano family may have been slightly less wealthy than the de Berrios but it was more prominent, probably the most prominent in New Spain. Family prosperity originated in encomienda rights to Indian labor in the Valley of Toluca granted, some years after the conquest, to Juan Gutiérrez Altamirano, a relative of Cortés. The title, Conde de Santiago de Calimaya, was granted in 1616 to Fernando de Altamirano y Velasco, a grandson of the second Viceroy Velasco. Through intermarriage and inheritance the family acquired three other titles: Adelantado of the Philippines, originally granted in 1569 to Miguel López de Legazpi who initiated the conquest of the islands; Marqués de Salinas, originally granted in 1609 to the second Viceroy Velasco himself; and Marqués de Salvatierra, granted in 1708 to Juan Bautista Luyando, the founder of the town of Salvatierra in the Bajío near Morelia. By the late eighteenth century the family owned ten major agricultural estates, thirteen lesser haciendas, and a number of smaller ranchos.

The old house dating back to the sixteenth century—and incorporating as literal cornerstone the head of a feathered serpent with gaping mouth and powerful fangs probably taken from the Aztec sacred precinct—was in poor shape by the middle of the 1760s. Abortive efforts to initiate reconstruction were made in 1764 and in 1768. Seven years later Guerrero was given the task, which was substantially completed on June 5, 1779, the date recorded on a balcony at the street corner.

It is impossible to determine to what extent the old building constrained Guerrero's design, but certain features of the present structure reflect the earlier one. Glenn Patton detected evidence of blocked-in windows in the upper walls. The massive portal crowds the lower openings, flanking it in a way that suggests that they were retained from the older structure and that Guerrero's portal ornamentation required more space than the original arrangement (Figs. 6.23 and 6.24). The principal patio is located north of the middle of the structure. Consequently the portal, which is centered on it, is placed to the north, that is the left, of the midpoint of the western facade. Along the face of the building on the street to the south is an extra tier of rooms which lack direct communication with the front patio and which were probably originally used as shops.

The structure is lower than the Valparaíso house, giving the appearance of a solid block of dark red *tezontle*, relatively much less marked by *chiluca* ornamentation. There are two stories instead of the three of the original Valparaíso house. There is no tower at the corner nor a series of strong finials to add verticality. The horizontality of the strikingly plain upper cornice is broken

6.22 House of the Conde de Santiago de Calimaya, Mexico City.

only by the powerful ornamentation above the portal and by small scrolls placed above the waterspouts that are shaped as wheeled cannons. The modest additional verticality, once furnished by iron grillwork and stone figures of soldiers standing over the cannon and between the scrolls, was lost when they were removed in 1826 in response to republican prohibitions of symbols of nobility.

Two features of the exterior recall the formal organization of the Valparaíso structure. Broad pilasterlike strips provide a similar vertical accent at the corner of the building. These are emphatically bare of ornament. The south facade is organized in a fashion generally similar to that of the Valparaíso house. Eleven pairs of superposed openings are enclosed in pilaster frames, in this case, doors below and French doors above. The design also sets an isolated unit on the left, next to the corner, against the other ten units which are grouped together. In the Santiago house the frames are notably plainer and, more important, in the lower story the ten units on the right are separated by small pilaster-framed windows and in the story above by ample expanses of *tezontle* wall.

On the west side Guerrero faced the problem of creating a coherent facade incorporating a portal which had to be placed off-center because the interior patio was off-center. He devised a unified design, asymmetrical but balanced and giving a sense of symmetry to the casual viewer through inventive handling of the elements which he had used on the south facade. The portal, which is left of center, is strongly emphasized. At the right end of the wall, counterweight is provided by an emphasis on the corner similar to that which he had created on the south facade. Guerrero reinforced the broad strip of undecorated pilaster by placing the nearest pilaster-framed ensemble of superposed openings close against it. Only a thin strip of *tezontle* separates the elements. He also used two additional pilaster-framed ensembles on the right side of the facade. They are placed so that the areas of *tezontle* wall between them increase gradually and appreciably as they approach the portal. In addition he places three small windows, of varying width and enclosed in pilaster frames like those of the south facade, irregularly in the lower story. Guerrero placed one between the doors constituting the lower elements of the second and third pilaster-framed ensembles, and paired two near the portal, under the broadest expanse of plain *tezontle* wall. At the other end of the facade beyond the portal, he filled the lower wall with a network of alternating, closely aligned windows and doors, similar to the articulation used on the south facade. Only

6.23 House of the Conde de Santiago de Calimaya, portal.

two pilaster-framed French doors interrupt the wall above this network. Like those of the opposite side of the facade, they are spaced to satisfy the eye's sense of needed balance rather than a system of mathematically determined intervals.

The portal is much more prominent than that of the Valparaíso house, pushing powerfully out from the contained block of the structure. Pairs of engaged, fluted columns—Ionic below and Corinthian above—stand on substantial bases at the sides. They are framed by curving, linear ornamentation reminiscent of that surrounding the pilasters of the portal of the Valparaíso house. The most striking features of the ornamentation of the lower level, apart from the handsome Baroque doors, are decorations resembling claw-and-ball chair legs at the corners of the bases of the columns; a row of ten bosses suspended curiously from the cornice over the doorway; and, just below them, an extraordinary flat arch, composed of swinging curves and countercurves, deeply angled indentations, and, at its center, a dropped keystone. A smaller double door opening onto the balcony is at the center of the second level. A three-layered linear molding frames the door, becoming a flattened three-lobed arch over the opening. An outer, rectangular frame is constructed of powerful interwoven linear ornament suggestive of three flattened strands of chain that share their oval links. Pushing into this frame over the central arch is the suggestion of a large decorated keystone. At the attic level, above the cornice, the ornamentation spreads out and up into a three-arched, many-angled parapet. At the center cupids standing on scrolls brace a rectangular frame enclosing the family escutcheon. At the sides, above the paired columns, are powerful finials, suggestive of urns.

The house is large, probably the largest constructed in Mexico City, except for the palace of the viceroy and the house on the Zócalo owned by the descendants of Cortés. It has approximately forty-eight rooms at ground level and approximately thirty-nine on the principal floor above. Except for the range along the south flank, the plan is normal, with the rooms arranged around two patios: one for family living, entertaining, and ceremonial functions; and the other for the kitchen, services, and servants. The prin-

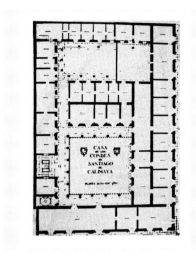

6.24 House of the Conde de Santiago de Calimaya, plan, from Glenn Neil Patton, "Francisco Antonio Guerrero y Torres and the Baroque Architecture of Mexico City in the Eighteenth Century," Pl. IV.

most interesting feature of the patio is a fountain of rococo flavor, which is placed at the base of the wall on the fourth side. A large shell form, bordered by floral ornament and small figures of cupids and mermen, creates a niche for a sprightly, double-tailed, guitar-playing mermaid of doleful countenance.

The stair, which has simple iron railings, is a modest version of the great Baroque stairs of

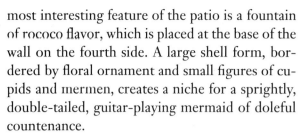

6.26 House of the Conde de Santiago de Calimaya, grand stair.

cipal suite of rooms is placed inside the west facade with no rational relationship to its formal organization. The "gran salon" occupies the area behind slightly more than half the facade, extending from the northern corner of the building past the portal.

The principal patio lacks the structural drama of the smaller one of the Valparaíso house. Superposed arcades of five bays of somewhat flattened arches face three of the sides. The

central Europe, containing seven flights and six landings. It is framed, bottom and top, by three great lobed arches which hover suspended over the openings, appearing to lack the intervening structural supports needed to sustain them. Curious doglike lions guard the bottom of the lower flight; they suggest some of the charming animal figures created by sixteenth-century Indian carvers who had only partially mastered the European idiom. At the first landing the single flight separates into two and spreads to the outer walls of the stairwell. There the flights turn back at right angles in reverse direction until they turn again to reunite just as they reach the principal floor above.

To the right of the top of the stairs, near

6.25 House of the Conde de Santiago de Calimaya, fountain in patio.

6.27 House of the Conde de Santiago de Calimaya, portal to chapel.

the northwest corner of the building and adjoining the grand salon, is a small chapel covered by an octagonal dome. The ornamentation of the entrance is the finest decorative ensemble Guerrero created for the house. Single-fluted Corinthian columns supported by high bases, which are decorated by standing figures of naked cupids, flank the opening. The columns and the portal are bordered by a diverse, yet harmonious combination of geometric and floral ornamentation. Above the door opening is a variety of curved and layered elements. The arch is intricately angled and three-lobed, with the central lobe larger and higher than the other two. The waving three-lobed pattern is repeated by two sturdy bands of vibrant floral ornamentation and, with increasing complexity, by two superposed cornices, the uppermost one strikingly layered. In contrast to the decorative complexity below, the attic level is flattened and powerfully simple. Broad scrolls at the sides curve up and then straighten, forming the outer sides of a rectangular frame which breaks open at the center of its upper margin to create an

oval. The star and crown of the knightly order of Carlos III now contained in the oval were added in 1816.

In early 1779 while the rebuilding of the Santiago house was still under way, Miguel de Berrio asked Guerrero y Torres to design a second house for his family. Construction probably began in the middle of June. The building is located on the present Calle de Madero, not far from the House of Tiles and a few blocks northwest of the earlier house. The grandest domestic structure of viceregal Mexico, it is known both as the Palace of Iturbide and, more properly, as the House of the Marqués de Jaral de Berrio. Miguel de Berrio had been granted that title five years before initiating construction of the house. The building would later be occupied as the official residence of General Agustín Iturbide, during his brief reign as emperor of Mexico between 1821 and 1823.

Miguel de Berrio's decision to construct a second great city house when he was sixty-three years old, and had less than a year to live, seems to have been the result of the marriage eleven years earlier of his only daughter, María Guadalupe Ana, or Mariana, to a handsome, artistically gifted Sicilian soldier and nobleman, Pedro de Moncada, Marqués de Villafont and son of the Prince of Larderia.

The Moncadas were originally Catalan, with a castle near Barcelona, but several generations earlier had moved to Palermo following the Spanish, or Aragonese, assumption of power in Sicily. Although Pedro had little personal wealth, his lineage, manner, and attainments made him a very desirable husband for the sixteen-year-old Mariana. The Berrios cushioned their daughter's fiscal future with a dowry of 200,000 pesos. Ultimately she could expect a great inheritance. A son and two daughters were born, the last as late as 1785, but Pedro made lavish use of the dowry and Mariana's developing troubles with her husband were known throughout their circle of acquaintances.

The difficulties of life under one roof, even one as broad as that of the Valparaíso House, seem to have been a factor in Miguel's decision to construct for himself and his wife a new house and to turn the old one over to Mariana and her husband. A legend passed down in the family concerning the circumstances of the construction of the second house attributes the decision to the wish of the parents to put funds, approximately 100,000 pesos, into real estate which could be secured through an entail from their free-spending son-in-law. We know that Pedro's squandering of the 200,000 dowry infuriated the parents, and that, after Miguel's death, Pedro took the countess to court and successfully contested a *mayorazgo* that excluded his wife from inheritance and named his son as heir. Ultimately the countess took her grandchildren to the country to live at the Hacienda de Jaral, leaving her daughter in the city with her husband. In 1792, after six years of delaying action by Pedro, Mariana was granted a legal separation and her husband returned to Sicily.

We have no knowledge of the influence or the wishes and tastes of Miguel de Berrio or his wife Ana María upon the design of the house. Family legends have attributed aspects of the design to Pedro Moncada's knowledge of palatial residences in Palermo, but he was in Sicily when the building was begun. Heinrich Berlin discovered documents recording the effort of Agustín Durán, the foreman in charge of construction, to secure additional wages because of increased responsibilities taken on after Guerrero y Torres was discharged as architect as a result of differences with the marqués. The foreman was turned down with the marqués's express statement that Durán made no special contribution beyond that of any other foreman because he simply followed the plans of Guerrero. The house was still under construction when Miguel de Berrio's will was settled in 1782. At that time 78,852 pesos had been expended, and it was estimated that an additional 28,220 would be needed for completion, which occurred by 1784. We know that in designing the Jaral house, contrary to his situation in the Valparaíso and Santiago houses, Guerrero was not constrained by pre-existing construction. Only some foundations, and possibly some internal walls of an earlier dwelling, were retained.

The house is tall, incorporating a mezzanine within the considerable height of its first story and, unlike other residences in the city, includes a full third story. Once again, the build-

ing materials are those generally favored in eighteenth-century Mexico City: *tezontle*, in this case gray-pink in color, for the walls; and cream-colored *chiluca* for the ornamentation. The house, which is located in the interior of the block rather than on a corner, is symmetrical, centered on a giant portal. The symmetry does not entail simplicity. Guerrero's interweaving of decorative motifs produced an intricacy greater than his asymmetrical designs for the Valparaíso and Santiago houses. A feature of the design, which links it to his earlier houses which had incorporated

6.28 House of the Marqués de Jaral de Berrio, Mexico City.

construction of earlier centuries, is a marked evocation of the fortified houses of the conquistadors. A more remote antecedent, as Diego Angulo suggested, is Rodrigo Gil de Hontañón's sixteenth-century Monterrey Palace in Salamanca.

The formal organization of the facade involves a complex interpenetration of vertical and horizontal elements. There are at least three major and four lesser vertical accents and at least three major and two lesser horizontal accents. At the ends of the tall lower story, pairs of vigorously ornamental pilasters lift in a vertical thrust that is carried up through the cornice line by other pilasters and finials in the stories above to define tower-like elements. The thrust of a similar pair of giant pilasters flanking the portal is also carried through the upper stories, with a nearly comparable vertical emphasis, by sharp-edged pilasters and by half-columns and atlante figures. (Fig. 6.30). In between these expressive elements, the grouping of openings within superposed frames provide lesser vertical accents. The cornices and balconies which define the upper floor levels and the diverse features which accent the skyline create the principal horizontal accents.

flanked by bays of varying width containing small sculptured panels of rococo design which are framed by large rectangles of geometric ornamentation. The rhythm of the pilaster frames enclosing the windows is complicated, if not disrupted, by the placing of the more strongly emphasized pilasters on high bases, which define the tower motifs at the ends of the floor and enclose the large French door at its center.

The third story contains a central arcade of five flattened arches, the middle one broader than the others. Fluted Corinthian half-columns ornamenting their sustaining piers support atlante figures, which uphold gargoyle waterspouts

6.29 *House of the Marqués de Jaral de Berrio. Lithograph of Casimiro Castro from* México y sus alrededores.

6.30 *House of the Marqués de Jaral de Berrio, center of facade.*

The balconies defining the mezzanine level and, below them, the strongly marked line of the powerfully ornamented upper frames of the openings along the sidewalk create lesser horizontals.

Guerrero created a coherent facade which incorporates remarkable diversity. He treats all three floors differently. The principal middle floor seems the most conventional with eleven bays and five symmetrically placed windows or French doors enclosed by pilaster frames similar to those used on the Valparaíso and Santiago houses. But the straightforward arrangement of the fenestration is placed within a total decorative pattern that is not simple. The windows are

160

in the form of monster fish. At the ends of the story, flanking the arcade, are two bays suggesting the top stages of fortified towers. The solidity of these bays contrasts with the graceful openness of the arcade. The expansion of the tower motif in this story, from the single bay defined in the stories below into two bays, is visually disconcerting, creating an uneasiness regarding the support of the added bay. The skyline's ornamentation is varied, with finials and irregularly ruffled moldings above the tower bays, and arcs swinging broadly from finial to finial in the central section, echoing in reverse the curves of the arcade below.

The lowest story has heroic scale and

6.31 House of the Marqués de Jaral de Berrio, facade, lower left side. See also Plate X.

considerable complication. It constitutes half the building's total height and suggests both a single great story by the giant pilasters at its center and ends, and two stories of modest dimensions by the tightly composed intervening elements. The giant order and the two-story elements are linked together by related decoration in the area over the portal and in the panels under the mezzanine windows. Surmounting the low arch of the portal is a closely packed, T-shaped area of grotesque ornamentation with heavily muscled figures grasping powerful clubs on both sides, standing above large softly rolled scrolls. Echoing this design is the broader, looser ornamentation of the rectangles under the mezzanine windows. There Guerrero wittily uses cupids to replace the substantial athletic figures, and dynamic, springlike scrolls to replace the soft toothpastelike ones.

The delicacy of the sculptural ornamentation of the building is unsurpassed in Mexico. The execution of Guerrero's complex interplay of contrasting moldings is more refined than in his other structures. Particularly striking are the two-tailed mermaids placed in the midst of the grotesque ornamentation of the six giant pilasters of the lower story, and the rococo carving of the small figurative plaques set in the middle of the unadorned bays of *tezontle* wall, at the sides of the main portal and between the windows of the central section of the principal story above.

In 1850 the building was converted into a hotel. A few years later, renamed the Hotel Iturbide, it had 170 rooms and was for decades the most imposing hostelry in the city. Substantial modifications were made for its use as a hotel and for its subsequent use as a residence and as a bank building. No evidence remains of the structure's original interior arrangement and appearance except for the principal patio. Recent restoration by Ricardo Legorreta allows us to fully comprehend Guerrero's handling of this area, the most architecturally significant of the interior spaces.

In surprising contrast to the complexity of the outside face of the building, the patio appears simple. One passes through the strong giant order of the portal and then becomes aware of a graceful arcade (Fig. 6.32) of semicircular arches supported by tall, delicate columns standing on ornamented bases of full human height. Five arches

6.32 House of the Marqués de Jaral de Berrio, patio.

One feature of the patio's design demonstrates Guerrero's delight in expressive contrast, his love of setting delicacy against strength. This characteristic of his decorative sensibility is usually shown on flat surfaces, in areas such as portals where delicate, curving, linear moldings frequently frame powerful pilasters or columns. In the patio the contrast is of one plane set against another. The visitor sees the graceful, tall arcade against a background of powerful rectangular forms, the frames of the doors and windows of the inner wall behind it. The wide frames resemble the forceful decorative ensembles of the outer facade and constitute an expressive foil to the slim verticals of the arcade's columns.

The treatment of the portal in the north wall leading back into the passage to the street provides another variation of Guerrero's decorative vocabulary. A tall, semicircular arch is framed by heavy geometric moldings similar to the rectangular framing of the openings of the opposite wall of the patio and of the exterior facade. This tall frame provides a fitting transition to the exterior. It shares the height and semicircular form of the tall arches of the interior patio and is decorated with the forceful geometric ornamentation of the exterior.

swing across the south side of the patio, opposite the entrance, with a straightforward stair of double flights in the southeast corner. Four arches line the shorter east and west sides and five, again, line the north side inside the entrance. On the upper level, corresponding with the principal story of the facade, there are flattened arches on the south side and windows set in pilaster frames on the other three sides.

VII
Baroque Religious Architecture II

The churches constructed in the middle decades of the eighteenth century have been particularly admired by modern Mexican scholars concerned with their nation's colonial past and by foreign travelers with an interest in architecture. The work that first acquainted North Americans with Mexican buildings, Sylvester Baxter's *Spanish Colonial Architecture in Mexico of 1901*, devoted most of its excellent photographs by Henry Greenwood to eighteenth-century Baroque churches. In his summary of his life's work, *Colonial Art in Mexico*, the leader of the Mexican effort to conserve the colonial artistic heritage, Manuel Toussaint, entitled the chapter devoted to these churches simply "The Great Religious Architecture." Sacheverell Sitwell included enthusiastic descriptions of the churches of Taxco, Valenciana, Tepotzotlán, and Ocotlán in his study of *Spanish Baroque Art*, stating that Taxco was "better than anything in Spain, with the exception of the Cathedral of Santiago de Compostela," and, with marked hyperbole, that all four churches "have a supremacy that no other buildings can challenge" (see Fig. 7.18).

Despite the celebrity of these churches and the growth of professionalism among Mexican architects, documented information regarding these and other important eighteenth-century churches is scanty. Thirty years ago Margaret Collier suggested the title "The Case of the Missing Architect" in discussing several of the finest church facades in Mexico City. In recent decades Efraín Castro Morales, Guillermo Tovar de Teresa, and others have worked diligently to identify the names of the designers of many important structures, but the documentation remains tantalizingly limited and attribution regarding several significant structures must of necessity be made on the basis of stylistic affinities alone and is therefore uncertain and frequently disputed.

The practice of architecture had been officially recognized when the Guild of Masons and Architects was established in 1599 in order to improve building practices and to ensure the prosperity of the master builders who passed the guild's examinations. The guild's regulations apparently did not limit the architectural activities of members of religious orders and seem to have had only limited success in controlling secular construction. Architectural writing in Mexico probably began with the treatise written by the Carmelite friar Andrés de San Miguel, which survived in manuscript from the 1630s or early 1640s and has been edited by Eduardo Báez Macías.

The author had earlier designed several establishments for his order, including one in the capital, a college in San Angel nearby, and the original church and convento in the Desert of the Lions, a place of solitude in the ridge of mountains west of the Valley of Mexico. Recently a second architectural manuscript, anonymous and of the late colonial period, has been discovered and has been edited by Mardith E. Schuetz. This is a naive work, less coherent and less learned than that of Fray Andrés. Yet it provides considerable information about the functioning of the architects' guild and about other matters ranging from architects and construction workers' salaries to the ideal proportions for the planning of churches and the various rooms of houses.

During the eighteenth century until the foundation of the Royal Academy of San Carlos in 1785, the most prestigious architectural position in New Spain was maestro mayor of the Cathedral of Mexico. Frequently the office also included responsibility for the royal palace as well. In a few instances the title was enlarged to maestro mayor of New Spain. That was exemplified in the appointment of the first incumbent, Claudio de Arciniega, who was named *Maestro Mayor de las obras de Cantería de la Nueva España* by Viceroy Luis de Velasco I in 1559. In the seventeenth century the normal salary was five hundred pesos a year, and in the eighteenth it had been increased to six hundred pesos until suspension of work on the cathedral in the late 1750s. A partial list of the maestros mayores subsequent to Claudio de Arciniega includes: Diego de Aguilera (1593–c. 1601?), Andrés de Concha (1601?–12?), Alonso Pérez de Castañeda (1612?–14?), Alonso Martínez López (1614?–26), Juan Gómez de Trasmonte (c. 1632–47?), Juan Serrano (1651–52 or 1653), Melchor Pérez de Soto (c. 1653–55?), Luis Gómez de Trasmonte (1656–84), Cristóbal de Medina Vargas Machuca (1686–99), Felipe de Roa (1699–1709), Francisco Antonio de Roa (1709–20?), Pedro de Arrieta (1720–38), Luis Díez Navarro (1739–42), Miguel Espinosa de los Monteros (1743–c. 60), Lorenzo Rodríguez (c. 1760–74?), Isidoro Vicente de Balbás (1772–?) and Francisco Antonio Guerrero y Torres (1774?–92). José Damián Ortiz de Castro was appointed maestro mayor of the cathedral in 1786 or 1787, and Ignacio Castera became maestro mayor of the palace after the death of Guerrero y Torres.

Another position, that of maestro mayor of the city, involved responsibility for inspecting the Desagüe, projects on public lands, bridges, and ditches for irrigation. The salary ranged from sixty to three hundred pesos in the sixteenth century and sometimes reached five hundred subsequently. Architectural appointments were also made by institutions such as the Inquisition and the Mint and by the convents of nuns. Annual salaries for convent architects averaged approximately one hundred pesos.

Some of these positions might be held concurrently. Lorenzo Rodríguez was appointed architect to the Inquisition within a few years of his appointment as maestro mayor of the cathedral and the royal palace. The author of the late colonial manuscript states that the guild never admitted more than eight maestros of architecture at one time and never allowed their number to drop below four so that architects were sufficient for the professional work available and competition was limited. There were, however, nine certified architects in 1746.

The Guild of Masons and Architects, which continued to exist, despite the competing authority of the new Neo-Classical Academy of San Carlos, until 1813, was an anachronistic remnant of medieval social organization surviving in an era increasingly shaped by capitalism. All guilds had a cofradía, a religious mutual aid society. The Guild of Masons had two; those who worked on the cathedral belonged to the cofradía of the Holy Cross which held its services in the Chapel of the Virgin of Solitude in the cathedral; and the other workers belonged to the cofradía of the Holy Angel which met in a chapel in the Church of Santo Domingo and which was patronized by Our Lady of Delights and by the Archangel Gabriel. The cofradías aided impoverished and sick associates and buried the dead. Guild members marched in religious processions clad in their particular colors. The cofradía of the Holy Cross carried both a representation of the Archangel Gabriel and instruments of the crucifixion, the crown of thorns and the lashes. In theory the guild was obligated to march as a unit to war.

In 1735 six architects, including the Pedro de Arrieta and Miguel Custodio Durán, and possibly constituting the entire roster of current maestros of the guild, drew up for approval of the city government a new set of ordinances which prescribed a six-year apprenticeship for journeymen and a series of examinations for the mastership. A written examination was required in cut-stone construction, in rubble-masonry construction, or in drafting. Candidates had to demonstrate practical and theoretical knowledge of drafting plans and elevations of buildings to scale, and of the ability to compute volumes. These examinations were conducted in the presence of the secretary of the city government by two overseers who were elected annually from among the maestros.

Modifications and additions to the ordinances were proposed eleven years later by nine architects, including Miguel Custodio Durán, again, and Lorenzo Rodríguez, the current overseers of the guild; Miguel Espinosa de los Monteros, maestro mayor of the cathedral and the royal palace; José Eduardo de Herrera, maestro of works of the Inquisition; Manuel Alvarez, maestro mayor of the city; and Custodio Durán's nephew, Ildefonso de Iniesta Bejarano y Durán. Most of the proposals related to the internal organization and operations of the guild, but two are of more general interest. One addition made explicit the admission, with minor limitations, of Indians to the examination for the rank of maestro and the exclusion of those of mixed blood. Representative of the growing conception in the mid-eighteenth century of the design of buildings as a fine art and the growing concern of their designers for professional prestige was a provision for changing, after a century and a half, the name of the ordinances from *Albañilería* (Masonry), to *Arquitectura* (Architecture).

We know that favoritism toward family members was shown in awarding apprenticeships. The late colonial manuscript informs us that the ordinances were successfully challenged in a suit brought by an auditor of the cathedral, Diego Dávila. The audiencia decreed that subsequent candidates would not be required to serve an apprenticeship. At the end of the colonial period the written portion of the examination centered on the mathematics of architecture, but candidates were still asked to demonstrate practical competence by constructing a personally designed pilaster or length of cornice.

The manuscript describes a secondary level of examination, commonly called the black

to distinguish it from the white, or maestro's, examination. Candidates for certification at the lower level were not expected to have mathematical knowledge or even the ability to read and write. They were examined in practical matters only and were authorized to build adobe structures but not to make fiscal calculations or complex plans. With the exception of the provision requiring an apprenticeship, the ordinances as modified in 1746 remained in force until the guild was abolished.

Particular ordinances were devoted to building standards concerning the correct proportion of lime for mortar, the minimum dimensions for structural beams and planks, and the proper types and dimensions of cut stones. The manuscript distinguishes two qualities of *tezontle* stone for wall construction (hard and soft), and two qualities of lighter stone for cutting for ornamental work (the harder *chiluca* and the softer *cantería*).

Several of the ordinances attempted to enforce a monopoly for the maestros of architecture. Ordinary individuals and the mayordomos of religious establishments were prohibited from building on their own, and stonecutters, masons, and carpenters were specifically warned against supervising construction projects while declaring that they were merely making repairs. Craftsmen were allowed to initiate on their own only minor jobs such as whitewashing walls or patching leaks. Members were required to record their professional activities with the guild, and they were prohibited from accepting any commission until it was registered.

It is unlikely that the modifications of the ordinances proposed in 1735 and 1746 made them more successful in ensuring the standards of the guild or the monopoly of its maestros. Yet the specificity of the regulations suggests the impressive growth of professionalism that underlies the achievements of Mexican architecture of the eighteenth century. Comparable professionalism was not initiated in the United States until after the arrival from England of Benjamin H. Latrobe in 1796.

The most prominent style that flourished in Mexico between mid-century and the establishment of the Academy of San Carlos in 1785 is widely called churrigueresque after a family of artists of Catalan birth who were prominent in Castile for some decades before and after 1700. The Churrigueras were generally conservative designers, but one member of the family, José Benito, pioneered in using the principal decorative motif of the style, the *estípite*, and the name has a fine rolling sound which has appealed to historians of architecture. Another term favored by several Mexican writers, *Ultra Baroque*, creates confusion if Mexican buildings are placed, as they deserve, in the context of the international Baroque style. For the major works of later Baroque religious architecture in Mexico, whatever term is used to describe them, are remarkable, rivaled in the Americas only by the churches of the great crippled mulatto artist of Brazil, Aleijadinho, and surpassed only by the supreme structures of the European Baroque.

The adaption of the *estípite*-decorated retablo to the adornment of church facades, which initiated the principal high Baroque style in Mexico, is an American development without substantial European precedent. Yet the creators of the style were two immigrants from Spain, Jerónimo de Balbás and Lorenzo Rodríguez. After nearly forty years of intermittent effort by the city government and the archbishops to procure a great retablo for the Chapel of the Kings, the compartment at the end of the nave of the Cathedral of Mexico, Balbás arrived from Spain in 1718, possibly dispatched as a result of action of King Philip V himself. Born in Zamora and resident for three years in Madrid, Balbás had moved to Andalusia. There he had designed a celebrated retablo for the *sagrario* of the Cathedral of Seville in 1706 in which he had introduced to that city the use of the *estípite*. This form was to be widely used in the architectural ornamentation of Andalusia and was to be even more pervasive in Mexico.

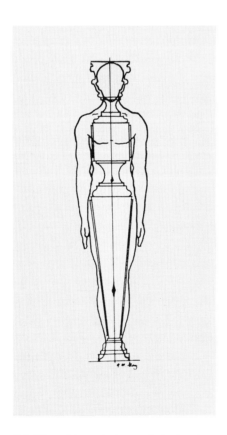

7.1 *The estípite as the human body, drawing of Manuel González Galván, from Francisco de la Maza,* El churrigueresco en la ciudad de México, *p. 9.*

7.2 *Cathedral of Mexico, Retablo de los Reyes.*

The *estípite* is a Mannerist variant of the classical column consisting of a variety of angular, faceted elements; it suggests in its lower sections an upside-down obelisk and in its entirety an abstract version of an atlante or caryatid figure, as it ascends from its feet at the base through swelling legs, tight waist, broadened shoulders, and narrow neck, to its substantial head, or capital.

The Retablo de los Reyes, designed by Balbás immediately after his sudden appearance in Mexico but not dedicated until 1737, contains at its center two large paintings by Juan Rodríguez Juarez. These paintings, *The Adoration of the Kings and The Assumption of the Virgin*, portray respectively the sacred events recalled in the titles of the chapel and of the cathedral. It is dominated by four glittering, tall *estípites* like the retablo designed by Balbás in the *sagrario* of the Cathedral of Seville which was demolished in 1824. Although the retablo is placed in an apselike chapel covered by a semicircular half-dome—a space similar to the concave facades of several prominent eighteenth-century Mexican churches such as Miguel Custodio Durán's San Juan de Dios—the impression made on the viewer is strikingly different. Rather than expressing the space-molding properties of curving walls, the retablo destroys them. The sense of firm enclosing surface in the half-dome at the top is disrupted by ascending patterns of pointed riblike frames. At the lower level, as the eye sweeps across the main portion of the retablo from corner *estípite* to corner estípite, no sense of curving wall remains. Space-moulding surface has been shattered into a myriad of faceted forms, glittering projections, and shadowed recessions. The elements of the traditional classical entablature, supported by columns and containing sculptural figures set in niches, are still present but they are virtually unrecognizable. Instead, as Elizabeth Wilder Weismann has written, the whole chapel has been transformed into an immeasurable golden cave. All rational sense of solid, weight-supporting classical order and entablature has disappeared,

swept away by soaring three-story columns that burst like skyrockets before our eyes, broken into polyphonic rhythms, dissolved in dynamic shadow. Everything is in movement, in flight. Cherubs hover suspended, angels flutter, stirring the garments of the royal saints by the wind from their wings. The very walls disintegrate, and heaven opens up . . . to receive the worshiper.[1]

Balbás remained in Mexico until his death in 1748, continuing for many years to work for the cathedral. Among his assignments was in 1725 or 1726 to travel to Acapulco to meet the Manila galleon to inspect and supervise the transportation of the choir screen. The screen had been manufactured to Mexican design in Macao, the Portuguese enclave off the coast of south China. He then directed the trimming of the screen so that it would fit properly between the piers of the nave of the cathedral. The soaring, pyramidal, *estípite*-covered tabernacle which he designed to stand farther along the nave was demolished in the mid-nineteenth century. It is visible in the background of a painting of the coronation of Agustín Iturbide as emperor of Mexico. The Retablo del Perdón, which faces visitors entering the cathedral and which has been carefully reconstructed since the fire that consumed much of the choir in 1967, is attributed traditionally to Balbás. He also worked for the Franciscans, designing three-sided altarpieces for the Chapel of Zuleta of the Church of San Francisco, which was demolished in the nineteenth century, and the principal retablo for their church of the Third Order, which was demolished also.

In the 1730s he was engaged in full-scale architectural design, although no works of his are known to survive. He was appointed architect for the church of the missionary college of San Fernando west of the Alameda but was dismissed for being too extravagant in construction. Nothing of the existing church suggests his hand. A description of his entry in the competition of 1733 for a new building for the *Casa de Moneda*, or Mint, is of great interest. In the words of another architect the design was "beautiful but decorated in such a strange manner that it would require a great expenditure to construct, and when completed it would resemble an altarpiece in a church more than the facade of a house." To the architect it seemed "more suited for carving [in wood] than for stone sculpture."[2] Luis Díez Navarro won

7.3 Church of the Compañía, Guanajuato, facade.

facade of the cathedral with its suggestions of waving movement in the concavity of its buttresses. A few years later, while still in his twenties, he served as overseer of construction of the cathedral of Cadiz, Acero's more ambitious exercise in the design of angled and curving surfaces. We are ignorant of the reason for Rodríguez's departure for America after beginning a promising architectural career in Spain. It may have come some time after Acero was replaced in Cadiz by another architect from Gaudix, the undistinguished Torcuato Cayón. By 1731 Rodríguez was in Mexico working, despite his Spanish experience, as master carpenter in the mint. He may have done some work in collaboration with Balbás. Only after nine years of employment in the mint did he take and pass the maestro's examination in architecture in 1740. Two years later he was involved in a heated dispute with one of his examiners, Miguel Custodio Durán, the senior architect of the city and son of another Mexican architect, José Durán. Custodio Durán regarded Rodríguez as a brash Spanish upstart, a know-it-all who was insufficiently respectful of the established architects and practices of Mexico. His extended attack on Rodríguez's character and professional failings concluded, after some thirty pages of enumerating offenses, with the statement that the young Spaniard was a "vino de otra clima," a vine from another continent, a foreigner alien to Mexican ways.

Both Balbás and Rodríguez, the principal creators of the *estípite* style in Mexico, were favored by influential patrons within the cathedral hierarchy, but they suffered from substantial native resistance. Despite his celebrated arrival in the city as the designated designer of the long anticipated retablo for the Chapel of the Kings, Balbás endured increasing professional disappointment, losing a major competition to a native-born architect and being replaced as architect of an important church. Rodríguez ultimately became the most influential of mid-century architects. Yet he had to wait nine years to be admitted as an architect of the guild, and another nine before construction began upon his first major work. Native Mexican suspicion of immigrant Spaniards and their foreign ideas had a substantial effect upon the decline of Balbás's career and the delay of

the competition; he who would later design the now demolished oval Church of Santa Brígida. Balbás's unbuilt design anticipated the type of retablo facade prevalent in Mexico City and other architecturally sophisticated areas after mid-century, embodied first in the facades of the Jesuit church in Guanajuato of Felipe de Ureña and of the *sagrario* of the cathedral which Lorenzo Rodríguez erected between 1749 and 1768 (Figs. 7.23 and 7.24). Rodríguez worked as master carpenter in the Mint between 1731 and 1740. He would have been alert to the revolutionary implications of Balbás's idea of ornamenting a facade with the intricacy appropriate to wood carving so that it resembled an altarpiece. But the retablo designs of Rodríguez, Ureña, and their contemporaries were used entirely for churches. No one followed Balbás in using a retablo ornamentation for a secular structure.

The careers in Mexico of both Balbás and Rodríguez illuminate the resistance of the conservative creole architectural establishment to innovations from Europe. Rodríguez had been born about 1704 in Gaudix, a city in Andalusia northeast of Granada, the son of a man who served as architect of the local bishopric. During the years after his tenth birthday, he had observed the beginning of construction of Vicente Acero's new nearly eighteen years before Rodríguez's really began.

The eighteenth-century adoption of the *estípite* as a substitute for the classical column in supporting a decorative architectural entablature seems to have begun in Spain in a temporary monument designed in 1689 by José Benito de Churriguera for the funeral of Queen María Luisa de Orleans. Early Andalusian examples include Balbás's retablo for the *sagrario* of the cathedral of Seville and the retablo of Santiago designed by Francisco Hurtado for the cathedral of Granada, both before 1710. The latter work also anticipated the flatness characteristic of much Mexican architectural ornamentation. The designers of these works seem to have discovered the *estípite* in architectural engravings which had been published in Flanders in the sixteenth century by Vredeman de Vries and Wendel Detterlin.

The greatest retablo designers of the succeeding generations in Andalusia, Pedro Duque Cornejo (1678–1757) and Cayetano da Costa (1711–80), created altarpieces more powerfully ordered and more imaginatively decorative than any in Mexico. But in Spain the *estípite* retablo remained a spectacular piece of interior ornamentation, of church furniture. The great Mexican innovation of Felipe de Ureña in the Jesuit church in Guanajuato and of Lorenzo Rodríguez in the *sagrario* of the Cathedral of Mexico, perhaps anticipated by Jerónimo de Balbás's design for the *Casa de Moneda*, was to move the *estípite* retablo to the exterior. In churches the decoration of the stone facade would provide the worshipper with an anticipatory suggestion of the ornamentation within, especially of the great golden retablo above the principal altar which would come into view once the portal was passed.

Initially the *estípites* were used as replacements for columns in entablatures, arranged in a generally classical manner as the earlier Baroque generation had substituted twisting, vine-encrusted, Salomonic columns for conventional classical ones. The horizontal line of the entablature might be altered and made more dynamic by indentations or curves, but it remained clearly identifiable as an entablature. The gilded *estípites* might enliven the composition with the sparkling edges of their faceted forms but all the elements followed the measured order of the post-and-lintel construction of the classical entablature. The verticals of the *estípites* rose to capitals and entablature blocks to support the horizontals of real or implied cornices. At regular intervals between the *estípites* were statues of saints placed in niches much as they were in a retablo facade such as that of early seventeenth-century Yanhuitlán. In *Mexico in Sculpture* Elizabeth Wilder Weismann indicated that mid-eighteenth-century writers saw clearly the classical pattern in contemporary retablos and used descriptive language that emphasized the familiar underlying structure rather than the departures from it. A work of great complexity that would strike an inexperienced twentieth-century observer as a mass of glittering incoherence would be described by a contemporary simply as designed "in the Composite Order." Traditional elements such as friezes, capitals, and bases were described as though they were as easily recognizable as the corresponding parts of a Renaissance entablature. Eighteenth-century writers were keenly aware of the particular esthetic qualities of the retablos. Weismann writes that their "very vocabulary vibrates with words like *crespo y delicado, desplantadas al aire, brillante, tremuloso.*"[3]

Gradually the architectonic character of the *estípite* retablo and of the *estípite* facade weakened. From the beginning the substitution of the *estípite* for the column had substantially lessened the weight-bearing appearance of the classical entablature. Later the crisp vertical and horizontal elements emphatically present in Rodríguez's *sagrario* portals (Fig. 7.27) were softened by increasing decorative complexity. An important development was the growing emphasis given to pilasterlike forms enclosing statue-containing niches. These forms, called niche pilasters by Joseph A. Baird, the leading student of Mexican eighteenth-century retablo design, had in the *sagrario* portals constituted an alternative order behind the *estípites*, filling the spaces between them. Increasingly they were broadened, brought forward to prominence, and decorated with motifs of greater complexity (Fig. 7.26).

In both the gilded interior retablos and the exterior facades, *estípites* were frequently reduced to ornamental accessories framing the niche pilasters but conveying little sense of architectonic vigor. In addition to the growth to swelling dominance of the niche pilaster, there came a general loosening of overall design most apparent in the treatment of the upper level of retablos and facades. The *sagrario* portals had consisted of two clearly defined stories enclosed within a firmly defined rectangular frame. After 1765 many major designs loosened, abandoning Rodríguez's tautness. A second story treated similarly to the first became rare. Above the entablature line decorative arrangements frequently narrowed as they rose, thinning as they spread to the edges of the design. Instead of the elements of the classi-

7.5 *San Francisco, Mexico City, facade of the Balvanera Chapel.*

7.4 *San Francisco, Mexico City, facade of the Balvanera Chapel before iconoclastic stripping by North American Protestants, photograph c. 1855, from Guillermo Tovar de Teresa,* La ciudad de los palacios, *Tomo II, p. 24.*

cal entablature, the principal ornamental motifs were curving and angling moldings, scrolls, statues placed so as to create diagonal, emphasis and broad, niche-containing finials. The facade of the Balvanera chapel of the convent church of San Francisco in Mexico City is the most impressive of such designs. An extraordinary provincial example in the remote north is the facade of the mission Church of San José in San Antonio. Swaying statues standing at their ease on pedestals assume the role filled traditionally in classical architectural arrangements by sturdy, load-bearing columns.

Ultimately designers of interior retablos, in Querétaro, Salamanca, San Miguel Allende, and elsewhere, began to abandon the form of

7.6 *San José Mission, San Antonio, facade.*

the architectural entablature entirely, substituting freer and flatter patterns of organization. Against shining gilded backgrounds, frequently suggestive of basketry work or textiles, a few large elements were disposed, most often statues in glazed niches flanked by paintings in oval frames or by statues in elaborate gilded settings. Frequently

Manrique suggested that Guerrero y Torres was but one of a number of architects intent on saving the Mexican Baroque from the tendency toward formal dissolution and incoherence implicit in the *estípite* style. Manrique dated the beginnings of this final phase of the Baroque to the years between 1770 and 1775, making it contemporary

7.7 *Church of San Agustín, Salamanca, retablo of the nave.*

7.8 *Church of San Agustín, Salamanca, transept retablo of San José.*

figures at the top were silhouetted against light coming from an outer window. Decorative motifs included crowns and theatrical curtains, which were prominent in retablos of the Spaniards Hurtado and Duque Cornejo, and scrolls, shells, and fronds, frequent in the decorative patterns of the rococo.

Architectural historians have long recognized that the last great architect of the Mexican Baroque, Francisco Antonio Guerrero y Torres, rejected the flatness, disintegration of forms, and general looseness of design favored by his contemporaries and developed an architectonic style involving a replacement of the *estípite* by the firmly rounded column. Two decades ago in an article in *Historia Mexicana* in 1971, Jorge Alberto

7.9 *Convento Church of Santa Rosa, Querétaro, screen of nuns' choir.*

7.10 Cathedral, formerly Parish Church, of San José, Tlaxcala, facade.

the mature Baroque were retained. The *interestípite*, or niche pilaster, was frequently used in combination with classical columns, and the decorative vocabulary continued to draw from the rococo. The moving molding, *la moldura movil*, assumed new importance, undulating in unexpected ways, zigzagging here and slithering like a serpent there. Perhaps the most important characteristic of this architectonic Baroque, called by Manrique *New Style Baroque*, was its interest in space-shaping forms. Guerrero y Torres's late work, the Chapel of the Well, displays many of these elements; its interplay of curving walls, tiled parapets and domes, and the shifting forms and directions of its interior spaces make it a structure unparalleled in Hispanic architecture.

JOSÉ DE LA BORDA AND THE PARISH CHURCH OF SANTA PRISCA AND SAN SEBASTIÁN IN TAXCO

with the culmination of the *estípite* style. He related a number of facades ornamented with expressively articulated, decorated columns to Guerrero y Torres's ecclesiastical designs, the Chapel of the Well at Guadalupe and the Church of the Enseñanza in Mexico City (Fig. 7.36). Among those mentioned were San Lorenzo in the Capital, the parish church (now the Cathedral) in Tlaxcala, San Felipe Neri (now the cathedral) of Querétaro, and the awkwardly powerful columnar facade of the Guadalupe church in San Luis Potosí. Manrique also described two facades notable for their use of twisting Salomonic columns, the parish churches of Santiago Tianguistenco (Fig. 7.20) and Taxco (Fig. 7.13 and Plate XIV). Both were paid for by the miner, José de la Borda, and are traditionally dated in the 1750s. For the church in Taxco, Manrique suggested a date of approximately 1770.

Manrique argued that the architectonic phase of the late Baroque did not mark a transition to the Neo-Classicism of the future. The informing sensibility was quite different. Although the *estípite* was abandoned, many other features of

Taxco is mentioned in 1524 in the fourth letter from Cortés to Charles V as a source of tin needed for casting cannons of bronze. Silver was discovered in the next decade, but Taxco never equaled in importance the mining centers to the north until José de la Borda's bonanza in the late 1740s. Borda informed the Inquisition that he was born in Jaca in Aragón. His mother seems to have been a local girl and his father was from the Oloron area in France, just north of the Pyrenees. The de la Bordas or de la Bordes were active on both sides of the mountains. A relative also born in Jaca, Jean Joseph de la Borde, was a French financier guillotined in Paris during the Reign of Terror. At seventeen José joined his older brother Francisco in Taxco where he had established himself as a miner. José developed the requisite knowledge of technological processes and management that would lead to his providing expert advice to Visitor General Gálvez and Viceroy Croix, when they wished to revive the Mexican mining industry, and to his being identified by the knowledgeable Francisco de Gamboa as "the first miner of the world."[4] Financed by Manuel de Aldaco, the leading silver merchant of Mexico City, he made his first great strike at Tlalpujahua in 1743. After his brother Francisco's death in the following year, he inherited the La Lajuela mine near Taxco and by 1748 was extracting great quantities of ore from the San Ignacio vein.

In February 1751 Viceroy Revillagigedo and Archbishop Rubio y Salinas approved Borda's request to be allowed to construct a new parish church for Taxco to replace the existing one which was in poor condition. The eagerness of the great entrepreneur to repay God for His generosity to him, recalled in a famous phrase in José Antonio Ximenez y Frias's funeral oration, "Dios a darle a Borda, y Borda a darle a Dios,"[5] led to extraordinary acknowledgment in a papal letter from Benedict XIV in 1754. The origin of Santa Prisca in Borda's desire to honor God in his home city with a splendid new church is beyond dispute, but much less certain is the source of its design. Assessing Borda's personal contribution is difficult; he was an intelligent miner whose architectural preferences are unknown. Names of several of the artists who worked for him are recorded, but some of the most important are names with which few other surviving works can be associated. Manuel Toussaint believed that he had discovered the name of the principal architect, Durán, in a witty five-line poem which was painted on an interior wall of the north tower. The poem, now lost, alluded to the Cave of Montesinos episode of *Don Quixote* and set in juxtaposition the words *arte*, *Durán*, and *Durán-darte*.

Toussaint believed that "Durán" was unlikely to have been the prominent earlier architect, Miguel Custodio Durán, and discovered in the census list of 1754 a Spanish-born architect, Diego Durán Burruecos. In 1973 Efraín Castro Morales discovered in the Archivo de Notarias in Mexico City a contract between Borda and an otherwise uncelebrated architect, Cayetano de Sigüenza, suggesting that he had primary responsibility for the structure. The architect Juan Caballero served as master of works and may have had some role in design. Isidro Vicente de Balbás, the adopted son of Jerónimo, is recorded as designer of retablos in the church. He seems to have resided in Taxco between November 1752 and November 1757. Baptismal records of his children place him in Taxco between 1753 and 1756. He is also recorded in Taxco in 1773. He is known as the designer of the principal retablos of the *sagrario* of the cathedral of Mexico, of the Rosario Chapel of Santo Domingo also in Mexico City and of the cathedral of Morelia, all demolished in the nineteenth century. His Baroque project for the completion of the cathedral is preserved in a drawing (Fig. 8.1). On the basis of stylistic affinity, Joseph A. Baird has attributed to him the retablos of the nave of another of the major decorative ensembles surviving from mid-century, the interior of the Jesuit church in Tepotzlán.

On December 3, 1758, according to an inscription placed over the basin in the sacristy, the church in Taxco was completed after approximately seven years of work. During the following spring, dedicatory ceremonies were organized, and the son of the patron, Manuel de la Borda, who had been awarded a doctorate in philosophy by the University of Mexico, was installed as parish priest. Despite the father's great skill, energy, and willingness to move from mining camp to mining camp, even for a time to Real del Monte to collaborate with the Conde de Regla, he achieved mixed results from his mining activities in the late 1750s and the 1760s. By 1767 he was sixty-eight years old and close to bankruptcy. He had spent approximately half a million pesos on the construction of Santa Prisca and owed almost as much to creditors, 112,000 pesos to Manuel de Aldaco alone. In that year the viceregal government, following a policy Borda himself had recommended earlier to Visitor General Gálvez, offered him very substantial financial incentives to go north to Zacatecas to drain and restore the difficult Quebradilla mine, which had recently cost a local group 300,000 pesos in an unsuccessful effort. Borda was granted a full exemption from the government's tithe on production during the costly period of renovation, a half-exemption for twenty more years, and a sharply reduced price for the mercury needed in refining, roughly equivalent to an outright grant of 100,000 pesos. Despite these governmental concessions and his immense reputation, Borda was unable to secure sufficient financial backing to attempt the Quebradilla. He used 30,000 pesos borrowed from friends to initiate less difficult operations on the Veta Grande vein of silver. He later managed to borrow an additional 18,000 from the government itself, and in 1772 raised substantial funds through an action he had considered and put off for several years, selling the sacred vessels, jewelled decorations, and other church furnishings of Santa Prisca to the Cathedral of Mexico. Despite his generosity in endowing his church, Borda had prudently retained ownership of these precious objects, some of which ultimately reached Notre Dame in Paris. The sale was expedited by Viceroy Bucareli, who was eager to stimulate mining, and approved by Archbishop Núñez de Haro y Peralta. The very considerable sum of 110,000 pesos received from the sale was essential to Borda's continuing and expanding activities in Zacatecas. By 1775 he had made 1.75 million pesos from his seven mines on the Veta Grande and had constructed the largest refining mill in the north. At that time it was clear that these mines were losing profitability, and he used accumulated capital to begin a prolonged campaign in the Quebradilla. Borda delighted in the success of his mule-

7.12 *Santa Prisca, Taxco, view from the northwest.*

powered whims in pulling to the surface water from the seams of ore, writing that "everyone must agree that water which was insuperable to them [his predecessors in the mine] is like a toy to me."[6] He remained in Zacatecas long enough to sense his success but not to see the completion of the operations he had initiated. Failing health

7.11 *Taxco and the Church of Santa Prisca, view from the northeast.*

7.13 *Santa Prisca, Taxco, facade. See also Plate XIV.*

174

caused his removal to Cuernavaca in late 1776 or early 1777 to be close to his son Manuel, who had taken a clerical post in that city and who constructed there the well-known Borda Gardens. At the time of José de la Borda's death on May 30, 1778, he had been able to repay all his creditors. Twenty-two years later, in 1790, Manuel estimated his inherited wealth at approximately a million pesos.

Santa Prisca dominates Taxco, rising at its center from an elevated base. The silhouette, composed of tall towers of complex outline and a simpler dome of colored tile which floats above a smoothly rippling balustrade, changes from viewing point to viewing point. The front, side, and rear elevations, visible from differing distances and angles of sight, are diverse but constitute a harmonious whole. The Latin-cross volume of the church proper rises high above the low forms of the subsidiary structures surrounding it—baptistry, archive, sacristy, and Chapel of Padre Jesús—which fill out the roughly rectangular plan.

The square twin towers of Santa Prisca, which inspired Hart Crane's powerful poem "The Broken Tower," were unusual in a parish church of its time but had precedent in the major Mexican cathedrals. Relative to the main body of the church they are shorter than those of Puebla, but their slim proportions make them seem unusually lofty. Their height may reflect the influence of the tall single towers of Andalusian churches such as San Juan of Ecija (1745). The towers at Taxco are placed in advance of the central facade. The rectangular austerity of their lower sections, broken only by the decorative framing of four superposed oval windows, sets off the elaborate ornamentation of the central facade and increases the apparent height. Above a strongly shaded line of cornice, two complex belfry stages seem to swell out and up, dissolving into the blue of the sky. The effect of swelling is caused by the addition at the corners of the belfry stages of an *estípite* flanked by columns which are knobbed, beaded, and fluted at the lower level and banded diagonally at the upper. The stages are generally similar in design, with the smaller upper story more elaborately ornamented. In mid-eighteenth century Andalusia, towers were usually altered in form and reduced sharply in size as they mounted stage

by stage. At Taxco there is no substantial change in form, and the diminution in scale in the upper story is disguised by its increased ornamentation. The towers are crowned by concavely curved pyramidal elements, associated by George Kubler with an unexecuted design of 1742 by Jaime Bort for the Cathedral of Murcia in southeastern Spain.

The richly decorated central section of the facade is framed by an arch and, like the interior volume of the church and the towers in their relationship to the total structure, is governed by the simple geometrical proportion of the double square so that its height doubles its width. Vertical emphasis is provided at its sides by superposed paired columns which are set out from the plane of the facade. All the columns have elaborately decorated capitals, composite or Corinthian, and unadorned shafts. Those below are simple cylinders, those above smoothly spiraling Salomónicas. The intervals between the columns are occupied by niche pilasters which are crisply edged and adorned with restrained curving ornamentation. They contain at the lower level statues of Saint Peter and of Saint Paul and at the upper,

7.14 *Santa Prisca, Taxco, central facade, upper level.*

statues of the church's patrons, Santa Prisca and San Sebastián.

The area enclosed by the tall framing columns contains elements traditional in Mexican Baroque church facades: a round arched doorway below; a nearly rectangular window above, just below the framing arch; and, in between, a sculptural representation of the baptism of Christ placed within a frame which approximates an oval. These elements are related in a design of surging energy unprecedented in Mexican architecture (Fig. 7.14). The horizontals of the major and secondary lower cornices are broken upward in a series of angles and facets, scrolls and layers. The oval frame of the sculptural relief is broken out into angular projections and spread by a variety of scroll and shell forms. The horizontals of the lower and upper margins of the window dip and rise in swinging curves. A stunning decorative element crowns the center of the facade, midway between the towers. Its base, set below the layered center of the framing arch, is a large shell which seems supported by the curve of heavily layered molding above the window. Just above the arch, thrusting through the horizontal of the balustrade, is an ornamental ensemble containing a clock. At its sides are large swirling scrolls which support the bases of statues of the evangelists, John and Matthew; its pinnacle, above, is a representation of the Virgin of the Immaculate Conception.

The overall pattern of the ornamentation of the facade of Santa Prisca resembles a great Y (Fig. 7.13), with the strongly decorated central area surrounding the portal constituting the trunk, and the even more powerfully decorated belfry stages of the towers constituting the upper branches. Supporting and compressing these ornamented sections is the tan masonry of the lower towers, contrastingly austere in sharp-edged geometry. The design of the elevation of the open, south side is also based upon a contrasting pattern of ornamented and plain surfaces which constitutes a Y, here broader and looser in outline. One upper branch is again formed by the belfries of the tower, or towers, and the other is formed by the dome, with its drum and its lantern. The trunk is formed by the axial alignment of important decorative features at the center of the flank

of the nave. The strongly decorated side portal is the base and above it is the carved relief of the assumption and coronation of the Virgin and the tall, deep-set central window of the clerestory. Particularly noticeable are the substantial areas of plain surface which project on either side, the base of the nearer tower and the broad end of the transept. These surfaces are entirely unadorned, except for discrete indications of their terminations and divisions in the cornice of the tower and in a string course and the swinging curve of the balustrade of the transept. The dome is more ornamented (Fig. 7.12) but it depends for expressiveness primarily upon its simple geometric shape and upon its covering of glazed tile. Its octagonal drum is soberly decorated. There are low-arched windows, starkly simple pilasters, small brackets, and finials. The most prominent feature is a frieze of colored tile with the inscription, "Glory to God in the highest and peace on earth to men of good will." Each of the eight segments of the dome proper contains a white tile star of eight points, or rays, sparkling in a circle of blue, suggestive of the dome of heaven.

The admirable rear elevation is sparely ornamented and is organized in pyramidal form with the lantern of the dome as apex (see Fig. 7.11). The base, the broad stretch of wall of the lowest story housing the sacristy, is divided by plain buttresses into four bays, each perforated by two windows, a rectangular one below capped by a scroll pediment, and a small oval opening above to light the vault inside. The wall is terminated by a thin undulating cornice. Set well back from this dynamic horizontal is the plain mass of the main body of the church, its high shoulders marked by the more ponderous swing of the balustrade. Still higher and farther back is the dome with its finials and ribs and culminating lantern.

The interior of Santa Prisca is one of the few in Mexico to retain its eighteenth-century decoration substantially intact. The stone surfaces have absorbed a rosy tint from the application and subsequent removal earlier in this century of a marbleizing coating of paint, added at the direction of the parish priest, Lorenzo Rodríguez. But Santa Prisca, unlike almost all its contemporaries, was altered little during the period of Neo-Classical taste, and it was splendidly re-

176

stored in the years after 1928 and more recently between 1988 and 1990 so that it now looks much as it did when it was completed by José de la Borda's artists over two hundred years ago.

The interior consists of a choir to the west, a nave of three bays, a substantial transept, and a rectangular sanctuary. The feeling of height derived from the double-square proportions is increased by the decorative treatment. Up to the

relatively delicate decoration of the drum stage above is incongruously juxtaposed to the heaviness of the rusticated stonework below.

Santa Prisca contains twelve retablos, nine in the church proper and three in the Chapel of Padre Jesús. The chapel occupies the area north of the nave and is entered through a doorway in its central bay, opposite the external side portal in the south wall. Isidro Vicente de Balbás is the

7.15 *Santa Prisca, interior, facing choir.*

7.16 *Santa Prisca, interior, area above the south portal.*

cornice line the ornamentation is heavy and rich, surrounding the gilded retablos, the paintings, and the window bases with assertive mouldings and rusticated pilasters constructed in three broad layers. The rustication consists of pairs of parallel bars alternating between vertical and horizontal. The contrasting treatment of the vaulted ceiling above creates a feeling of openness and lift. Almost all the surfaces of the groin vaults of the nave and choir and of the octagonal interior of the dome are now light-colored and undecorated. Traces of delicate painting reinforcing the structural lines of the vault have been discovered and restored in the bay before the choir. The massiveness of the stonework below is echoed only by comparatively slight rusticated arches swinging across the vaults from pilaster to pilaster to define the individual bays. Unhappily, the transition at the crossing is less successful than in the nave. The massive entablature blocks of the piers are surmounted by pendentives which are modest in scale and uninteresting in ornamentation. The

only designer of retablos known to have worked in Taxco, but he probably was not responsible for all twelve retablos. They differ in style and very likely in date, and although he is recorded as resident in Taxco in 1773 as well as in the middle 1750s, the stylistic variation makes his authorship of all the retablos improbable. Joseph A. Baird attributes to Balbás the three retablos dedicated to the Virgin which stand against the end walls of the transepts and of the sanctuary.[7] The retablos in the transepts dedicated to the Our Lady of Guadalupe and Our Lady of the Rosary are virtually identical in design, and the central retablo of the Immaculate Conception is composed similarly (Fig. 7.17). All three are tall, reaching almost to the vaults, and strongly vertical in emphasis. The verticality is reminiscent of the proportions of the exterior, but the ornamental detailing bears no resemblance to the strongly outlined decorative patterns of the facade. The forms of the principal elements of the retablos, the towering *estípites* and niche pilasters, are designed with such elaborate complexity that they are almost un-recognizable. In the principal retablo, especially, the tectonic sense of weight-bearing architectural entablature has been dissolved into a shimmering pattern of glittering fragments.

The church's other six retablos, which Baird dates in the 1770s, are less vertical and more formally coherent. The four placed in the nave are associated with those of the transepts by a common use of shell motifs in their frames. All are built out from a background of clearly defined, semicircular, arched, gilded surface to a prominent central tabernacle. The tabernacle contains a polychrome figure that is surrounded by other figures easily detached visually from the gilding. All are built upward from the central tabernacle toward a figure at the top that thrusts out and up from the gilded whole to push across the framing stone arch above.

These six retablos were designed as pairs. Those in the bay of the nave next to the transept and dedicated to the Virgin of Sorrows and St. Joseph have an emphatic horizontal line of cornice

7.18 *Santa Prisca, nave retablo dedicated to the Virgin of Sorrows.*

7.19 *Santa Prisca, nave retablo dedicated to Saint John Nepomuk.*

7.17 *Santa Prisca, main retablo.* Santa Prisca Restaurada, *p. 58 photograph of José Ignacio González Manterola and Pablo Osguera Iturbide, O G Fotógrafos Asociados.*

7.20 *Parish Church of Santiago Tianguistenco, facade.*

178

and are placed within clearly defined arched frames which are decorated with clusters of shells. They contain prominent figures of saints flanking their tabernacles and triads of figures at their tops, Christ and the two thieves on their crosses in the retablo of the Virgin of Sorrows. The bay at the other end of the nave, beyond that containing the portals to the sides, has retablos dedicated to the Virgin of the Pilar and to St. John Nepomuk, which are similar in overall design. Here the gilded framing arches consist of chains of rosettes flanked with shells at their outer edges and the figures flanking the tabernacle are arranged in more pyramidal form. The more modest pair of retablos on the walls of the bay under the choir, dedicated to Saint Lucy and Saint Isidor, have single flanking figures set in niches and putti carrying green fronds and gilded trees which form a sweeping mandorla around the central niche.

The three retablos of the Chapel of the Padre Jesús are more architectonic than those of the nave. The side ones, dedicated to Jesus and to the Virgin, have flanking niche pilasters and are organized about centrally placed frames of pictures. The larger lower ones are simple, rectangular with a round arched top, and the smaller upper ones complex, with a variety of curves and angles. The principal Retablo de Animas contains brilliantly faceted *estípites* flanking the complexly curved frame of a painting by Miguel Cabrera below the entablature, and three decorated ovals to frame three small paintings above.

The most celebrated of the painters employed by José de la Borda to decorate Santa Prisca, Cabrera contributed large semicircular canvases portraying the martyrdoms of San Sebastián and Santa Prisca. These canvases are placed above the south door and the door to the chapel, respectively, and face each other at the center of the nave (Fig. 7.16). Cabrera also painted for the sacristy a cycle of fourteen canvases narrating events in the life of the Virgin and her child Jesus, beginning with the Immaculate Conception and concluding with the Assumption.

Despite the prominence of its patron and the general excellence of its design and execution, Santa Prisca was not closely imitated. Its closest relative is Santiago Tianguistenco in the Valley of Toluca, also constructed with funding from José

7.21 *The Church of the Virgin of Ocotlán.*

de la Borda. There powerful swirling Salomonic columns are set on high, diagonally placed bases between conventional, sturdily decorated columns so that their function resembles that of particularly dynamic *interestípites*, or niche pilasters. Something of the formal arrangement of Santa Prisca is suggested by the towers and facade of the Sanctuary of the Virgin on the hill of Ocotlán east of Tlaxcala. The proportions, however, are broader and lower and the ornamentation in whitewashed stucco, set against unglazed red tile, is entirely different. Santa Prisca's tall proportions are reflected in the great shell facade of the Church of Lagos de Moreno in eastern Jalisco, but the upper stages of the twin towers there are of modern construction.

The *Sagrario* of the Cathedral of Mexico

During the years Santa Prisca was being erected in Taxco, work was under way on the most influential building of eighteenth-century Mexico, the sacramental chapel and parish church set beside the cathedral at the corner of the great plaza in the capital. Among the striking differences between these contemporary structures are

7.22 Sagrario, Mexico City, interior (facing northwest).

the sources of their funding. Cathedral buildings were customarily built with monies from the royal treasury, but little had been made available to Mexico in the half-century before construction was begun on the *sagrario* in 1749. The upper stages of the cathedral's towers were still unbuilt, and its interior had proved unsuited to providing properly for those who lived nearby and depended on two side chapels for their parish services. Crowds of worshippers blocked the aisle and much of the nave in an effort to see and hear the mass and other religious ceremonies. Efforts to secure funds to construct a *sagrario* had been made in 1693, in 1701, again in 1728, and more recently by Archbishop Juan Antonio de Vizzarón. Some time before the death of the archbishop in January 1747, Lorenzo Rodríguez was asked to prepare designs for a *sagrario*, which the prelate approved. At the beginning of 1749 an extraordinary decision was made to proceed illegally with construction without seeking royal funding or approval. Upon being informed some years later when the structure was nearing completion, Ferdinand VI made clear his kingly displeasure with such proceedings. Central to the decision to go ahead must have been Dean of the Cathedral Moreno de Castro, who was acting *en sede vacante* until the arrival of the new archbishop late the following summer. But there was widespread sup-

port for proceeding independently of Spanish authorization.

Another design for the *sagrario*, prepared by Ildefonso Iniesta Bejarano y Durán, followed the traditional three-nave plan of Mexican cathedrals. Both Iniesta Bejarano and Rodríguez participated in the deliberations of a committee constituted to examine the plans. The committee included a representative of the chief engineer of the viceroyalty and the maestros of architecture of the royal palace and the cathedral and of the city, and it voted unanimously for the adoption of Rodríguez's centrally planned design. The plan was then approved by the cabildo of the cathedral, the viceroy's fiscal adviser, and by the viceroy, the first of the two condes de Revillagigedo who held that office. The first Viceroy Revillagigedo, known popularly as Don Juan Tobago for his investments in the tobacco trade, was an able administrator willing to risk royal displeasure in supporting a project critically important to his Mexican subjects.

So rapid was the approval of all parties in the city that work on the foundations was begun within five weeks of the initiation of the process. A contemporary account of the ceremony staged for the laying of the cornerstone in May suggests the strong local civic pride in the project demonstrated by the representation of the dean and priests of the cathedral, the viceroy and his administration, and the officials of the city government. Also attending were members of the *archicofradía* of the Santísimo Sacramento, a religious confraternity supporting the work and consisting of the great merchants of the consulado and other rich and powerful citizens.

Despite the enthusiasm for the project and the breadth of support in the largest and richest city in America, maintaining an adequate flow of cash to sustain construction during the ten years of major effort between 1750 and 1760 proved difficult. A surviving income book lists the names of the many individual donors and records the alms collected, day by day, by Padre Sarmiento, who solicited support from ordinary people by riding through the streets on his mule. Lotteries were organized to supplement the funds donated, and, for a period in 1756, a shortage of money forced the suspension of work on the ornamentation of the portals if not on the main work of construction. But ultimately the community succeeded in its effort to go it alone, to construct without any dependence on royal funds a splendid new *sagrario*, costly and stylish in a new Mexican way. When the king was finally informed of its impending completion, he was assured that it would be "the wonder of America."

For the *sagrario*, Rodríguez adopted a plan without precedent in Mexico. It involved setting a short-armed Greek cross within a square. *Sagrarios* in Spain were conceived primarily as sacred spaces for sacramental ritual and frequently were given the ideal geometric forms preferred in Renaissance Italy. Rodríguez's plan (Fig. 3.12) bears some resemblance to the cross-in-square scheme used by Francisco Hurtado in 1704 for the *sagrario* of the Cathedral of Granada. Both have a major dome at the center and four peripheral domes. Rodríguez differs from Hurtado in placing his four subordinate domes in the corners between the barrel-vaulted arms of the cross rather than over the arms themselves. Margaret Collier located the source of Rodríguez's conception of the *sagrario* in the plan, elevation, and section of a "Tempio Quadrato in Croce" included in the fifth book of Sebastiano Serlio's sixteenth-century volume of architectural designs. Serlio's model church, which was not set within a square, reflects a celebrated original; it seems a simplified version of Bramante's plans for a centrally ordered St. Peter's in Rome.

Collier demonstrated through juxtaposition of drawings that the very close relationship between the *sagrario* and the "Tempio Quadrato in Croce" extended beyond the plan to the proportions of both the interior and exterior elevations. She also suggested that Rodríguez, who had received his architectural training in Andalusia, was responsive to Mexican precedents in modifying Serlio's design. The greater height and greater openness of the *sagrario*'s interior reflect an awareness of two interiors of Pedro de Arrieta, the basilica at Guadalupe and the Jesuit church of La Profesa in the city, and, especially, of the interior of the cathedral itself. Serlio's corner chapels had been virtually closed off from the main volume of the interior. Those in the *sagrario* have been opened to the barrel-vaulted arms of the

structure by high arches so that space and light flow freely around the four piers of the crossing. The principal decorative features of the austere interior—fluted Doric half-columns, similarly fluted transverse ribs and arches, and lunettes above the entablature that are pierced with windows over the chapels—resemble those of the sixteenth-century cathedral and of the early eighteenth-century interiors of Arrieta. Nothing of the *sagrario*'s conservative interior structure suggests the Baroque. Although the proportions are less steep than those of the cathedral, there continues to be, despite the sober Renaissance ornamentation, a suggestion of Gothic skeletal construction and of Gothic light flooding down from high windows at diverse levels. The *sagrario* now contains at the end of its northern arm a sober Neo-Classical retablo of white and gold which was designed in 1829 by an Indian artist, Pedro Patiño Ixtolinque, who had been a student of Manuel Tolsá. The present retablo seems adapted to the general austerity of the interior, but it violates Rodríguez's conception of the interior. He had commissioned Isidro Vicente de Balbás to design and supervise the carving, gilding, and painting of a retablo during 1763 and 1764. The retablo constituted a blaze of gold and color, scintillating in the light flooding in from the many windows, and standing in dramatic contrast to the austere geometry of its surroundings.

Rodríguez's design for the *sagrario*'s exterior seems, like Balbás's retablo, intended to contrast with the sober simplicity of the interior. Viewed frontally (Fig. 7.24), the walls on the building's southern, eastern, and northern outer sides are decorative screens, attracting the eye to their varying patterns of surface and tumbling silhouette and suggesting little of the building's plan and structure. Viewed from the corners (Fig. 7.23) where the screening walls have dropped to little more than a third of their height, the *sagrario* reveals behind them its construction in solid, right-angled walls of exposed rubble which climb pyramidally toward dome and lantern. At the lowest level, just above the top of the wall, is the projecting cube of the corner chapel with its flat dome. The next surfaces are receding walls marking the tall arms of the interior cross, and above them is the projecting corner of the angular

7.23 *Sagrario, Mexico City, view from southeast corner.*

7.24 *Sagrario, Mexico City, south facade.*

7.25 *Sagrario, Mexico City, south facade, side portal, upper level.*

cube which serves as base for the curving drum and dome.

The curtain walls reveal Rodríguez's awareness of the development of a distinctly Mexican type of Baroque wall in structures such as the Church of Santo Domingo and the colleges of San Ildefonso and Las Vizcaínas. As in these earlier works (see Figs. 6.16 and 6.17), the walls are organized in contrasting patterns of light and dark, with hard-edged *chiluca* ornamentation set against a background of dark, plain red *tezontle*. The customary cornice which terminates a European wall has been replaced by a delicate cap moulding, and the wall's organization is a division into vertical bays rather than horizontal stories. Rodríguez found the elements of his *sagrario* design in existing walls in Mexico City but he transformed them. Díego Angulo Íñiguez, director of the Prado and pioneer historian of Latin American art, stressed the heightened dynamism of the *sagrario*, and its new forcefulness in contrasting elements and in confining and seeming to compress ornament within strongly vertical, plain buttresses. Angulo drew particular attention to the treatment of the wall's terminal cap molding, "curvetting down to each corner of the facade" in an ingenious interplay of angles and curves so that what traditionally was a sober horizontal cornice has completely disintegrated. "This cascading of the main cornice," he wrote, "entirely ignoring its traditional function, is the final step in the liberation of the wall from any responsibility to reflect interior structure."[8]

Two of the *sagrario*'s facades contain portals and are elaborately decorated in generally similar fashion. The most complete and complex is on the south, facing the great plaza, in line with the facade of the cathedral. Ornamentation is concentrated in the tall frontispiece at the center and in the bays at the ends, where the lesser entrances are surmounted by candelabralike masses of powerful decoration which nearly fill the entire

7.26 *San Felipe Neri el Nuevo, Mexico City, facade (top completed in the 20th century).*

wall surface. The intervening bays are plain, faced by soft blankets of dark *tezontle* which are broken only by low windows. Tall, two-tiered buttresses frame the frontispiece; short, thick ones surmounted by powerful finials flank the end bays. Against the strength of the buttresses is set the delicacy of the parapet moldings, especially during their precipitate, rippling, diagonal descent

7.27 *Sagrario, Mexico City, south facade, portal, lower level.*

over the intermediate bays from the tall to the short buttresses.

Rodríguez's design for the totality of the *sagrario* is unique, unimitated in Mexico, but the *estípite*-type ornamentation of the frontispieces of the southern and eastern facades inspired rapid and wide emulation. A contemporary account describes artisans studying and sketching sculptural details while the building was under construction. In 1751, long before it was completed, Ildefonso Iniesta Bejarano, who had followed the sober style of the cathedral in his competing project for the *sagrario*, adopted a design patterned on Rodríguez's in his facade for a new church of San Felipe Neri.

Rodríguez abandoned the traditional form of the eighteenth-century Mexican church front, with central portal surmounted by sacred scene carved in stone and a window to bring light into the choir, which had been retained and transformed into a powerful vertical surge in Santa Prisca in Taxco. His invention was a precisely bounded, mathematically ordered, sculptural composition of superposed *estípites* and niche pilasters inspired by the retablos of carved and gilded wood which were being created for contemporary church interiors. The two-to-one proportion of height to width, which is a determinant of the central facade at Taxco, was followed in the *sagrario*, and the geometrical basis for the design was made more evident. The vibrant patterns of light and shadow produced by the carving of the *estípites* and niche pilasters are confined within sharply defined rectangular areas by the thin, austere buttresses, which separate the frontispieces from the softly curving *tezontle* walls on their flanks. Within the rectangles the strong vertical thrust of the buttresses is countered by the horizontal accents of the jagged shadowed lines of both entablatures and, less emphatically, by shadowed horizontals created by the tops of the bases of the upper and lower orders of *estípites*.

Dominating the tall order flanking the portal in the lower story are tactilely vigorous pairs of *estípites* which surround recessive niche pilasters. The complex shorter order of the upper story (Fig. 7.28) appears broader. A central niche, six *estípites*, and four intermediate niche pilasters are arranged in a syncopated rhythm. No motif is

7.28 *Sagrario, Mexico City, south façade, portal, middle and upper level. See also Plate XI.*

7.30 *Church of the Jesuit establishment at Tepotzotlán, façade.*

7.29 *Church of La Santísima Trinidad, Mexico City, façade.*

dominant, but emphasis is placed upon broad niche pilasters at the sides which echo the form of the niche at the center. The attic stages of the south front and of the incomplete east front are similar but different. Both push free from the rectangular confinement of the two lower stories and suggest, through alternation of finials, sta-

tues, and rising curving elements, the loosely rippling silhouette of molding surmounting the outer sections of wall. The acceleration evident in the skyline seems to result from a surging vertical energy expressed along the central axis of the composition. A thrusting force seems to push a powerfully articulated frame up from the round-arched portal and to bend the restraining horizontal line of the entablature into an upward curve. From a notch at the center of the curve ascends a flowing form which lends support to a statue in the central niche. In the south frontispiece analogous forms push up through a broken curve of pediment at the upper entablature line to support the culminating image of the *sagrario*'s vertical axis, the eucharist.

The underlying principle of Rodríguez's design is the setting of elements in dynamic tension. Initially the effect seems less dramatic than the soaring verticality of Santa Prisca but, once understood, it is at least equally impressive. None of the celebrated *estípite* façades that followed—

the three attributed to Iniesta Bejarano, the incomplete one for San Felipe Neri (Fig. 7.26), the Santísima Trinidad (Fig. 7.29), and San Francisco Xavier at Tepotzotlán (Fig. 7.30), or even the anonymous Balvanera Chapel of San Francisco (Figs. 7.4 and 7.5)—rival its complex power.

El Pocito: the Chapel of the Well at Guadalupe

On June 1, 1777, sixty-eight years after the dedication of Pedro Arrieta's basilica, the cornerstone was laid for another structure at Guadalupe. In Luis Becerra Tanco's powerful narrative of 1675 a spring of mineral water was associated with the site of the most significant of the apparitions of the Virgin, the one during which she sent Juan Diego to the barren hilltop to cut miraculous roses. An account written by a visitor to Guadalupe, English captive sailor Miles Philips, informs us that as early as 1568 an association had been made between the "very fair church, called our Lady's church, in which there is an image of Our Lady of silver and gilt, . . . as high . . . as a tall woman" and the effects of "certain cold baths, which arise, springing up as though the water did seeth: . . . somewhat brackish in taste, but very good for any that have any sore or wound, to wash themselves therewith, for as they say, it healeth many."[9] After over two hundred years of reverent use of the spring waters and widespread faith in their divine power to heal, a campaign was organized to mark their source with a monumental structure.

We lack information regarding the initiation of the project which attracted wide-based interest and support. Both private and public funds were used to pay the costs of construction. Citizens of Guadalupe and artisans and guilds of the city contributed labor and materials. Two influential citizens, Calixto González Abencerraje and, later, the Cadiz-born merchant Nicolás Zamorátequi, promoted the project; Archbishop Alonso Núñez de Haro y Peralta encouraged artisans to volunteer their services by granting indulgences of eighty days to those who worked for four hours on holy days. Francisco Antonio Guerrero y Torres, who had grown up nearby and had recently

succeeded Lorenzo Rodríguez as chief architect of the viceroyalty, designed the structure and directed the work of construction without accepting any remuneration for the fourteen years needed for its completion.

By the time construction was formally begun on the Chapel of the Well, another religious edifice designed by Guerrero y Torres was almost finished. His church for the teaching order of nuns of the Compañía de María Santísima y la Enseñanza is unique among the churches for nuns in Mexico City (Fig. 7.31). It has a single entrance on the longitudinal axis, and its interior is rectangular with the corners cut off so as to form a stretched-out octagon. A stimulus to the plan was the need to place the church in the midst of pre-existing convent buildings. The design may reflect the influence of the interior of the now-demolished nun's Church of Santa Brígida with its flowing ovals, which was designed by Luis Díez Navarro and constructed between 1740 and 1745. The interior of the Church of the Enseñanza provides a dramatic, some have said theatrical, experience for the visitor. One passes from the entrance between retablo-clad walls under the shadow of the choir (Fig. 7.32) to enter the light-filled central space under the dome through a great tri-lobed arch. At the end of the vista is a tall, layered, golden retablo flanked by paintings covering the truncated corners of the interior which dissolve all sense of solid wall into airy spaciousness.

In formulating his design for the Chapel of the Well, Guerrero y Torres wanted to provide a monumental shelter for the miraculous spring and a chapel to accommodate congregations for daily, if not hourly, masses, and for other religious ceremonies on the site. The need to consider two purposes led Guerrero to conceive a structure more complex spatially than the Church of the Enseñanza, its precursor Santa Brígida, or any other building of viceregal Mexico. Guerrero was probably aware of the spatial innovations of mid-century Madrid, of the flowing plans of the late Baroque churches of the Italian Santiago Bonavía, and of Ventura Rodríguez. But the direct inspiration for his design was not a recent Spanish conception or a work of one of the masters of the Italian Baroque of the previous century but, as Diego

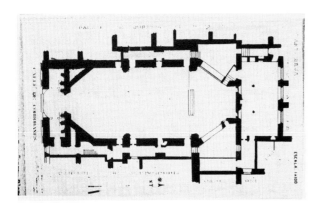

7.31 *Church of the Enseñanza, Mexico City, plan, from Glenn Neil Patton's "Francisco Antonio Guerrero y Torres."*

running from the center of the portico at the front to a concave niche at the rear. In Serlio's temple the alternating trapezoidal and circular chapels rimming the interior periphery of the rotunda, which in the Pantheon are contained within a thick circular wall, burst free of the confining circle to create a powerful rhythm of curves and angles on the exterior. In addition, the apse-like niche at the end of the longitudinal axis of the Pantheon is expanded into a separate chamber, circular on the exterior and consisting in the interior of alternating segments of straight, concave, and convex wall.

The December 27, 1791, edition of the *Gaceta de Mexico*, which recorded the dedication

7.32 *Church of the Enseñanza, Mexico City, interior.*

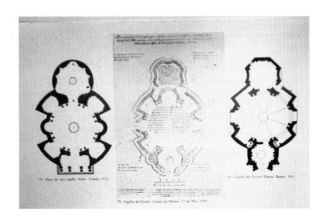

7.33 *Chapel of the Well, plans and plan of Serlio's ruined Roman temple, from Manuel Toussaint,* Paseos coloniales, *figs. 78–80.*

Angulo discovered, a proto-Baroque building of imperial Rome. Lorenzo Rodríguez had discovered the germ of the *sagrario*; in a plan for a centralized church of High Renaissance-type included in Serlio's architectural treatise. Guerrero found stimulus from a much more ancient structure, a temple outside Rome already ruined in the sixteenth century, the plan of which was included in the same work.

Serlio's "ruinous temple" (Fig. 7.33, left) represented a loosening of the plan (Fig. 7.33, center) of the Pantheon and its extension into two chambers. A central rotunda is fronted by a pillared portico and a linear axis bisects the rotunda,

of the Chapel of the Well, included an engraving of a plan (Fig. 7.33, center) of the structure attributed to Guerrero y Torres. Despite its being published after the building was completed, the plan represents an intermediate rather than the final stage of Guerrero's thinking. The essential features of the rotunda of Serlio's Roman temple remain without substantial modification to constitute the principal chapel of Guerrero's design. The two large trapezoidal chapels on each side have been retained and would be devoted to the four apparitions of the Virgin that appeared to Juan Diego. The smaller semicircular chapels, or niches, which occupy the center of each flank have

7.34 Chapel of the Well, Guadalupe, view from the east. See also Plate XII.

In 1933 Diego Angulo published several drawings portraying the front and side elevations of the exterior of the Chapel of the Well and the processional stair to the chapel above it on the hill. These drawings are in the Archive of the Indies in Seville and were sent in a letter by Viceroy Matías de Gálvez to Charles III in January 1782 in accordance with a royal directive of May 1780. The pairs of drawings of the front and side elevations seem to represent different stages in the conceptual evolution of the structure, but uncertainties in the foreshortening make definitive interpretation of some features difficult.

The drawings reveal the principal features of the completed structure, three domes crowning the curving, angled, complexly interrelated walls, which extend upward into parapets masking and buttressing the bases of the domes which have no drums. The parapets terminate in a swinging molding of ascending and descending profile and are punctuated by columns and finials. Like the walls below them, they are pierced by window frames in the form of Moorish six-pointed stars. The walls of the projecting subsidiary chapels at the sides of the principal chapel swing out beyond the circular walls of the chamber of the well and stand out several feet from the base of the central dome. The drawings reveal Guerrero's effort to provide a graceful transition between the projecting walls of the subsidiary chapels and the set-back parapet and dome of the main chapel that was essential to his adaptation of the plan of Serlio's temple to his three-domed structure. He experimented with different combinations of finial, column, and lantern set on top of the projecting chapels. At this stage of his conception the structure would have had five lanterns, three crowning the domes and two flanking the point of intersection of the first two domes. Ultimately he eliminated the flanking lanterns and found a more satisfactory final solution to the problem of transition in the secondary frontal parapets, pierced with three arched openings for bells, which he placed at the top of the curving exterior walls of all four projecting chapels.

Some details of the ornamentation are indicated in the drawings but important elements are not. Rather fully suggested is the form of the side portals (Fig. 7.35) with their undulating pi-

been converted into side entrances. The most striking change in this part of the design was on the axis opposite the center of the portico, where the entrance to the subordinate chamber at the rear was blocked with a curving, apselike enclosure for an altar. More significant changes were made to the other parts of Serlio's temple. A third interior element was added by the transformation of the rectangular portico into a circular chamber to contain a small chapel surrounding the well of the sacred spring. The secondary chamber at the rear of the "ruinous temple" was converted into an octagonal sacristy with an undulating wall constructed of alternative sections of concavity and convexity.

The completed structure (Fig. 7.23, right), which was dedicated at Christmas time in 1791, was similar to the published plan in regard to the front and rear chambers but significantly different in regard to the central chapel. Guerrero decided to extend the Roman rotunda into a Baroque oval and to place its axis at a right angle to the main axis of the building. He also made several lesser modifications in the design: what had been deep and approximately trapezoidal chapels became rather shallow rectangles, but with curving exterior walls; the semicircular curves of wall at the side entrances were reduced to rounded spurs; and the enclosing apselike space for the altar was replaced by a retablo recessed only slightly from the broadly curving sweep of the oval.

7.35 *Chapel of the Well, Guadalupe, side portal. See also Plate XIII.*

7.37 *Chapel of the Well, Guadalupe, parapets and domes.*

lasters, rusticated multilobed arches, and powerfully sweeping scrolled pediments. There is no indication that Guerrero had yet conceived the upper section of the main portal, with its soft carpet of arabesque ornamentation surrounding the powerful moldings of the frame of the six-pointed star-window against which a statue of the Virgin would be set. He had determined to set pairs of

7.36 *Chapel of the Well, Guadalupe, view from the front.*

7.38 *Chapel of the Well, interior chamber of the well, from the east.*

188

generally orthodox fluted Corinthian columns on the flanks of the star-window and on the flanks of the entrance below with its characteristic Guerreroesque multilobed archlintel suspending three bosses.

The drawings provide no suggestion of the bands of geometric fret ornamentation that frame, in buff *chiluca*, segments of brownish-pink *tezontle* wall. They provide an inadequate sense of the shape of the central dome, which dwarfs the others with a steeply rising silhouette closer in spirit to Brunelleschi's medieval dome (Fig. 7.34) in Florence than to the classical domes of ancient Rome or the Renaissance. Even more striking, despite a suggestion of scrolled ribs on the central dome, there is no hint of the rippling sheathing of blue and white tiles that Guerrero applied to his domes and parapets to create a fantastic, shimmering, tentlike covering for his monument to the appearance beside the spring of the Virgin to the poor Indian, Juan Diego.

Regrettably little remains of the original interior decoration. In the early 1880s the building was refurbished in Neo-Classical taste. A res-

7.40 *Chapel of the Well, interior, the sacristy, upper level.*

7.39 *Chapel of the Well, interior, oval chapel.*

toration in the 1960s undid much of the damage. The chamber of the well is covered by a flattened domical vault decorated with powerful rippling rays of gold that emanate from the dove of the Holy Spirit suspended from a boss at the center directly above the sacred well. The background of

the vault is painted a deep blue. Six pairs of fluted Corinthian columns encircle the plain walls of the chamber. The only remaining decoration is a floral frieze and a cluster of child angels over the arch that leads into the central chapel. That oval space is divided into eight bays which are framed by arches and divided by powerful pairs of fluted Corinthian columns, set on bases like those of the other chamber. A balustrade swings around the base of the oval dome. Limited Baroque dynamism is created by breaking the balustrade forward over the entablature blocks; by varying the width of the bays, which are narrowest at the side entrances and widest at the openings to the four chapels; and by creating a modest flow of space into the chapels, and more substantially into the chamber of the well and into another chamber which is placed above it. But in the chapel's present state only the two tiers of star-windows, set high in the arches and in the dome just over the balustrade, and the eight undulating ribs of the dome suggest the decorative exuberance of the exterior, or of the interior of Guerrero's previous Church of the Enseñanza. The original retablos, which seem to have resembled those of the Enseñanza, and the original decoration of the walls must have had an enlivening effect, yet the handling of space of the major chapel is akin to that of grand classicistic Baroque works such as Bernini's Jesuit Church in Rome, San Andrea al Quirinale.

The tall sacristy, the most spatially dynamic of the three interior chambers, is wholly separate, entered through the back side chapels and a small exterior doorway. The eight segments of wall, alternatively convex and straight, are now without ornamentation. As in the oval chapel, two tiers of star-windows pierce the exterior walls. Polygonal arches supported by columns and by corbels support an entablature which circles the interior at the springing of the dome, decorated with a pattern of closely placed ribs making it resemble the underside of a parachute.

The Chapel of the Well was the last important building of the Mexican Baroque to be completed. Guerrero y Torres was nearly sixty-five years old and had less than a year to live. He must have felt considerable satisfaction at the dedication of his building, the most inventive and charming of Mexican structures, completed at a time when he, despite retaining the title maestro mayor, was reduced to designing bakeries; all the important commissions went to younger architects, exponents of the rising Neo-Classical style.

VIII

Neo-Classicism and Beyond in New Spain and in Mexico

In the spring of 1803, twelve years after the dedication of the Chapel of the Well, the Prussian polymath Alexander von Humboldt entered Mexico. He had been exploring the jungles along the Orinoco and climbing Andean peaks near Quito. He anticipated making a short sojourn before returning to Europe by way of Philadelphia and Monticello, where he would be entertained by President Jefferson. The pleasantness of life on the Mexican plateau (in contrast to the rigors of South America) combined with his interest in the land's geographic diversity, its volcanoes, its mines, and its Aztec past caused Humboldt to prolong his stay to just over a year. In 1811, he wrote the *Political Essay on the Kingdom of New Spain,* one of thirty volumes recording his discoveries and a book that has caused his name to be continuously revered in Mexico.

Humboldt's description of the valley of Mexico from the hill of Chapultepec on a summer morning reminds us of Bernal Díaz del Castillo's account of the lost magical city of the Aztecs. It also may disturb us with a fresh awareness of the deprivations our century has brought to this scene and to other urban places of the world. He first mentioned the cloudless sky, of an azure peculiar to dry mountain air, and then directed the reader's eye to sweep

over a vast plain of carefully cultivated fields, which extends to the very feet of the colossal mountains covered with perpetual snow. The city appears as if washed by the waters of the lake of Texcoco, whose basin, surrounded with villages and hamlets, brings to mind the most beautiful lakes of the mountains of Switzerland. Large avenues of elms and poplars lead in every direction to the capital; and the two aqueducts, constructed over arches of very great elevation, cross the plain. . . . The magnificent convent of Nuestra Senora de Guadalupe appears joined to the mountains of Tepeyac. . . . Towards the south, the whole tract between San Angel, Tacabaya and San Agustin de las Cuevas, appears an immense garden of orange, peach, apple, cherry, and other European fruit trees. This beautiful cultivation forms a singular contrast to the wild appearance of the naked mountains which enclose the valley, among which the famous volcanoes . . . Popocatepetl and Ixtaccihuatl are the most distinguished. The first of these forms an enormous cone, of which the crater, continually inflamed and throwing up smoke and ashes, opens in the midst of eternal snows.[1]

In the city itself, like travelers since the sixteenth century, Humboldt praised the uniform levelness of the site, "the regularity and breadth of the streets and the extent of the public places."[2]

He found the architecture generally pure in style and particularly noted the principal plaza in front of the cathedral and the palace, the ornamentation of which had been conceived as part of the refurbishing of the city directed by Viceroy Conde de Revillagigedo II and in 1796 executed under his successor the Marqués de Branciforte. Humboldt was impressed by the plaza's "vast circumference paved with porphyry flagstones, and enclosed with an iron railing, richly ornamented with bronze, containing an equestrian statue of King Charles IV placed on a pedestal of Mexican marble."[3] All in all, Humboldt believed the city was rivaled in general handsomeness only by St. Petersburg, Berlin, Philadelphia (which had no comparable architecture), and "some quarters of Westminster."[4] He explained that the city was admired by Europeans less for its edifices and monuments than for "its uniform regularity, its extent, and position."[5] But he singled out for praise several recent buildings including the School of Mines, which was still under construction, and the Neo-Classical house of the Conde de Pérez Gálvez (Figs. 8.5, 8.6, and 8.7), stressing the progress made in the arts in the thirty-odd years since the visit of the Abbé Jean Baptiste Chappe d'Auteroche. The Abbé had died in Baja California an international hero of science, persisting in his astronomical observations of a rare transit of Venus over the face of the sun in the midst of a typhus epidemic.

Humboldt attributed the improvements to the influence of the Royal Academy of San Carlos and declared that no city on the American continent, "without even excepting those of the United States, can display such great and solid scientific establishments as the capital of Mexico."[6] In addition to the academy, the other institutions mentioned were the School of Mines and the Botanical Garden.

Humboldt visited the studios of the academy at night and was impressed by the hundreds of students studying with the aid of the latest type of lamps. They were drawing from living models and from plaster casts of classical reliefs, and were copying drawings of furniture or bronze chandeliers. Particularly striking was the racial and social diversity of the students in a country where the prejudices of the upper classes against the castes of mixed blood were so ingrained. In the studios "we see the Indian and the Mestizo sitting beside the White, and the son of a poor artisan in friendly competition with the children of the great lords of the country."[7] Humboldt was appreciative of the spread throughout Mexico of the recent European taste for the Neo-Classic and cited as evidence of the salutary influence of the academy "the symmetry of the buildings, . . . the perfection with which the hewing of stones is conducted, and . . . the ornaments of the capitals and the reliefs of stucco."[8]

The Academy of San Carlos had been established between 1781 and 1785 primarily through the effort of Jerónimo Antonio Gil, who had come to Mexico in 1778 as chief engraver of the mint after having studied at the Royal Academy of San Fernando in Madrid. Although Gil initiated the academy and its principal teachers were Spaniards from the Academy of San Fernando—such as José Antonio González Velásquez, director of architecture; Rafael Ximeno y Planes, director of painting; and Manuel Tolsá, director of sculpture—there was widespread local enthusiasm for the enterprise. The Mexico City government promised to provide 1,000 pesos in support annually, the merchants of the consulado 3,000, and the miner's court 5,000. Other cities made annual contributions, and individuals outside the capital—such as the Conde del Valle de Suchil of Durango, and the Conde de la Valenciana, who was constructing a sumptuous late Baroque church beside his great mine above Guanajuato (Figs. 6.1 and 6.2)—provided significant initial gifts. Charles III—who as King of Naples had been responsible for excavating Herculaneum and as King of Spain brought to Madrid both the last great Baroque painter, Giovanni Battista Tiepolo, and Anton Raphael Mengs, the classicist—gave approval and generously established 13,000 pesos as the amount of the annual royal subsidy.

The Spanish artists appointed to teach in the academy had been educated in the Neo-Classical way of seeing, which had spread rapidly throughout Europe in the 1750s and 1760s. They found Mexico City old-fashioned architecturally, full of frivolous and inept Baroque buildings. The works of Guerrero y Torres, especially the house of the Marqués de Jaral de Berrio, were singled out for scornful condemnation. Characteristic of the new judgments was the report to the king prepared by the academy's director of architecture, Antonio González Velásquez, which criticized Mexican architects' "unwillingness to submit themselves to the rule of art"[9] and their rashness in building to heights dangerous because of the instability of the soil beneath the city. In all the public buildings of the city, wrote González Velásquez,

> there is a disregard of that selectivity and taste in facade decoration which determines the elegance . . . of a building. In many of them one perceives with horror a confused and disagreeable mixing of the Three Orders; doors and windows are placed arbitrarily, without balance or symmetry; the stairways are as perilous as they are unsightly, and the interior plan offers none of that ease and convenience which was the precise object of its invention. Finally . . . one can hardly find a single building in which the different members which should compose it can be distinguished clearly, and in none of them does one note the least sense of proportion, of that relationship of the whole with the parts, and of the part to the whole which constitutes the elegance of a good design. [10]

Like other Neo-Classicists, González Velásquez considered correct drawing the foundation for achievement in the arts, and he found the Baroque architects of Mexico inept in rendering and in mechanical drawing and, as a result, unaccustomed to putting their ideas down on paper before they initiated construction. "Precisely from this lack of composition . . . results the general monstrosity of the constructions which disfigure this fair capital and are a matter of ridicule in the eyes of every intelligent man, despite their having cost their owners great sums of money." [11]

There was little effective resistance to the determination of the leaders of the academy to transform the architectural practice of the city. Guerrero y Torres was allowed to complete the Chapel of the Well, but his plans for rebuilding Chapultepec Castle were rejected in 1784 and he subsequently received no important commissions. The viceroys succeeding Antonio María Bucareli

(1771 – 79), who had been a friend and supporter of his, fostered the founding of the academy. On more than one occasion the last great architect of the Mexican Baroque was in difficulty for failing to adhere to the procedure imposed by that institution to ensure that public structures were designed with proper regard for classical principles. All of the master architects recognized by the city government were honored with the title of academician, *Académico de Mérito*, and then were obliged to adhere to the "absolute stipulation that before beginning any work, whether church, convent, or other considerable building they must present the plans to the Junta Superior de Gobierno [the governing body of the academy] and submit, without objection or excuse whatsoever, to the corrections made in them, and with the warning that in case of resistance they will be severely chastised." [12]

The victory in 1786 of José Damián Ortiz de Castro's design for the completion of the ca-

8.1 *Cathedral of Mexico, competition designs for its completion by Isidro Vicente de Balbás and José Damián Ortiz de Castro, from Manuel Toussaint,* La Catedral de Mexico, *figs. 2 and 3.*

thedral marked the triumph of the taste of the academy, which had been formally organized only the year before and had waited until that year to receive the first artists sent from Spain to constitute its faculty. Guerrero y Torres apparently did not enter the competition sponsored by the cathedral chapter, despite retaining the title of maestro mayor, but drawings of two Baroque projects have survived. One was a relatively restrained design by José Joaquín García de Torres, the other a fanciful concoction by Isidro Vicente de Balbás, designer of the principal retablos at Taxco, who had died in 1783. Balbás provided alternate versions of the towers and central section of the facade with a rich variety of curves and counter curves, projections and recesses (Fig. 8.1, left). Ortiz de Castro was a native, born in the area of Jalapa in eastern Mexico. Although only in his middle thirties in 1786, he seems to have achieved some prominence as an architect despite the absence of known works of importance before the competition. His classical taste may have been developed through working as an assistant to Miguel Constanzo, a Spanish-born engineer and cartographer who later became a professor of architecture in the academy. Ortiz de Castro was abreast of contemporary architectural developments in Spain and probably modeled the bell-like concluding stages of his towers upon those designed by the great Ventura Rodríguez for the Cathedral of Pamplona, which had been completed in 1783.

Ortiz de Castro's sober plans were remarkable for their structural inventiveness as well

8.3 *Cathedral of Mexico, upper facade, center.*

as for their precocious Neo-Classicism. Fearfulness regarding the likely effect of the heavy stones of the upper stages' towers upon an already settling structure had been one cause of the protracted delay in completion of the cathedral. Designing light second-belfry stages, which appeared as ponderous as those below, and using veneers of stone held together by metal hoops and braced by beams of cedar in the seemingly solid construction of the bell-shaped top stages helped reassure those responsible for proceeding with construction of the building. Ortiz de Castro's original scheme had also provided simple iron crosses at the tops of the towers to minimize the weight. Ultimately they were replaced by stone crosses set upon substantial stone globes in order to improve the appearance and to reduce the threat from lightning. A report on the construction work written in 1796 conveys a sense of the state of mind of the commissioners who undertook the "alarming project" and their gratitude for the "ingenuity and architectural inspiration" of Ortiz de Castro, who had satisfied them that the "harmonious aspect of stone crosses on globes of stone" could be secured without "danger in winds or earthquakes" by devising "rings four inches thick on which rests the unbelievable weight of the globes . . . and the crosses."[13]

8.2 *Cathedral of Mexico, towers, upper facade, and dome.*

Ortiz de Castro was recognized by the leaders of the academy and their supporters as an important ally in the campaign against Baroque taste. Manuel Toussaint suggested that members of the academy circle played a crucial role in the selection of his project over the Baroque alternatives. Even before the choice was made, Ortiz de Castro was named *Académico de Mérito*, and by 1787, the year following the competition, when he and two associate architects submitted the official estimate, he had acquired half of Guerrero y Torres's title, maestro mayor of the cathedral. In order to qualify to be an academician, Ortiz de Castro submitted a design for the rebuilding of the parish church of Tulancingo. The handsome, restrained Neo-Classical structure now standing, roughly sixty miles northeast of Mexico City, probably derives from his project.

Ortiz de Castro died in 1793 at forty-two, having hastened his death by pushing on with the completion of the towers despite failing health. His successor as architect of the cathedral, Manuel Tolsá, had arrived in Mexico two years earlier to assume leadership of the Mexican academy's department of sculpture with more than seventy-five chests of books and other artistic materials and a large assortment of plaster casts from the Academy of San Fernando and the Vatican, including the Apollo Belvedere and the Laocoön. Tolsá had no formal training in architecture but he succeeded in completing the cathedral harmoniously, if a trifle awkwardly. He altered Ortiz de Castro's competition design by adding the large cubic clock-case and statues of Faith, Hope, and Charity above the center of the facade, and by placing the tall lantern above the existing dome, which he refaced. Ortiz de Castro's competition drawing seems to have called for replacing the dome and drum with a taller and more massive structure adapted to the height and strength of his towers.

Tolsá's creative achievement in Mexico was more notable in architecture than in sculpture. Relatively few known sculptural works exist. They include the three statues of the theological virtues for the cathedral, two other figural pieces, and the large equestrian bronze of Charles IV, placed in the center of the great plaza facing the palace of the viceroy in 1803. Alexander von Humboldt admired the latter. In addition, Tolsá designed a retablo for Santo Domingo, an altarpiece for La Profesa, and the vigorous baldacchino for the high altar of the Cathedral of Puebla.

In May 1797 Tolsá submitted plans for the school which the Tribunal of Mines had been intending to erect for several years. The plans were accepted and construction was initiated on the huge structure, with its seven interior patios, three stairs, and eleven fountains (Figs. 8.7–8.9). Work continued for sixteen years at a cost of 1,596,435 pesos. Tolsá's submission to the academy of these plans, and his designs for a retablo and for a nun's cell for the Marquesa de Selva Nevada in the convent of Regina Coeli qualified him for the title of *Academico de Merito* in architecture. Tolsá's drawings exist of an unexecuted project for an austere convent of Santa Teresa in Querétaro and for a great portico-fronted rotunda for the Church of Nuestra Señora de Loreto in Mexico City. Both structures were built from the designs of others. Several distinguished Neo-Classical structures in the capital are attributed to Tolsá, including the church of the convent of Jesús María, and the houses of the Conde de Pérez Gálvez, now the Museo de San Carlos (Figs. 8.5 and 8.6), and of the Marqués del Apartado, now the Sub-Ministry of Culture. The extensive and handsome Hospicio Cabañas in Guadalajara, now frescoed with the heroic designs of José Clemente Orozco, are probably Tolsá's creation.

A third remarkable Neo-Classic artist, Francisco Eduardo de Tresguerras, was, like Ortiz de Castro and Tolsá, largely self-taught in architecture. Despite its emphasis on professional training, the academy made possible the rapid advancement of intelligent individuals who could educate themselves by studying architectural books. Such gifted beginners would have been blocked from architecture by the craft traditions of the guild system. Tresguerras was multitalented. He was a musician and a poet, as well as an engraver, a painter, and an architect. He was born in Celaya in 1759 and early in life tested a clerical vocation. His buildings are in his native city and in places nearby in the Bajío rather than in the capital, where he spent a year at the academy in 1794 while in his middle thirties. He petitioned for approval to exercise freely the profession of architecture stating that he had "complied with all the requirements, as is shown by the Plan and Elevation as assigned and executed by me in the Sala del Arquitectura of my own invention, without copying or fraud."[14] Tresguerras's language conveys something of his restless and prickly nature. There is no evidence that Tresguerras was honored by the title *Academico de Merito* but he later wrote that "the Academy recognizes me as its disciple and has licensed me for work of any kind."[15] The earliest known activity of Tresguerras was in the late 1780s at the church of the Convent of Santa Rosa de Viterbo in Querétaro, celebrated for its late Baroque nave retablos. Tresguerras was probably responsible for redesigning the tower, increasing its size, and modifying the ornamentation of the dome. He wrote contemptuously of Ignacio Mariano de las Casas, the designer of the church and almost certainly of some or all of the retablos, describing the altarpieces as being in the most diseased taste. Tresguerras's documented works include the restrained Neptune fountain in Querétaro (1797), his masterpiece, the Church of the Carmen in Celaya (1802–07) (Figs. 8.13–8.16), and the me-

morial chapel he designed for himself in the *atrio* of San Francisco, also in his native city. Attributions abound. Generally accepted as his are the Church of the Convent of Santa Teresa in Querétaro (1803), for which Tolsá had submitted a design and Ortiz de Castro initiated construction; a bridge over the Río de la Laja near Celaya; and the House of the Conde de Rul in Guanajuato, which Humboldt praised for its remarkable purity of style and described as a structure which would ornament the best streets of Naples or Paris. Rul was the second son-in-law of the Conde de Valenciana to construct a Neo-Classical building admired by Humboldt. The other, the Conde de Pérez Gálvez, had his house in the capital designed by Tolsá (see Figs. 8.5 and 8.6).

The exponents of the new taste associated with the Academy of San Carlos were scathing in their denunciations of the works of the Baroque architects of the preceding generation. They and their pupils were responsible for the redecoration of many church interiors and for the destruction of many of the finest Baroque retablos. Had Mexican prosperity continued after the outbreak of Father Hidalgo's revolutionary insurrection of 1810, their program of artistic reconstruction would undoubtedly have extended beyond refurbishing of church interiors to massive demolishing and rebuilding of Baroque structures.

The dislike of Neo-Classicists for the complexity and what they regarded as the irrationality of Baroque design was paralleled by enlightened clergymen's aversion toward popular Baroque religious observances. They were particularly offended by religious images that seemed omnipresent and all too often "indecent, ugly and ridiculous,"[16] more likely to rouse derision than genuine religious devotion. A priest in an Indian community attacked the custom of having a villager represent Christ in Holy Week with his "face, shoulders and body bathed in blood."[17] Archbishop of Mexico Francisco Antonio de Lorenzana (1766–72) prohibited, under threat of twenty-five lashes, "all live representations of the Passion of Christ our Redeemer, the Volador pole, all dances of Santiago . . . [, and] representations of Shepherds and Kings."[18]

Despite their relative simplicity and their uniform of chaste, light-colored building stone,

8.4 House of the Conde Rul, Guanajuato.

the best works of the Mexican Neo-Classicists display notable Baroque characteristics. The first major Neo-Classical design, Ortiz de Castro's project for the completion of the cathedral, is restrained if not severe (Fig. 8.1). But its bell-shaped tower tops, borrowed from Ventura Rodríguez, with their terminating balls and crosses, provide a Baroque note of upward curving aspiration

block of the School of Mines initially seems to be properly classical with the pedimental forms placed at the center of the three outer sides and the horizontal balustrade terminating the walls on either side of these forms (Fig. 8.7). Closer examination of the decorative detailing discloses broken pediments and Baroque verticality, in projecting elements over the side entrances of the

8.5 House of the Marqués de Pérez Gálvez, now the Museum of San Carlos, Mexico City, patio. See also Plate XV.

8.6 House of the Marqués de Pérez Gálvez.

(Fig. 8.2) quite similar to that struck by the towers designed by Christopher Wren for St. Paul's and more distantly akin to that of the towers of Jacob Prandtauer's Abbey church of Melk on the Danube. The works of Manuel Tolsá reflect a personality attracted to Baroque unity and movement despite training in Neo-Classical separation of parts and clarity of definition (Fig. 8.2). The junctions between drum and dome proper and between dome proper and lantern in his cathedral dome are blurred by curving pediments and a finial-topped balustrade in the first instance, and by upswinging ribs, rhythmically draped swags, upcurving buttresses, and another finial topped balustrade in the second. His house for the Conde de Pérez Gálvez, although restrained in ornamentation, is built around an oval patio and is fronted by a concave facade. The massive three-story

main front to the west (Fig. 8.8), and odd shelflike bracketed projections over the windows and below the blind arches of the principal story. Above the horizontal balustrades at the top of the walls are pairs of bell-like finials which alternate rhythmically, two facing the sky and two facing the ground. The principal patio is distinguished by a delicate rhythm of flattened arches swinging between paired Ionic columns at its upper level and by a powerful divided Baroque stair (Fig. 8.9).

The most striking Neo-Classical church in Mexico City is the Church of Our Lady of Loreto, which was designed by Ignacio Castera and Agustín Paz and constructed between 1809 and 1816. The facade is restrained and planar, decorated by a pediment and pilasters, either austerely fluted or austerely rusticated. The belfry stages of the towers are topped by small Baroque domes,

197

8.7 *School of Mines, Mexico City.*

8.9 *School of Mines, Mexico City, grand stair. See also Plate XVI.*

but their most prominent features are pedimented edicules which house the bells. Rearing up behind the chaste facade is a massive Baroque dome decorated by riblike projections of varying width and a diminutive lantern topped by a large ball and cross. The six bays of the round drum stage contain tall glass windows framed by Serlian, or Palladian, motifs with their central arches crowned by pediments, alternately triangular and arched. Set between the bays are paneled buttresses that support finials shaped as curving obelisks terminating in star-topped balls. The plan of

8.10 *Church of Loreto, Mexico City, central facade and portal.*

8.8 *School of Mines, Mexico City, side portal.*

8.11 *Church of Loreto, Mexico City, view of the dome from the rear.*

198

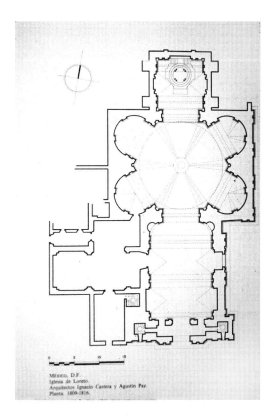

8.12 *Church of Loreto, Mexico City, plan, from* Cuarenta Siglos.

8.13 *Church of the Carmen, Celaya.*

the interior is the most spatially dynamic in vice-regal Mexico. The dark nave contracts before one enters the bright area beneath the dome. There huge niches burst from the central space, and, below the springing of the arches, an angled and curving entablature swings around the entire area, linking the niches and the intervening piers to the nave and to the deep chancel.

The frontal tower of Francisco Eduardo de Tresguerras's Church of the Carmen in Celaya is a prime example of the Mexican Neo-Classicists' tendency to fuse classical and Baroque forms in a whole which seems more Baroque than Neo-Classical. The entrance porch is assertively classical with its pedimented frontispiece, fluted columns, severe pilasters, and full Doric entablature. Above the porch, traces of the Baroque appear in the scroll brackets, which ease the transition from its breadth to the tall cubic stage of the tower, and in the paired brackets of the clock stage. The tower seems to swell out into its two belfry stages and to contract in a final stage

capped with a bell-shaped dome of glazed tile. The orders of the belfry stages are regularly classical, Ionic and Corinthian, but the overall effect is Baroque. This is most apparent in the upper of the two stages with its inverted, upward-curving scroll brackets at the four corners and its broken pediments on the four faces which serve to frame oval openings in the ultimate stage above.

Other elements of the church also display Baroque characteristics. The elegant dome over the crossing (Fig. 8.14) is comparatively regular, inspired by the Michelangelo–Della Porta dome of St. Peter's, and decorated with ribs and shimmering chevrons in yellow glazed tile. As at St. Peter's, paired Corinthian columns buttress the drum. Swag-draped ovals and Michelangelesque brackets decorate the eared frames surrounding the windows. The most Baroque feature of the exterior is the handsome and spatially com-

199

8.14 *Church of the Carmen, Celaya, dome.*

plex portal on the south side. Strikingly Baroque is the diagonal arrangement of columns subtly suggesting both convexity and concavity at the portal level and strongly suggesting convexity at the level above. The upper stage recalls to some extent the formal arrangement of Borromini's façade of the Church of San Carlo alle Quatro Fontane in Rome, with its strongly projecting niche set in a recessed arc defined by the concave swing of the upper balustrade against the sky.

In general appearance the surviving portion of Tresguerras's interior, that below the

8.16 *Church of the Carmen, Celaya, interior, the crossing.*

level of the vaulting, is wholly classical, brilliantly white and gold with only touches of color. But a study of the eleven handsome retablos reveals the Baroque animation they share with the tower and the south portal. In his greatest work Tresguerras, savage polemicist against the earlier architects of the Mexican Baroque, reveals himself to be, even more strikingly than Manual Tolsá, a belated exponent of the style.

In the decades following the completion of the cathedral and the School of Mines in 1813 and of the Church of Loreto three years later, few buildings of any distinction were constructed in Mexico even though Tresguerras lived on until 1833. Political instability and economic uncertainty discouraged ambitious architectural under-

8.15 *Church of the Carmen, Celaya, side portal.*

takings and led to the extinction of the distinguished line of native-born architects. The most notable structures of mid-century were designed by foreigners, the Spaniard Lorenzo de la Hidalga, and the Italian Javier (Severio) Cavallari. Hidalga designed the grand, columned National Theater, originally the Gran Teatro de Santa Anna, and a Neo-Classical main altar for the cathedral. They were demolished in 1900 and 1943, respectively. His principal surviving work is the powerful double-tiered dome of Santa Teresa la Antigua, just east of the cathedral. Cavallari, a Sicilian who had studied in Göttingen and served as director of the academy in Milan, came to reestablish the program in architecture of the Academy of San Carlos and to link it to civil engineering. He redesigned the building housing the academy, providing it with its present facade, reminiscent of Italian Renaissance palaces.

The principal civic structures constructed toward the end of the long regime of Porfirio Díaz were also designed by Italians: the central post office in 1902 by Silvio Contri, and another national theater, now known as the Palace of Bellas Artes, begun in 1904 by Adamo Boari. Three of the most interesting buildings of the Díaz period were the work of native-born masons; the Church of San Antonio in Aguascalientes with its three-towered frontispiece and amply colonnaded dome was designed by J. Refugio Reyes, and the superstructure of the parish church and the dome of the convent church of La Concepción in San Miguel Allende were both designed by Ceferino Gutiérrez, an Indian without formal training who is reported to have illustrated his ideas for workmen by sketching on the ground. In the years after 1880 the eighteenth-century parish church was entirely covered with a toy Gothic tower composed of rounded buttresses, pointed arches, and pyramidal pinnacles. The dome of La Concepción, constructed in 1891, is more orthodox with a double-tiered drum and ten sides. Another striking double-tiered dome, with oval window openings cut through the curving upper slope, was added to Felipe de Ureña's Church of the Compañía in Guanajuato between 1881 and 1884.

The political upheavals of the early twentieth century inhibited architectural develop-

8.17 *Palace of Bellas Artes, Mexico City.*

8.18 *Parish Church, San Miguel Allende.*

201

8.19 *National University of Mexico, Library Book Stack.*

8.21 *Church of the Miraculous Virgin, Mexico City, from Paul F. Damaz,* Art in Latin American Architecture, *p. 74, photograph of Erwin Lang.*

8.20 *House of Juan O'Gorman, Mexico City, from Paul F. Damaz,* Art in Latin American Architecture, *p. 229, photograph of Annie Damaz.*

ments between 1910 and the early 1920s. The revival of a vital Mexican architecture can be attributed primarily to the modernist teaching of José Villagrán García in the National Academy beginning in 1926. Among his pupils was Juan O'Gorman, designer of the first "functional" houses in Mexico, which included the house and studio of Díego Rivera. O'Gorman is now better

known for his mosaic-covered book stack for the National University library and for the extraordinary house he designed for himself. The house suggests a kinship to the fantastic designs of Antoni Gaudí and even to the spirit, if not the forms, of the grotesque statuary of the sixteenth-century garden of Bomarzo in Italy. Mexican structures which make dramatic use of thin concrete-shell roofing are internationally known. Among the most striking are the Church of the Purísima in Monterrey (1946) and the Chapel of the Padres del Espíritu Santo in Coyoacán (1957) by Enrique de la Mora, and the works of the Madrid-born engineer Félix Candela, who had served with the Spanish Republican forces and who later emigrated to the United States. Candela designed or collaborated in the design of several churches, including that of the Miraculous Virgin in Mexico City (1955); markets and diverse industrial structures; a Palace of Sports for the 1968 Olympics; a restaurant on a canal in Xochimilco (1958) with rippling parabolic shells; and a soaring open chapel in Cuernavaca (1959).

Approximately 150 architects, engineers, painters, and sculptors collaborated in designing structures between 1949 and 1954 for University City, a new campus of the National University on the southern fringe of Mexico City. Of particular interest, in addition to O'Gorman's library, are structures created by Alberto Arai for athletics; the designs for their outer walls, which contain courts for handball and related games, were inspired by Indian pyramid structures. The Olympic Stadium of Augusto Pérez Palacios, Raúl Salinas, and Jorge Bravo is also of great interest, with its floating cantilevered upper tier of seating. Another notable arena is Aztec Stadium (1965) designed by Pedro Ramírez Vázquez, Rafael Mijares, and Luis Martínez del Campo. Dramatic structural technique is also a feature of Ramírez Vazquez's Museum of Anthropology (1964) with

8.22 National University of Mexico, Fronton Courts.

8.23 National Archeological Museum, Mexico City, fountain in court.

8.24 Horse Exercise Area, San Cristóbal, house of Mr. and Mrs. Folke Egerstrom, Los Clubes subdivision, Mexico. The Architecture of Luis Barragán, pp. 94-95, photograph of Armando Salas Portugal.

8.25 Plaza and Fountain del Bebedero, Las Arboledes subdivision, Mexico City, from Emilio Ambasz, The Architecture of Luis Barragán, p. 69, photograph of Armando Salas Portugal.

its aluminum canopy, or umbrella, in the central court supported by a single sculpted pillar splashed by cascading water.

The great master of landscape and domestic architecture was Luis Barragán who died at eighty-six in 1988. In his one convent and in the houses, gardens, and fountains located in the lava beds of the Pedregal section of southwestern Mexico City, Barragán created an intensely personal and Mexican version of European minimalist modernism which recalls a wide diversity of sources: Mies van der Rohe's Barcelona Pavillion, the gardens and whitewashed North African

8.26 Ricardo Legoretta Hotel Camino Real, Mexico City, forecourt.

buildings of the Moors, and the ordinary structures of rural Mexico which he knew as a boy. By the simplest of means Barragán created serene spaces (Fig. 8.24) which have been associated with

the visions of surrealists like Magritte and De Chirico. His walls, both warmly colored and white, and cut by a few rectangular openings, are placed with an assured sense of interval and of the effect of subtle variations in height and width. Simple constructed forms are masterfully related to natural elements, to trees, to the broad Mexican sky, and to patterns of light and shadow. Particularly
dramatic is Barragán's handling of water, jetting up and cascading down from fountains and spread in shimmering mysteriously sheeted pools (Fig. 8.25).

Ricardo Legoretta, like O'Gorman a student of José Villagrán and, later, his partner, shares Barragán's love of strong colors and stark wall surfaces and his respect for the Mexican vernacular and colonial traditions. Legoretta's buildings extend from houses and resorts to offices and factories. He respectfully restored the house José Antonio Guerrero y Torres designed for the Marqués de Jaral de Berrio.

The Mexican architectural tradition was obliterated during the protracted upheavals of the nineteenth and early twentieth centuries. Many colonial structures, particularly churches, hospitals, and conventos in the capital, were casually obliterated. More recently the immense growth of Mexico City has resulted in problems that seem nearly beyond management. Yet an imaginative vitality has been rekindled in Mexican architecture in recent decades, distinct from international modernism or post-modernism. Figures such as O'Gorman, Barragán, and Legoretta exemplify this creativity which has restored to Mexico an architectural distinction reminiscent of the eighteenth century when Lorenzo Rodríguez and Francisco Antonio Guerrero y Torres were without peers on this continent.

Notes

Chapter I

1. Díaz del Castillo, *The True History of the Conquest of New Spain*, in the edition of the Hakluyt Society Series 2, Vol. 24 (London, 1910), Book 5, Ch. 87, p. 37.

2. Ibid, p. 38.

3. William Bradford, *Of Plymouth Plantation 1620–1647* (New York, 1952), Ch. 9, pp. 61–62.

4. *Hernán Cortés: Letters from Mexico* (New Haven and London, 1986), Second Letter, p. 56.

5. Díaz del Castillo, *The True Conquest of New Spain*, Ch. 92, p. 73.

6. Ibid, p. 76.

7. Ibid, p. 77.

8. Motolinía, *Motolinía's History of the Indians of New Spain* (Berkeley, 1950), Book 1, Ch. 2, p. 86.

9. Ibid, p. 88.

10. *Letters from Mexico*, Third Letter, p. 223.

11. Ibid, p. 270.

12. Ibid.

13. *Motolinía's History of the Indians of New Spain*, Book 1, Ch. 1, pp. 41–42.

14. Kubler, George, *Mexican Architecture of the Sixteenth Century* (New Haven, 1948), p. 73.

15. *Letters from Mexico*, Fourth Letter, p. 322.

16. Ibid, p. 323.

Chapter II

1. Quoted in McAndrew, John, *The Open-Air Churches of Sixteenth-Century Mexico* (Cambridge, 1965), p. 83.

2. Ibid, p. 77.

3. *Motolinía's History of the Indians of New Spain*, Book 1, Ch. 13, p. 92.

4. *The Open-Air Churches of Sixteenth-Century Mexico*, p. 175.

5. McAndrew, John, *The Open-Air Churches of Sixteenth-Century Mexico* (Cambridge, 1965), p. 176.

6. Palou, Francisco, *Historical Account of the Life and Apostolic Labors of the Venerable Father Fray Junípero Serra* (Washington, 1955), p. 33.

7. Quoted in Toussaint, Manuel, *Colonial Art in New Mexico* (Austin, 1967), pp. 23–24.

8. There is a 1934 photograph showing the neoclassical tabernacle. I've found no date for its removal.

Chapter III

1. *Escritos sueltos*, p. 92, quoted and translated by John McAndrew, *The Open-Air Churches of Sixteenth-Century Mexico*, p. 93.

2. Prescott, William H., *History of the Conquest of Mexico* (New York, 1843), Vol. 3, Appendix 2, No. 15, p. 478.

3. Fourth Letter, p. 333.

4. Motolinía's *History of the Indians of New Spain*, Book 3, Ch. 17, p. 261.

5. Ibid, p. 262. Later the Indian community of Tlaxcala attempted to resist supplying labor drafts for construction and agricultural work in Puebla.

6. *Life in the Imperial and Loyal City of Mexico in New Spain, Dialogues for the Study of the Latin Language* (Austin, 1953), p. 40.

7. Ibid, p. 48.

8. Ibid, p. 54.

9. Ibid, p. 40.

10. Hakluyt, Richard, *The Principal Navigations Voyages Traffiques & Discoveries of the English Nation* (London, New York, 1910), Vol. 6, p. 287.

11. Weismann, Elizabeth Wilder, *Art and Time in Mexico* (New York, 1985), p. 37.

12. Archivo General de la Nación (Mexico City) Reales Cédulas, duplicado vol. 47, folio 427, translation by Elizabeth Wilder Weismann in Manuel Toussaint, *Colonial Art in Mexico* (Austin & London, 1967), p. 110.

13. Ibid.

14. Ibid.

CHAPTER IV

1. *The Mediterranean and the Mediterranean World in the Age of Philip II* (New York, 1973), Vol. 2, p. 835.
2. *The Open-Air Churches of Sixteenth-Century Mexico*, p. 89.
3. Paz, Octavio, *Sor Juana* (Cambridge, 1988), p. 467.
4. Ibid, p. 126.
5. Calderón de la Barca, Frances Erskine, *Life in Mexico* (Berkeley, Los Angeles and London, 1982), pp. 152–54.
6. "Respuesta a Sor Filotea de la Cruz," *Obras completas de Sor Juana de la Cruz* (Mexico City, 1957), Vol. 4, pp. 446–47, 450–51. Translations are available in Alan S. Trueblood and Octavio Paz, *A Sor Juana Anthology* (Cambridge and London, 1988), and Margaret Sayers Peden, *A Woman of Genius* (Salisbury, 1982).
7. Lafaye, Jacques, *Quetzalcóatl and Guadalupe* (Chicago and London, 1976), p. 239.
8. Brading, D. A., *The First America* (Cambridge, New York, Port Chester, Melbourne, Sydney, 1991), p. 236.
9. (Mexico City, 1969), Vol. 1, Prólogo general, the pages are unnumbered.
10. (New York, 1985), p. 60.
11. (Berkeley and Los Angeles, 1962), p. 105.
12. Quoted by Weismann, Elizabeth Wilder, *Mexico in Sculpture* (Cambridge, 1950), p. 125.

CHAPTER V

1. Pp. 198–200.

CHAPTER VI

1. *Political Essay on the Kingdom of New Spain* (London, 1822) Book 2, Ch. 6, p. 184.
2. *Colonial Entrepreneurs: Families and Business in Bourbon Mexico City*, (Albuquerque, 1983), pp. 16–17.
3. *The True History of the Conquest of New Spain*, Book 17, Ch. 210, p. 275.
4. Simpson, Lesley Byrd, *Many Mexicos* (Berkeley, Los Angeles, London, 1966), pp. 256–57.
5. Brading, D. A., *Miners and Merchants in Bourbon Mexico 1763–1810* (Cambridge, 1971), p. 21.
6. Letter to Admiral Andrés de Pez, Irving A. Leonard, *Don Carlos Sigüenza y Góngora* (Berkeley, 1929), Appendix B, p. 240.
7. Ibid, p. 275.
8. Quoted in *Miners and Merchants in Bourbon Mexico*, p. 39.
9. Probert, Alan, "Pedro Romero de Terreros," *Journal of the West*, Vol. XIV (1975), p. 70.
10. Diario del viaje que hizo a la América en el siglo XVIII 2 Vols (Mexico, 1964), quoted in *Miners and Merchants of Bourbon Mexico*, p. 276.
11. Ladd, Doris, *The Mexican Nobility at Independence 1780–1826* (Austin, 1976), p. 53.
12. Ibid, p. 63.
13. *Mexico in Sculpture*, p. 153.

14. Romero de Terreros, Manuel, *The House of Tiles* (Mexico City, 1934), p. 21.
15. Chevalier, François, *Land and Society in Colonial Mexico: The Great Hacienda* (Berkeley and Los Angeles), p. 82.
16. Baxter, Sylvester, "The Passing of the 'House of Tiles'," *Architectural Record* 46 (1919): 493–95.
17. *Artes de México* 79/80 (1966): 17, 35.
18. *Land and Society in Colonial Mexico*, p. 296.
19. Robinson, William Davis, *Memoirs of the Mexican Revolution* (Philadelphia, 1820), p. 151.
20. Ibid, p. 153.

CHAPTER VII

1. *Mexico in Sculpture*, p. 130.
2. Quoted by Berlin, Heinrich, "Three Master Architects in New Spain," *Hispanic American Historical Review* 27 (1947): 378.
3. *Mexico in Sculpture*, p. 212.
4. *Miners and Merchants in Bourbon Mexico*, pp. 198–99.
5. Vargas Lugo, Elisa, *La Iglesia de Santa Prisca de Taxco* (Mexico City, 1974), p. 27.
6. *Miners and Merchants in Bourbon Mexico*, pp. 199–200.
7. *The Churches of Mexico 1530–1810* (Berkeley and Los Angeles, 1962), p. 114.
8. "Eighteenth-Century Church Fronts in Mexico City," *Journal of the Society of Architectural Historians* 5 (1945–46): 30.
9. *The Principal Navigations Voyages Traffiques & Discoveries of the English Nation*, vol. 6, pp. 314–15.

CHAPTER VIII

1. *Political Essay on the Kingdom of New Spain*, Book 3, Ch. 8, pp. 32–33.
2. Ibid, p. 29.
3. Ibid, p. 30.
4. Ibid, p. 29.
5. Ibid, p. 31.
6. Ibid, Book 2, Ch. 7, p. 212.
7. Ibid, p. 214.
8. Ibid, p. 213.
9. Carrillo y Gariel, Abelardo, *Datos sobre la Academia de San Carlos* (Mexico City, 1939), pp. 33–36. The translations are by Elizabeth Wilder Weismann in Manuel Toussaint, *Colonial Art in Mexico*, pp. 405–6.
10. Ibid.
11. Ibid.
12. Ibid.
13. Report of Juan José de Gamboa quoted in *Colonial Art in Mexico*, p. 410.
14. *Datos sobre la Academia de San Carlos*, p. 34, translation *Colonial Art in Mexico*, p. 422.
15. *Colonial Art in Mexico*, p. 422.
16. *The First America*, p. 494.
17. Ibid.
18. Ibid, p. 495.

GLOSSARY

acolyte one who assists at the mass and other religious services.

alcalde mayor the chief magistrate of a province or district.

alfarje a ceiling constructed of small wooden pieces forming an interlacing pattern, of Moslem derivation.

alfiz a rectangular frame enclosing an arch, of Moslem derivation.

apse the polygonal, or curved, extension of a church which contains the principal altar.

archivolt a broad moulding curving around an arch.

artesonado a wooden ceiling containing sunken coffers.

ashlar masonry of dressed stone laid in horizontal courses with square edges.

atlante human male figure used in place of a column or pilaster.

atrio the area, usually walled and raised on a platform, in front of church.

audiencia a high court with administrative and judicial authority.

barrel-vault an arched ceiling or roof which is undivided so that it resembles a tunnel or the inside of a barrel.

barrio a section of a town or city, a ward.

basilica a type of church with a nave flanked by lower aisles and lighted by windows above them.

boss an ornamental projection dropped from the center of a vault or an arch.

bracket a small supporting element of stone or another material often attached to a wall.

buttress a projecting vertical element which supports a wall or a vault.

cabildo the governing council of a town, or the building in which it meets.

capital the head or crowning element of a column or pilaster.

cartouche an ornamental panel formed to resemble a scroll or a sheet of paper with curling edges.

cédula a royal decree.

chiluca a gray-white stone, like limestone.

clerestory the upper level of a wall with windows.

coffer a sunken panel, square or polygonal, used to decorate an arch, vault or ceiling.

cofradía a religious confraternity or sodality.

composite a classical order combining in its capital the icanthus leaves of the Corinthian order and the volutes of the Ionic.

confraternity a society organized for a religious purpose.

consulado the organization, or guild, of the principal merchants of Mexico City.

convento an establishment of friars or nuns, signifying both what are called in English friaries, or monasteries, and convents.

Corinthian a classical order, originally taller than the Doric or the Ionic, with a fluted shaft and a capital decorated with stylized icanthus leaves.

cornice the projecting moldings at the top of a structure; the topmost element of a classical entablature.

corregidor a royal official governing a district.

crenelation a battlemented top of a wall with alternating blocks and empty spaces, embrasures.

Creole a person born in America of Spanish parents or ancestry.

crossing the area of a church where the nave and transept intersect.

dado the ornamentation of the lower part of an interior wall.

dome a vault of even curvature built upon a circular or polygonal base.

dorador a craftsman who applies gold leaf to retablos or other forms of ornamentation.

Doric a classical order with a simple capital consisting of carved cushion and a block, and, normally, a fluted shaft.

drum a polygonal or circular section of wall supporting a dome; also a cylindrical block constituting a section of the shaft of a column.

encomendero the holder of an encomienda, a grant of Indian tribute, or Indian service with a responsibility, in theory, for the welfare of the Indians.

encomienda the grant of Indians who were required to perform services or pay tribute to the encomendero.

entablature the portion of a classical architectural order above the columns, normally including an architrave, a frieze, and a cornice.

escutcheon an architectural ornament in the form of a shield.

estípite a type of column or pilaster consisting of a base, an inverted obelisk, various blocky and sharp edged forms and an unorthodox capital roughly resembling a Corinthian one.

estofador a craftsman who coats wooden carvings with coatings of fine gesso to provide a basis for gilding and painting.

fiero a privilege of members of corporate bodies such as the clergy and the military, particularly the right to be tried in their own courts.

fillet a narrow band partially filling a flute on a column or pilaster.

finial an ornament placed at the top of a roof, gable or other architectural element, usually designed to provide a striking silhouette.

flute a vertical groove or channel on a column or pilaster.

flying-buttress a flying buttress is based some distance from the wall it supports and is linked to it by a "flying" arch.

fresco mural painting on plaster; in true fresco the pigment mixed with water is applied to fresh plaster; in dry fresco pigments bound in various substances are applied to dried plaster.

gargoyle a waterspout projecting from a wall or roof, or the parapet of a wall or tower, carved to resemble a grotesque figure, animal or human.

governor the elected head of an Indian community.

hacienda a large landed estate.

hall church a structure with aisles of the same height as the nave.

intendent the administrator of one of the twelve districts into which New Spain was divided by the Bourbon government. The responsibilities included fiscal and judicial as well as political matters.

Ionic a classical order with a capital containing spirals, or volutes, at its corners.

jamb the side pier or wall of a doorway or window, especially the surface along the opening.

keystone the center stone of an arch or vault, sometimes carved ornamentally.

lambriquin a pendant ornamental motif with a scalloped edge, originally a cloth ornament, a pinjante.

lantern a small turret, polygonal or circular, with windows all around designed to bring light into a dome or roof.

lunette the curved upper surface of a wall partly surrounded by a vault which intersects with the wall, often occupied by one or more windows.

mayorazgo an entailed estate passing wholly to the eldest (usually) male child.

mayordomo the manager of a landed estate.

merlon a solid section of a battlemented wall, often with a pyramidal top.

mestizo a person of mixed ancestry, Indian and Spanish.

mudéjar a style developed by Moslems in Christian Spain, or, more generally, by Moslems.

nave the central longitudinal area, or aisle, of a church.

niche a recess in a wall, or retablo, often containing a carved figure.

niche pilaster a decorative element which developed from the pilaster form and contains a niche, usually placed between and behind columns or estípites.

oidor a judge on the audiencia.

open chapel a chapel constructed in one of a variety of forms and styles which was open on one side for worshippers in the open air.

patio an inner courtyard of a secular building open to the sky, frequently surrounded by colonnades or arcades like a cloister.

pediment a low pitched gable over a portico, or a similar form used decoratively.

pendentive a concave triangular spandrel used to provide a transition from a squared space to a circular drum or a dome.

pilaster a flattened columnar shape attached for decoration to a wall.

pinjante a pendant ornamental motif with a scalloped edge, a lambriquin.

plateresque a flattened ornate decorative style of Spanish origin, literally like the work of a silversmith.

portal doorway.

portería the entrance to a friary or convento, frequently an arcaded porch.

portico a roofed space, often colonnaded, constituting an entrance or the centerpiece of a facade.

posa a chapel-like structure usually placed at a corner of an atrio, or forecourt, at which religious processions would pause.

retablo a decorative arrangement of painted panels and/or carved figures, usually placed in an architectural framework and rising behind an altar.

rib vault a section of arched ceiling supported or decorated by diagonal and, in many cases, other arched ribs.

Salomonic column or salomonica, a twisting column, named from the supposed use of such columns in the temple of Solomon.

segmental arch an arch consisting of a segment of a circle drawn from a center below the springing line, an arch which is flatter than a semi-circle.

spandrel the triangular space between two arches and the horizontal line drawn between their apexes.

squinch an arch or niche carried across the corner of a square to support a drum.

strapwork decorative interlacing bands, usually of stucco and with curving edges, of north European origin.

string course a continuous projecting horizontal band running across an external wall, usually used to mark off the level of a story or floor.

tecpan a large Indian structure including areas for domestic and governmental functions.

teocalli an Indian temple and its supporting pyramid.

tequitqui decorative work reflecting an Indian sense of form and pattern.

tezontle a reddish, or brownish, or purplish building stone of volcanic origin.

Tuscan order the barest of the classical orders, similar to the Doric but without fluting or other ornamentation, supposedly based on Etruscan temples.

tympanum the area between the lintel over a doorway and an arch above it.

villancio a popular song sung on religious occasions.

voussoir a wedge shaped stone or brick forming a section of an arch.

BIBLIOGRAPHY

BIBLIOGRAPHIES

Particularly useful bibliographies are included in the following works:

Angulo Íñiguez, Diego, Enrique Marco Dorta, and Mario J. Buschiazzo. *Historia del arte hispanoamericano.* 3 vols. Barcelona, 1945–56.

Baird, Joseph Armstrong. *The Churches of Mexico, 1530–1810.* Berkeley and Los Angeles, 1962.

Handbook of Latin American Studies. 1935–. Humanities bibliographies are published every other year, in even years.

Kubler, George. *Mexican Architecture in the Sixteenth Century.* 2 vols. New Haven, 1948.

Kubler, George, and Martin Soria. *Art and Architecture in Spain and Portugal and Their American Dominions: 1500–1800.* Baltimore, 1959.

Lockhart, James. *The Nahuas After the Conquest.* Stanford, 1992.

McAndrew, John. *The Open-Air Churches of Sixteenth Century Mexico.* Cambridge, 1965.

Smith, Robert C., and Elizabeth Wilder. *A Guide to the Art of Latin America.* Washington, 1948.

Toussaint, Manuel. *Colonial Art in Mexico.* Edited by Elizabeth Wilder Weismann. Austin, 1967.

Tovar de Teresa, Guillermo. *Bibliografiá novohispana de arte.* 2 vols. Mexico City, 1988.

———. *México barroco.* Mexico City, 1981.

Weismann, Elizabeth Wilder. "The History of Art in Latin America, 1500–1800: Some Trends and Challenges of the Last Decade." *Latin American Research Review* 10 (1975): 7–50.

GENERAL WORKS

Altman, Ida, and James Lockhart, eds. *Provinces of Early Mexico.* Los Angeles, 1976.

Anales del Instituto de Investigaciones Estéticas. Mexico City, 1937–.

Angulo Íñiguez, Diego, Enrique Marco Dorta, and Mario J. Buschiazzo. *Historia del arte hispanoamericano.* 3 vols. Barcelona, 1945–56.

Angulo Íñiguez, Diego. *Planos de monumentos arquitectónicos de América y Filipinas.* 3 vols. Seville, 1933–40.

Artes de México. Mexico City, 1953–.

Atl, Dr., José R. Benítez, and Manuel Toussaint. *Iglesias de Mexico.* 6 vols. Mexico City, 1924–27.

Baird, Joseph Armstrong. *The Churches of Mexico, 1530–1810.* Berkeley and Los Angeles, 1962.

Bargellini, Clara. *La arquitectura de la plata.* Mexico City, 1991.

Baxter, Sylvester. *Spanish Colonial Architecture in Mexico.* 1 vol. text, 9 vols. plates. Boston, 1901.

Berlin, Heinrich. "Three Master Architects in New Spain." *Hispanic American Historical Review* 27 (1947): 375–83.

Bethell, Leslie, ed. *History of Latin America.* Vols. I and II. Cambridge, 1984.

Brading, D. A. *The First America.* Cambridge, 1991.

Catálogo de construcciones religiosas del estado de Hidalgo. 2 vols. Mexico City, 1940–42.

Catálogo de construcciones religiosas del estado de Yucatán. 2 vols. Mexico City, 1945.

Fernández, Justino. *A Guide to Mexican Art.* Chicago, 1969.

Gerhard, Peter A. *A Guide to the Historical Geography of New Spain.* Cambridge, 1972.

———. *The North Frontier of New Spain.* Princeton, 1982.

———. *The Southeast Frontier of New Spain.* Princeton, 1979.

Gibson, Charles. *The Aztecs under Spanish Rule.* Stanford, 1964.

Journal of the Society of Architectural Historians 5 (1945–47).

Keleman, Pal. *Baroque and Rococo in Latin America.* New York, 1951.

Kubler, George. "Architects and Builders in Mexico, 1521–1550." *Journal of the Warburg and Courtauld Institutes* 7 (1944): 7–19.

———. *Mexican Architecture in the Sixteenth Century.* 2 vols. New Haven, 1948.

Kubler, George, and Martin Soria. *Art and Architecture in Spain and Portugal and Their American Dominions*. Baltimore, 1959.

———. *Studies in Ancient American and European Art*. New Haven, 1985.

Lavrin, Asunción, ed. *Latin American Women: Historical Perspectives*. Westport, 1978.

Liss, Peggy K. *Mexico Under Spain, 1521–1556*. Chicago and London, 1975.

Lockhart, James. *The Nahuas After the Conquest*. Stanford, 1992.

López Guzmán, Rafael, Lázaro Gila Medina, Ignacio Henares Cuéllar, and Guillermo Tovar de Teresa. *Arquitectura y carpintería mudéjar en Nueva España*. Mexico City, 1992.

Maza, Francisco de la. *Los retablos dorados de Nueva España*, Mexico City, 1950.

Maza, Francisco de la, Felipe Pardinas Illánez, Juan de la Encina, Luis Ortiz Macedo, and Xavier Moyssen. *Cuarenta Siglos de plastica mexicana: Arte colonial*. Mexico City, 1970.

MacLachlan, Colin M., and Jaime E. Rodríguez O. *The Forging of the Cosmic Race*. Berkeley and Los Angeles, 1980.

Mexico, Splendors of Thirty Centuries. New York, 1990.

Moreno Villa, José. *Lo mexicano en las artes plásticas*. Mexico City, 1948.

Parry, J. H. *The Spanish Seaborne Empire*. New York, 1966.

Rojas, Pedro. *Historia general del arte mexicano: Época colonial*. Mexico City-Buenos Aires, 1963.

Rosell, Lauro E. *Iglesias y conventos coloniales de la Ciudad de México*. Mexico City, 1946.

Simpson, Lesley Bird. *Many Mexicos*. Berkeley and Los Angeles, 1966.

Toussaint, Manuel. *Colonial Art in Mexico*. Edited by Elizabeth Wilder Weismann. Austin, 1967.

———. *Paseos coloniales*. Mexico City, 1962.

Tovar de Teresa, Guillermo. *Bibliografía novohispana de arte*. 2 vols. Mexico City, 1988.

———. *La ciudad de los palacios: Crónica de un patrimonio perdido*. 2 vols. Mexico City, 1990.

———. *México barroco*. Mexico City, 1981.

Vargas Lugo, Elisa. *Las portadas religiosas de México*. Mexico City, 1969.

Weismann, Elizabeth Wilder, *Mexico in Sculpture* Cambridge, 1950.

Weismann, Elizabeth Wilder, and Judith Hancock Sandoval. *Art and Time in Mexico*. New York, 1985.

SUGGESTED WORKS RELATED TO CHAPTER ONE

Bray, Warwick. *Everyday Life of the Aztecs*. London, 1968.

Broda, Johanna, Davíd Carrasco, Eduardo Matos Moctezuma. *The Great Temple of Tenochtitlan*. Berkeley, Los Angeles, London, 1987.

Calnek, Edward C. "The Internal Structure of Tenochtitlán" in Eric R. Wolf, ed. *The Valley of Mexico*. Albuquerque, 1976.

Clendennen, Inga. *Aztecs: An Interpretation*. Cambridge, New York, Port Chester, Melbourne, Sydney, 1991.

Coe, Michael D. *Mexico*. New York, 1977.

Cortés, Hernán. *Letters from Mexico*. Translated and edited by Anthony Pagden with an introduction by J. H. Elliott. New Haven, 1986.

Davies, Nigel. *The Aztecs*. London, 1973.

Díaz del Castillo, Bernal. *The True History of the Conquest of Mexico*. Vols. 23–25, 30, 40. Hakluyt Society. London, 1908–1916.

Gómara, Francisco López de. *Cortés: The Life of the Conqueror*. Berkeley and Los Angeles, 1964.

Hardoy, Jorge E. *Precolumbian Cities*. New York, 1973.

Kubler, George. *The Art and Architecture of Ancient America*. Baltimore, 1962.

León-Portilla, Miguel. *Broken Spears: The Aztec Account of the Conquest*. Boston, 1962.

Madariaga, Salvador de. *Hernán Cortés, Conqueror of Mexico*. London, 1942.

Matos Moctezuma, Eduardo. *The Aztecs*. New York, 1989.

Motolinía Toribio de Benevente. *Motolinía's History of the Indians of New Spain*. Washington, 1951.

Padden, Robert C. *The Hummingbird and the Hawk: Conquest and Sovereignty in the Valley of Mexico*. Columbus, 1967.

Pasztory, Esther. *Aztec Art*. New York, 1983.

Prescott, William H. *The History of the Conquest of Mexico*. New York, 1843 and many later editions, including Chicago, 1985, and editions paired with *The History of the Conquest of Peru*. New York, 1979, and New York, 1989.

Soustelle, Jacques. *The Daily Life of the Aztecs on the Eve of the Spanish Conquest*. Stanford, 1970.

Todorov, Tzvetan. *The Conquest of America*. New York, 1984.

Valliant, George Clapp. *Aztecs of Mexico*. New York, 1941.

Wagner, Harry Raup. *The Rise of Hernán Cortés*. Los Angeles, 1944.

SUGGESTED WORKS RELATING TO CHAPTER TWO

Borah, Woodrow. "The Spanish and Indian Law: New Spain." In George A. Collier, Renato I. Rosaldo and John D. Wirth eds., *The Inca and Aztec States, 1400–1800, Anthropology and History*. New York, 1982.

Edwards, Emily, and Manual Alvarez Bravo. *Painted Walls of Mexico*. Austin, 1966.

Gante, Pablo C. de. *La arquitectura de México en el siglo XVI*. Mexico City, 1954.

Kubler, George. *Mexican Architecture in the Sixteenth Century*. 2 vols. New Haven, 1948.

McAndrew, John. *The Open-Air Churches of Sixteenth Century Mexico*. Cambridge, 1965.

McAndrew, John, and Manuel Toussaint. "Tecali, Zacatlán and the Renacimiento Purista in Mexico." *Art Bulletin* 24(1942): 311–325.

MacGregor, Luis. *Actopan*. Mexico City, 1955.

Martínez del Sobral y Campa, Margarita. *Los conventos franciscanos poblanos y el número de oro*. Puebla, 1988.

Mendieta, Gerónimo de. *Historia eclesiástica indiana*. 2 vols. Madrid, 1973.

Mullen, Robert J. *Dominican Architecture in Sixteenth-Century Oaxaca*. Tempe, 1975.

Palou, Francisco. *The Historical Account of the Life and Apostolic Labors of the Venerable Father Fray Junípero Serra*. Washington, 1955.

Perry, Richard. *Mexico's Fortress Monasteries*. Santa Barbara, 1992.

Phelan, John Leddy *The Millenial Kingdom of the Franciscans in the New World: A Study of the Writings of Gerónimo de Mendieta*. Berkeley and Los Angeles, 1956.

Ricard, Robert. *The Spiritual Conquest of Mexico*. Berkeley, 1966.

Salas Cuesta, Marcela. *La iglesia y el convento de Huejotzingo*. Mexico City, 1982.

Toussaint, Manuel. *Acolman, guía oficial*. Mexico City, 1949.

Suggested Works Relating to Chapter Three

Benítez, Fernando. *The Century after Cortés*. Chicago, 1965.

———. *La Ciudad de Mexico, 1325–1982*. 3 vols. Mexico City, 1981–82.

Cervantes de Salazar, Francisco. *Life in the Imperial and Loyal City of Mexico in New Spain . . . . as Described in the Dialogues for the Study of the Latin Language*. Austin, 1953.

Chauvet, Fidel de Jesús. "The Church of San Francisco in Mexico City." *The Americas* 7 (1950–51): 13–30.

Fernández, Martha. *Arquitectura y gobierno virreinal: Los maestros mayores de la Ciudad de México, siglo XVII*. Mexico City, 1985.

Greenleaf, Richard E. *The Mexican Inquisition of the Sixteenth Century*. Albuquerque, 1969.

Hardoy, Jorge E. "European Urban Forms and their Utilization in Latin America." In *Urbanization in the Americas from its Beginnings to the Present*, edited by R. P. Schaedel, J. E. Hardoy, and N. S. Kinzer. The Hague and Paris, 1978.

Hardoy, Jorge E., and Carmen Aranovich. "The Scale and Function of Spanish American Cities around 1600." also In *Urbanization in the Americas from its Beginnings to the Present*, edited by R. P. Schaedel, J. E. Hardoy, and N. S. Kinzer. The Hague and Paris, 1978.

Leonard, Irving *Baroque Times in Old Mexico*. Ann Arbor, 1959.

Marco Dorta, Enrique. *Fuentes para la historia del arte Hispano-Americano*. I. Seville, 1951.

Marroqui, José María. *La ciudad de México*. 3 vols. Mexico City, 1900–1903.

Morse, Richard M. "Latin American Cities: Aspects of Structure and Function." *Comparative Studies in Society and History* 4 (1962): 473–93.

———. "Some Characteristics of Latin American Urban History," *American Historical Review* 67 (1962): 317–338.

Powell, Philip Wayne. *Soldiers, Indians and Silver: The Northward Advance of New Spain, 1550–1600*. Berkeley and Los Angeles, 1952.

Toussaint, Manuel. *La catedral de México*. Mexico City, 1948.

———. *La catedral y las iglesias de Puebla*. Mexico City, 1954.

———. Federico Gómez de Orozco, and Justino Fernández. *Planos de la Ciudad de México, Siglos XVI, XVII*. Mexico City, 1938.

Tovar de Teresa, Guillermo. *Bibliografía novohispana de arte*. 2 vols. Mexico City, 1988.

———. *La ciudad de los palacios: Crónica de un patrimonio perdido*. 2 vols. Mexico City, 1990.

Suggested Works Relating to Chapter Four

Berlin, Heinrich. "Salvador de Ocampo, A Mexican Sculptor." *Americas* IV (1947–48): 415–428.

Brading, D. A. *The First America*. Cambridge, New York, Port Chester, Melbourne, Sydney, 1991.

Braudel, Fernand. *The Mediterranean and the Mediterranean World in the Age of Philip II*. New York, 1973.

Calderón de la Barca, Frances Erskine. *Life in Mexico*. Berkeley, Los Angeles, and London, 1982.

Castro Morales, Efrain. "El santuario de Guadalupe de México en el siglo XVII." In *Retablo barroco a la memoria de Francisco de la Maza*, edited by Clementina Díaz y de Orando. Mexico City, 1974.

Chance, John K. *Race and Class in Colonial Oaxaca*. Stanford, 1978.

Fernández, Martha. *Arquitectura y gobierno virreinal: Los maestros mayores de la Ciudad de México, siglo XVII*. Mexico City, 1985.

———. *Artificios del Barroco*. Mexico City, 1990.

Gage, Thomas. *Travels in the New World*. Norman, 1958.

Lafaye, Jacques. *Quetzalcoatl and Guadalupe*. Chicago, 1976.

Lavrin, Asunción. "The Role of Nunneries in the Economy of New Spain in the 18th Century." *Hispanic American Historical Review* 46 (1966): 371–393.

———. "Women in Convents: Their Economic and Social Role in Colonial Mexico." In *Liberating Women's History: Theoretical and Critical Essays*, edited by Bernice A. Carroll. Champaign Urbana, 1976.

Leonard, Irving. *Baroque Times in Old Mexico*. Ann Arbor, 1959.

Martin, Luis. *Daughters of the Conquistadors*. Albuquerque, 1983.

Maza, Francisco de la. *Arquitectura de los coros de monjas en México*. Mexico City, 1956.

———. *La ciudad de méxico en el siglo XVII*. Mexico City, 1968.

———. *El guadalupanismo mexicano*. Mexico City, 1953.

Muriel, Josefina. *Conventos de monjas en la Nueva España*. Mexico City, 1946.

Obregón, Gonzalo. *La capilla de los Medina Picazo en la iglesia de Regina Coeli*. Mexico City, 1971.

Paz, Octavio. *Sor Juana*. Cambridge, 1988.

Tovar de Teresa, Guillermo. *Bibliografía novohispana de arte*. 2 vols. Mexico City, 1988.

———. "Consideraciones sobre retablos, gremios y artífices de la Nueva España en los siglos XVII, XVIII." *Historia Mexicana* 133, no. 34 (1984): 5–40.

Suggested Works Relating to Chapter Five

Gustin, Monique. El barroco en el Sierra Gorda. Mexico City, 1969.

Kubler, George. "Indianism, *Mestizaje*, and *Indigenismo* as Classical, Medieval and Modern Traditions in Latin America." *Studies in Ancient American and European Art* (New Haven, 1985): 75–80.

McAndrew, John. *The Open-Air Churches of Sixteenth Century Mexico*. Cambridge, 1965.

Neumeyer, Alfred. "The Indian Contribution to Architectural Decoration in Spanish Colonial America." *Art Bulletin* 30 (1948): 104–121.

Reyes Valerio, Constantino. *Tepalcingo*. Mexico City, 1960.

———. *Trilogía barroco*. Mexico City, 1960.

Rojas, Pedro. *Tonantzintla*. Mexico City, 1956.

Tovar de Teresa, Guillermo. *Bibliografía novohispana de arte*. 2 vols. Mexico City, 1988.

SUGGESTED WORKS RELATING TO CHAPTER SIX

Borah, Woodrow. *New Spain's Century of Depression*. Berkeley, 1951.

Boyer, Richard. "Mexico in the Seventeenth Century: Transition to a Colonial Society." *Hispanic American Historical Review* 57 (1977): 455–478.

Brading, D. A. "The City in Bourbon Spanish America: elite and masses." *Comparative Urban Research* 8 (1980): 71–85.

———. *Miners and Merchants in Bourbon Mexico*. Cambridge, 1971.

Chevalier, François. *Land and Society in Colonial Mexico: The Great Hacienda*. Berkeley and Los Angeles, 1963.

Couturier, Edith B. "The Philanthropic Activities of Pedro Romero de Terreros, First Count of Regla 1753–1781." *The Americas* 32 (1975): 13–30.

Escobar de Rangel, Magdalena. *La Casa de los Azulejos*. San Angel, 1986, 1989.

Flores Marini, Carlos. *Casas virreinales en la Ciudad de México*. Mexico City, 1970.

Gamboa, Fernando and others. *Edificaciones del Banco Nacional de México*. Mexico City, 1988.

Gómez Serrano, Jesús. *El Mayorazgo Rincón Gallardo*. Aguascalientes, 1984.

González Polo, Ignacio. *El Palacio de las Condes de Santiago de Calimaya*. Mexico City, 1973.

"Haciendas de Mexico." *Artes de Mexíco* 79/80 (1966).

Hoberman, Louisa Schell. "Merchants in Seventeenth Century Mexico: A Preliminary Portrait." *Hispanic American Historical Review* 57 (1977): 479–503.

———. *Mexico's Merchant Elite, 1590–1660*. Durham, 1990.

Israel, J. I. "Mexico and the 'General Crisis' of the Seventeenth Century." *Past and Present* 63 (May 1974): 33–57.

———. *Race, Class and Politics in Colonial Mexico 1610–1670*. Oxford, 1975.

Kicza, John E. *Colonial Entrepreneurs, Families and Business in Bourbon Mexico City*. Albuquerque, c. 1983.

Ladd, Doris M. *The Making of a Strike*. Lincoln, 1988.

———. *The Mexican Nobility at Independence, 1780–1826*. Austin, 1976.

Leonard, Irving A. *Don Carlos de Sigüenza y Góngora*. Berkeley, 1929.

Obregón, Gonzalo. *El Real Colegio de San Ignacio de México*. Mexico City, 1949.

Probert, Alan. "The Pachuca Papers." *Journal of the West* 12 (1973): 85–125.

———. "Pedro Romero de Terreros." *Journal of the West* 14 (1975): 51–78.

Robinson, William Davis. *Memoirs of the Mexican Revolution*. Philadelphia, 1820.

Rojas, Pedro. *La Casa de los Mascarones*. Mexico City, 1985.

Romero de Terreros, Manuel. *The House of Tiles*. Mexico City, 1934.

Sánchez Navarro y Peón, Carlos. *Memories of an Old Palace*. Mexico City, c. 1975.

Seed, Patricia B. "A Mexican Noble Family: The Counts of the Orizaba Valley 1560–1867." Masters thesis, University of Texas at Austin, n.d.

Simpson, Lesley Bird. *The Encomienda in New Spain*. Berkeley, 1950.

Tutino, John. "Men and Women of the Mexican Elite 1750–1810." *The Americas* 39 (1983): 359–381.

Wagner, Henry R. "Early Silver Mining in New Spain." *Revisita de Historia de América* 14 (1942): 49–71.

SUGGESTED WORKS RELATING TO CHAPTER SEVEN

Angulo Íñiguez, Diego. "Eighteenth Century Church Fronts in Mexico City." *Journal of the Society of Architectural Historians* 5 (1945–46): 27–32.

Baird, Joseph Armstrong. "Eighteenth Century Retablos in the Bajio, Mexico: the Queretaro Style." *Art Bulletin* 35 (1953): 197–216.

———. "The Ornamental Niche Pilaster in the Hispanic World." *Journal of the Society of Architectural Historians* 17 (1956): 5–11.

———. "Style in 18th Century Mexico." *Journal of Inter-American Studies* 1 (1959): 261–276.

Collier, Margaret. "New Documents on Lorenzo Rodríguez and his Style." *International Congress of the History of Art* 22 (Princeton 1963): 203–218.

Fernández, Justino. *El Retablo de los Reyes*. Mexico City, 1959.

Flores Marini, Carlos. *Tianguistenco*. Mexico City, 1965.

Louchheim, Aline B. "The Church Facades of Lorenzo Rodriguez." Masters thesis, New York University, 1941.

Manrique, Jorge Alberto. "El 'Neostilo': La última carta del barroco mexicano." *Historia Mexicana* 20 (1970–71): 335–367.

Maza, Francisco de la. *El Churrigueresco en la Ciudad de México*. Mexico City, 1969.

Patton, Glenn Neil. "Francisco Antonio Guerrero y Torres and the Baroque Architecture of Mexico City in the Eighteenth Century." Ph.D. diss., University of Michigan, 1958.

San Miguel, Fray Andrés de. *Obras de Fray Andrés de San Miguel*. Mexico City, 1969.

Schuetz, Mardith E., ed. *Architectural Practice in Mexico City: A Manual for Journeyman Architects of the Eighteenth Century*. Tucson, c. 1987.

Toussaint, Manuel. *Taxco: Su historia, sus monumentos, características actuales y posibilidades turísticas*. Mexico City, 1931.

Tovar de Teresa, Guillermo. *Gerónimo de Balbás en la Catedral de México.* Mexico City, 1990.

———. *México barroco.* Mexico City, 1981.

Vargas Lugo, Elisa. *La Iglesia de Santa Prisca de Taxco.* Mexico City, 1974.

Villegas, Victor Manuel, *El gran signo formal del Barroco.* Mexico City, 1956.

SUGGESTED WORKS RELATING
TO CHAPTER EIGHT

Almela y Vives, Francisco, and A. Igual Ubeda. *El arquitecto y escultor valenciano Manuel Tolsá* 1757–1816. Valencia, 1950.

Ambasz, Emilio. *The Architecture of Luis Barragán.* New York, 1976.

Angulo Íñiguez, Diego. *La arquitectura neoclásica en Méjico.* Madrid, 1958.

Attoe, Wayne, ed. *The Architecture of Ricardo Legorreta.* Austin, 1990.

Carillo y Gariel, Abelardo. *Datos sobre la academia de San Carlos en Nueva España.* Mexico, 1939.

Cetto, Max L. *Modern Architecture in Mexico.* New York, 1961.

Charlot, Jean. *Mexican Art and the Academy of San Carlos.* Austin, 1962.

Fernández, Justino. *El arte del siglo XIX en México.* Mexico City, 1967.

———. *Arte Moderno y Contemporáneo de México.* Mexico City, 1952.

———. *El Palacio de Minería.* Mexico City, 1951.

Humboldt, Alexander von. *Political Essay on the Kingdom of New Spain.* 4 vols. London, 1811.

Mariscal, Federico E. *La arquitectura en México.* Vol. II. Mexico City, 1932.

Marley, David, ed. *Proyecto, estatutos, demás documentos relacionados al establecimiento de Real Academia . . . de San Carlos de Nueva España. 1781–1802.* Mexico City, 1984.

Salas Portugal, Armando. *Armando Salas Portugal Photographs of the Architecture of Luis Barragán.* New York, 1992.

Tibol, Raquel. *Historia general de arte mexicana, época moderna y contemporánea.* Mexico City-Buenos Aires, 1964.

Index